WHEN
THE WAR
CAME
HOME

WHEN
THE WAR
CAME
HOME

*The Inside Story of Reservists
and the Families They Leave Behind*

S T A C Y   B A N N E R M A N

continuum

NEW YORK • LONDON

2006

The Continuum International Publishing Group Inc
80 Maiden Lane, New York, NY 10038

The Continuum International Publishing Group Ltd
The Tower Building, 11 York Road, London SE1 7NX

www.continuumbooks.com

Printed in the United States of America

Library of Congress Cataloging-in-Publication Data

Bannerman, Stacy.
    When the war came home : the inside story of reservists and the families they leave behind / Stacy Bannerman.
    p. cm.
    Includes index.
    ISBN-13: 978-0-8264-1795-4
    ISBN-10: 0-8264-1795-7 (alk. paper)
    1. Iraq War, 2003—Personal narratives, American.   2. United States—Armed Forces—Reserves.   I. Title.
    DS79.764.U6B36   2006
    956.7044'3373—dc22   2005031732

To Lorin

That you could find your way to loving me is the best evidence
I have of God's grace in this world.

ACKNOWLEDGMENTS

I WOULDN'T BE WRITING THIS if my parents hadn't put the television set
in lockdown every summer, and given me a list of required reading to be
completed by season's end. I also want to acknowledge two of my teachers:
Carl Schmeider, Oak Grove Lutheran High School, and Jim Hale, University
of Minnesota. In addition to giving me tools for my mind, you opened
a door in my soul.

Thank you to Sorche Fairbank, my champion literary agent, my editor,
Henry Carrigan, and the crew at Continuum Publishing. Many thanks to
Russ, Jean, Christina, and Alisa for being there even when it wasn't pretty.
I am grateful beyond words to Nancy Lessin and Charley Richardson, and
each and every one of the members of Military Families Speak Out. I salute
all of the men and women who have ever worn a uniform for this country, as
well as the peacemakers of yesterday, today, and tomorrow. It is my deepest
conviction that we are ultimately working toward the same end.

CONTENTS

1

He Got the Call Today

OCTOBER 2003

"Please don't overreact if you read about soldiers being killed or wounded. If something happens to one of your soldiers, we will come to your house and inform you, don't worry."

I've got to believe the officer in the National Guard uniform intends for this to make people feel better, but predictably, it has the opposite effect and a palpable wave of apprehension rolls through the audience of Guardsmen and their family members. Can it be possible that he was completely oblivious to the impact that statement would have? As he continues speaking, a scrap of paper with a few hand-scrawled words is being passed down our row.

One of the guys in my husband's platoon has a phone gizmo with Internet access and he logged on for the day's news when the speakers bored him. Lorin looks at it before handing it to me.

SEVENTEEN KILLED IN IRAQ.

After reading the note taken from this morning's headlines, I search the stone faces of the men in my row who've seen this. Turning my attention back to the presenter, who's still trying to reassure us, it seems as though he's speaking another language.

I've been at the Kent National Guard Armory for nearly two hours, struggling to comprehend why I'm here.

———⟨∞⟩———

Normally, Sundays in Seattle are tailor-made for five pounds of newspaper and four cups of steaming dark roast. Between the *Seattle Times* and the

Post-Intelligencer there's enough material to occupy several hours scanning the headlines, being engrossed in the Op-Eds, flipping through glossy pages of ads for bargains on things I don't need.

That's what we usually do, but not today. The alarm blares at half past six, and I kiss Lorin's cheek as I roll out of bed. I press the button on the coffee pot and scoot outside to grab the paper. I drop five pounds of newspaper on the kitchen counter, not bothering to remove it from its bright blue plastic sleeve. We have to be at the Kent Army National Guard Armory by eight and won't have time to read it. A one-and-a-half-mile stretch of Military Highway lies between our house and the Armory, and my husband and I are quiet during the three-minute drive that will eventually take him to Iraq.

People are milling about outside when we arrive, and parking spaces are scarce. Lorin drops me off at the door and I walk quickly through the drizzling rain to wait for him inside. Leaning against the cinder block wall of the Armory's gymnasium, I watch two hundred men and a few dozen women in camouflage; their glossy black boots leave tire-track mud prints on the tile floor. Seriously, what am I *doing* here? I cannot shake the feeling that someone, somewhere, has gotten me mixed up with someone else. I've spent my career trying to change the conditions that create war; I never imagined my husband would be fighting one. But attendance at the Family Support Briefing is mandatory, so here I am. Lorin hurries through the double doors just in time to locate his platoon and find me a seat with the other wives and girlfriends.

He joins the sea of soldiers at the north end of the hall. They call out names and rank and I'm not sure what else because they're so far away and the buzz of a hundred conversations makes for too much background noise. A high, skittish energy permeates the room. It manifests in the men as a false bravado, but it shows, panicky, in the eyes of the women.

We studiously avoid looking at one another, for when we do we see ourselves reflected in the unvarnished fear of the other. The sanctuary that's so often found in the company of women is absent today. We know what this war holds for us, what it will take from us, and we are afraid.

Pulling my baseball cap down over my eyes, I slump against the back of the metal folding chair. A young woman with a beautiful dark-haired baby girl wearing a fuzzy pink onesie sits on my right. Two seats to my left, another woman, barely in her twenties, is rigid in her chair. I glance at her white-knuckled hands clutching the metal seat on either side of her body, and my heart goes out to her.

There are perhaps four hundred civilians in the gym, their loved ones now the property of the United States government. A week ago, their husbands and partners were computer programmers, Boeing engineers, delivery drivers, teachers, and realtors. Some were fire fighters, policemen, ambulance drivers, or part of the local Emergency Response Teams. They will not resume those roles and responsibilities for eighteen months, if then. It's illegal for companies to prevent their employees from returning to their jobs after extended periods of active duty service, but it happens.

What with the deployments being so long, and the economy so bad, it's happening more and more often, especially to the men and women who aren't employed by the government or by big companies. Although Guard and Reservists are paid regular military pay according to their rank, once they're federalized, it's a pretty significant pay cut for almost forty percent of them. Some generous corporations, like Microsoft and Safeco, are making up the difference, but the government won't fill the wage gap for federal employees, citing concerns about costs. There's nothing that can be done for the soldiers that are small business owners themselves, and many of them will be shut down.

Looking around, I see that a lot of the soldiers are puppies, young guys, barely in their twenties, but then there's a jump, dozens of people in uniform who are in their late thirties, forties, and even older. Scanning the faces of the men in formation, I think, *Grandpa's going to war*. Then an officer gives the order allowing the soldiers to break rank and find seats with their families.

Another officer steps up to the mike in the front of the room and makes a few announcements, telling people where the restrooms are, and inviting them to help themselves to refreshments. As Lorin settles in next to me, a tall man in a sport coat steps out from behind one of the tables laden with donuts. He's with a coffee distributing company and announces they've created a new Freedom Blend just for this group.

Sickened by the use of war as a marketing maneuver, I lean over to Lorin with a sarcastic remark, "Why not just call it Casualty Coffee?" It's this kind of thing that gets me in trouble.

Another man with a lot of hardware on his uniform takes the podium. He thanks us all for being there, and for supporting our soldiers.

"I know that up until now, being in the Army National Guard has meant just one weekend a month and two weeks a year."

I make a sound that falls somewhere between a snort and a laugh. Being in the Guard has almost always required more time than that from Lorin.

When we were living in Spokane, he requested a transfer to the HHC 1-303rd Armor, Mortar Platoon, which meant he had to drive to Kent for Guard at least twice a month. There were a handful of times where he made the six-hundred-mile round trip more than once in the same week.

I learned there were a number of ploys and even bait-and-switch tactics used by Guard and Reserve recruiters, tricks more disturbing than the actual amount of time they demand from their soldiers. One night after training, Lorin came home and told me about one of the new guys in his unit.

"I was talking to him, and he moved up here from California, and just wanted to transfer units, not be called for active duty. The recruiter waited until after he signed the papers, and then said, 'Oh, by the way, pack your stuff. The unit you just signed up for was mobilized a few weeks ago.'"

Apparently, the "Don't ask, don't tell" policy has a broader application than I'd thought.

Now, sitting next to Lorin at the Armory, I feel the heat rise to my face, embarrassed that I'd been loud enough for the people in the rows around us to hear. From the looks on the faces of the other wives who've turned to see the ill-mannered woman near the aisle, it appears they share my sentiments. Lorin sneaks a look at me and rolls his eyes, patting my knee as he does. I tell him I'll be quiet, and slink further down in my seat.

A huge screen drops down at the front of the room, and the speaker says the video is to remind us why we're here. The lights dim and a country western singer croons he's proud to be an American as the screen fills with the images of 9/11.

Jerking up in my chair, I watch footage of the planes flying into the Twin Towers, people jumping from the buildings and fleeing the scene. I cannot help but compare this with the propaganda films used by Nazi Germany, and I am ashamed by my lack of patriotism. And then I am ashamed to be an American.

The film ends, the lights come back on, and for the next couple of hours, we're briefed on what to expect in the upcoming months. Information about medical plans is provided, and we're told to make sure our papers are in order. Papers like wills, next-of-kin, and powers-of-attorney. I hear the words, but it feels less and less real to me. I don't belong here; this has nothing to do with me.

After the session breaks up, everyone in my husband's platoon is coming to our house for a barbeque so that the wives can meet before the guys are mobilized. Before heading out, I follow Lorin down a long hallway and out the back door to the building where his office is located. We pass by wire cages with platoon equipment and training rounds stacked floor to ceiling. He introduces me to a few of his superior officers, and I mumble hello as we shake hands, wondering if it'll make Lorin look bad if I ask if maybe he can just stay home. I don't care how *I* look; I will grovel for his safety.

By the time we pull up to the house, there are already ten or twelve young men in uniform pacing on our front lawn. It looks as if the yard is being searched for land mines, and I wonder what the neighbors must think. The house fills up rapidly, and people spill into the fenced backyard. I move back and forth between the kitchen and the living room, greeting new arrivals, tending to our guests, meeting the wives, trying to make sure they've got what they need and know where the bathrooms are.

Washing a few dishes, up to my elbows in warm soapy water, I glance out the large window that overlooks the deck. Flames leap out of the old, slightly tipsy black Weber kettle, and the guys stand in a circle around the fire, long-necked beer bottles dangling from their hands.

As I'm setting chips and dips and dishes on the wooden table in the dining room, my neighbor Alisa walks in, calling my name. At five feet ten, she stands just an inch taller than me. She has curly light brown hair that falls to the middle of her back—hair she keeps threatening to cut, but never does. Alisa's quick to laugh, or cry, and that transparency is one of the things I like about her most. She moved into the house next door with her new husband and kids just a week before we arrived. When our caravan of two cars and a U-Haul pulled into the cul-de-sac after seven hours on the road, they came over to introduce themselves and offered to help. As we unloaded the twenty-six foot truck, she and I talked about weddings and dresses and bridal showers. We've been friends ever since.

I give her a quick hug, and see her four- and six-year-old sons and a playmate of theirs hopping and bouncing behind her. They see the soldiers and are drawn to them, their little-boy dreams personified. Waving their toy guns in the air, the trio runs in between and around the men, yelling and shooting one another.

"You're dead!"

Falling and screaming with delight, this is *way* better than Sunday school.

Based on the current rate of casualties, at least two of the soldiers that I've seen today won't be coming home. They may even be two of the men that are now standing, living and breathing and laughing, in my backyard while the sun pours gold on their heads. Trying not to think about it, I offer up a silent prayer that one of them isn't mine.

It's been almost a month since I learned my husband is going to war. The man who was at my side for countless peace rallies and human rights marches will be deployed to Iraq in four months. And though he was frequently in the audience when I spoke about peace, nonviolence, and social justice, he'll still carry a gun for his country.

I was putting together a mailing for peace workshops when Lorin told me he got the call. After everything that had already taken place, I'd have been surprised if it had happened any other way.

He got the first call from his Guard commander about six months earlier, back in March of 2003, when we were still living in Spokane, Washington, but nothing ever came of it. I remember both of us standing, stunned, in the kitchen, trying to make sense of it. Lorin's Army National Guard unit hadn't been deployed since World War II; overseas combat wasn't what the Guard was for. Natural disasters and community service, yes. National readiness, sure. Not war.

Weeks later, we breathed a sigh of relief when it was announced that major military operations in Iraq were over. The alert expired, and I put it out of my mind as quickly as I could. And even though we hadn't talked about it in months, I instantly understand what he means when he shows up unexpectedly at my work on a perfect, sunny October afternoon, and says, "I got the call."

I know in my gut that this one is for real, but I cock my head like a dog who has heard a noise and isn't sure what it is. I know what he said, but those four words seem to have jammed up the gears in my mind, and I am unable to process them.

"What call?"

"Our unit is getting mobilized. I'm going to Iraq," he says, looking at me closely, trying to calculate the effect of his words.

"No. No. No, that can't be right."

He moves toward me and I push back in my chair. I don't want him to touch me, don't want any physical contact whatsoever that will cement the words laid out before me. In that instant, I understand how it is that people refuse to believe it when they're first informed of the death of a loved one.

He's scanning my face, trying to read my thoughts, concerned about what this is going to do to me. I had only recently begun climbing out of the depression that had defined my life for the past several years. He's worried about losing me again, worried maybe that this time, I won't make it back. The intensity of his expression is such that I've got to turn away.

I reach for another stack of envelopes and force-feed them with invitations for peace and poetry workshops. He steps toward me and I roll away in my chair. We do this dance until I've got nowhere left to go, and then he draws me to him, closing his arms around me, and I begin to weep.

There's only one other person in the office, so Lorin quickly tells her what's going on, and then we find an empty room, closing the door behind us. He sits, and I cry. Several minutes pass before I can ask him to tell me what he knows, exactly when he's supposed to go. What I want is for him to tell me why, to give me one impeccable reason for going to war. No, what I really want is for none of this to be happening.

"Right now, I don't know too much other than it looks like we'll get the formal mobilization orders in early November. By the middle of the month, we'll probably be going to a training camp somewhere."

"For how long?"

"A couple of months or so."

"Then what?" I ask, like I don't already know.

"We'll be deployed to Iraq. I was told to expect up to eighteen months, total, from the time we start training until we come back."

"Well, you tell them no, goddammit!" Fearful, furious, I continue, "You tell them that we just moved to Kent. Tell them this was our chance for a new start. Tell them how hard the last couple of years have been, and that things are finally starting to look up. You tell them *that*."

I know it's impossible. I know I'm being childish and desperate, and I don't care. All I care about is me and my beloved, all I care about is trying to have some sort of life with him that doesn't include such pain. But everything about him—his voice, his body, his eyes—tells me that he's already thinking about what to pack. Being a soldier is about honor and strength and courage for him.

I admire him for those values, though there have got to be a thousand better ways to express them. He says going to Iraq will give him a chance to find out if he's got what it takes, if all the years of training and preparation have paid off.

"Is there any way they'll let you go for the day?" he asks.

"I doubt it. I have to finish this mailing, and pretty much everyone else is already gone, so I've got to answer the phone."

I'd only been at the Institute for Community Leadership (ICL) in Kent, Washington, for about a month and a half, after struggling for over three years to find work in Spokane. If I'd just quietly resigned from the Martin Luther King Jr. Outreach Center back in 1999 and laid low for a while, maybe things would've been different. But once the legal claims and stacks of files documenting one of the country's earliest cases of racial discrimination against a white person became public record and fodder for the local media, my unemployment in the Spokane area was guaranteed. Publicly and professionally, I was an outcast, untouchable.

We first started talking about relocating in 2002, but Lorin had to get some time in as a food broker with Morton & Associates before he could request a transfer. As he was a professional chef when he was younger, the job suits him well, and it was such a significant advance that I said I'd wait; but the timeline we'd committed to had come and gone, and for the sake of my career, mental health, and our marriage, we had to move.

Shortly after getting settled in our new home, I signed a three-month contract with the Institute. It's just general office assistance, entry-level work that's a long freefall from my previous position as Executive Director, and part of me chafed at the demotion. I felt angry and a little humiliated, and I struggled with having to start over, unable to fathom how it could be that all of my years of experience and education had become irrelevant.

But after sending out hundreds of resumés, it's as though someone's thrown me a lifeline. I'm relieved to be getting regular paychecks again, and happy to have somewhere to go each morning. For the first time in ages, I remember, a least a little bit, what it feels like to be doing work that matters, The Work, capitalized, as I've come to think of it. It's all I know.

Will it be enough to sustain me when he's gone? Sitting across from Lorin, I want to pull him to me and never let go, to imprint my hands with the feel of his face. But rather than reach out, I retreat. Everything feels like too much, the sunlight too harsh, the silence unbearably loud.

Lorin holds me tight again before leaving. I watch him drive away in his brand new white KIA Sorento. Where I once saw a manufacturer's name, I now see the military's acronym for "Killed in Action." When he began pricing cars, I lectured him for wanting the mid-size SUV, but he was so excited about being able to buy a vehicle right off the dealer's lot for the first time in his life that my concerns about the environmental impact and our country's growing dependency on foreign oil didn't really register. Besides, I reminded myself, it's his money, not mine. Now, sitting back down at the reception desk in the front of the office, I wonder if the price he'll pay for that machine includes his life.

More than two thousand flyers promoting peace have to go out in the mail today, and it's my responsibility. It's a mindless task and I keep track of the numbers as I bend, fold, and paste. I start to cry on the forty-seventh envelope.

Looking back, I'd known something was coming; I just couldn't face that it be this. Several weeks earlier, as I was getting ready for work, I heard Lorin yelling from the deck in the backyard.

"Hey! HEY! Stacy, you've got to come out here and see this!"

After nearly three years of marriage, he only calls me by name when he wants to make sure he's got my attention.

"What? I'm trying to get ready."

"No. Come here, quick! Hurry!"

Oh, for cripes sakes, I think, sighing in exasperation as I set my mascara wand on the edge of the sink. Pushing aside the glass slider, I step out onto the deck and see him gesturing wildly toward the roof of the house next door.

"You won't believe it! A great blue heron just landed on the roof! It was like the sky turned a different color and this huge bird came out of nowhere. I didn't even see it fly in." His eyes are lit up, his words rushing out. "It just stood there and stared at me. You missed it! Have you ever seen one of those?"

And something within me just knew. I heard a warning voice in my mind say, *Get ready, it will be here soon.* Now it was here, the latest act in a series of events set in motion when Lorin first enlisted in the Army National Guard in 1983.

Like a lot of the civilian recruits, he joined shortly after graduating high school, as a way to set some structure in his life and help with a few college expenses. Lured by signing and affiliation bonuses, tuition assistance and reimbursement, and affordable life insurance, most people join the Guard hoping to serve their state and local communities, believing it holds minimal risk for them. Forty-six percent of those joining the Guard do so after at least four years of active duty service, looking at the Guard as a way to fulfill the eight-year service obligation that's in the fine print of every military contract.

The Guard also offers training and programs that can be translated into civilian careers, and many employers in private industry consider service in the Guard an asset, even if it's an occasional inconvenience. At least as important is the sense of camaraderie, the *esprit de corps* that the armed services both promotes and depends upon.

Lorin put in more than fifteen years before resigning, and then, a few months before we got engaged, a recruiter called and asked him to reenlist. I was a little taken aback when he told me that he was thinking about it. I hadn't known it was something he'd even consider, and I asked him why.

"Well, I guess I'd like to do it again, and they said I could choose my unit. Besides, it's just one weekend a month, and I'd only have to put in five more years before I'd be eligible for retirement benefits. It seems foolish to throw that away."

Grinning sheepishly, he says, "I like being in charge of a group of men, and playing war games. Besides, in the military, I can move up in rank. They have a regular promotion system, which I don't have at work."

"Well, I love a man in a uniform, but you know how I feel about war, and I guess I thought you felt that way, too. I figured anybody who's so opposed to domestic violence and child abuse wouldn't support killing for their country, either. And I *know* you don't think fighting is the way to solve problems. This is your choice to make, though, not mine, and I'll do my best to support you in whatever you decide."

For a few days, Lorin pretended he hadn't already made up his mind. Several weeks later, his status as one of 3,600 members of the 81st Armor Brigade, Washington Army National Guard, became official. Comprised of National Guard elements from Washington, Minnesota, and California, the Brigade hasn't been mobilized since the 1940s.

The governor has called up various Guard units from time to time in order to protect lives and property from natural disasters. They assisted during the 1975 Snohomish River Valley flood, the 1980 eruption of Mount Saint Helens, and the 1990 Thanksgiving Day Floods, when nineteen Washington State counties were declared federal disaster areas. At the height of "Firestorm '94," as massive forest fires were raging in eastern Washington, Lorin was one of the thousands of 81st personnel who were fighting fires and providing support for local, state, and federal agencies.

For more than half a century, unless you were an officer, being a member of the Army National Guard was just what the television ad promised: "One weekend a month, two weeks a year. Earn money for college and protect your local community." That's what the citizen soldiers thought they were signing up for when they registered, and little in the last sixty-plus years has indicated otherwise, even after the draft ended on June 30, 1973.

Shortly after the military became an all-volunteer force, the Nixon administration adopted the Total Force concept, which mandated the National Guard and Reserves as the primary source for augmentation of active duty troops. The new policy was strongly supported by the Pentagon, primarily because it significantly lowered the costs associated with recruiting, training, equipping, and maintaining a large standing military. The other rationale presented by the Pentagon was that it would ensure that a greater cross-section of America would be invested in overseas military operations.

In 2003, there were 351,089 people in the Army Guard and almost 107,000 in the Air Guard, a combined total of nearly 458,089 citizen soldiers. The U.S. Reserves total another 211,890. There are presently more personnel in the Guard and Reserves than active duty military, which had 493,563 personnel in 2003.

Since President Bush declared a national emergency three days after the September 11th attacks, approximately 157,600—nearly half—of the men and women in the Guard and Reserves have served as active duty military. In the days preceding the attacks, only 5,500 were on federal duty missions. In October 2003, as Lorin is actively preparing for deployment, the total number on active duty for the Army National Guard and Army Reserve is 121,215; Naval Reserve, 1,976; Air National Guard and Air Force Reserve, 19,274; Marine Corps Reserve, 10,947; and the Coast Guard Reserve, 1,191.

The Army National Guard and Army Reserves are two of the three components that, along with the Active Army, make up the U.S. Army, the biggest military group serving in Iraq. The Guard is a state force of civilians, federalized only in "a time of war . . . or national emergency declared by Congress," according to the National Guard Act of 1934. The Army Reserve also serves on a part time basis, but it's a federal entity intended to supplement the Active Army. In the first Gulf War, both the Guard and Reserve supplied service support for combat troops. In the war in Iraq, the Army Reserve is again providing support, but many of the Guard Brigades have been assigned to combat.

The Guard has been deployed before but, with the exception of the Persian Gulf War, in relatively small numbers. The National Guard was originally known as the state militia, under state control, until the Constitutional Convention of 1787 gave the national government the power to federalize the states' forces. The passage of the Dick Act, introduced by Congressman

Charles Dick (Ohio) in 1903, initiated the federalization of state militias for domestic use and introduced their new name, the National Guard.

Five years later, the act was amended to give Congress the power to authorize Guard mobilization for overseas action when essential to contain rebellions, to resist invasions, or to enforce the laws of the United States. In 1952, Congress passed an act allowing the president to call out the State Guard for fifteen days, but it also gave state governors the right the refuse their deployment.

During the Vietnam War, white middle-class males joined the Guard in droves, hoping to avoid combat. Demographic shifts, feminism, and legal changes are reflected in today's Guard, but it's still about seventy-five percent white, as compared to the sixty percent of regular military.

There are any number of distinct differences between full-time troops and citizen soldiers. For starters, the average age of Army National Guard personnel is thirty-two, in the Air National Guard, it's thirty-seven, but in the regular military, it's twenty-seven. Part-time Reservists and National Guard members frequently remain in their units until their fifties or beyond.

Right after Lorin receives word that his unit was being deployed, we go out to dinner with a coworker of his, Lynn. During the dinner, Lynn casually remarks to my forty-two year old husband, "Don't take this the wrong way Lorin, but aren't you kind of old to be fighting in a war?"

Lorin's eyebrows raise in astonishment. He swallows, clears his throat, and replies, "Gee, thanks. But I've got to tell you, I'm not the oldest one in the brigade. There are quite a few guys older than me. I know for sure that one of them is fifty-six, and another guy fought in the Vietnam War, too."

He pauses a moment, then continues, "So I was thinking the other day about that movie, you know, the war movie that was based on the book *We Were Soldiers Once, and Young*. For us, it's 'We Were Citizens Once, and Old.'"

Most all of the older Guard and Reservists say they've stayed in for the retirement benefits. But unlike members of the regular military, who receive benefits after twenty years of service regardless of their age at retirement, Guard and Reservists who've completed twenty years aren't entitled to full retirement benefits until they've reached sixty years of age.

The profile of weekend warriors also differs from regular military personnel in that they more often have some level of college education and are well into a civilian career track, leaving behind career jobs and their own businesses when they are called into action.

More than 79,000 citizen soldiers are currently stationed in the CENTCOM AOR (Central Command Area of Responsibility), which includes Iraq, Southwest Asia, Turkey, Romania, and Bulgaria. This figure doesn't include the approximately 32,000 Guard and Reserve troops directly involved in Operations Iraqi and Enduring Freedom.

The Guard and Reserves were a small segment of the initial Iraq invasion, which was led by active duty Army and Marines. When President Bush declared that major combat operations were over, the countries that contributed combat forces to the invasion began pulling out.

The "coalition of the willing" included Britain, Korea, Australia, Denmark, and Poland. Spain was one of ten other countries that provided small numbers of non-combat forces, primarily medical personnel and decontamination specialists, but in many of these nations, domestic opposition to the war was so intense (one Spanish poll reported ninety percent of citizens were against the war) that they withdrew as soon as President Bush announced, "Mission accomplished."

In the nearly seven months since, it's become evident that the active duty army doesn't have anywhere near the manpower needed for an extended occupation, something that top military officials were worried about prior to the invasion. Their concerns were largely ignored by the administration, and an increasing number of the Guard and Reserve have been called up for "peacekeeping and reconstruction" purposes, and to assist with policing, patrols, and transportation.

In the past, these types of missions required deployments of no longer than six months. Now, according to the *Boston Globe,* "Many are serving one-year tours in Iraq after already having completed long tours in Afghanistan, Kosovo, or elsewhere." After the massive troop rotation planned for March of 2004, near the one-year mark of the invasion, Guard and Reservists were nearly forty percent of the armed forces in Iraq. On November 15, 2003, the men and women of the Washington State Army National Guard's 81st Brigade Combat Team report for active duty, and begin training for a twelve-month deployment in Iraq.

The American occupation of Iraq has provoked a growing insurgency, and attracted terrorist cells from other countries. The Pentagon's assurance that 50,000 troops would be sufficient after the initial invasion has proven false. There are presently 138,000 American soldiers in Iraq, with plans to have 150,000 boots on the ground by April of 2004.

Attempts to stabilize Iraq are requiring considerably more manpower than anticipated, resulting in protracted deployments, in part because the small numbers of coalition forces from other countries have begun to with-draw. Unlike the quick, efficient strike of the first Gulf War, which is what many Americans had hoped for, and most Reservists expected, Operation Iraqi Freedom has become a guerrilla war where there are no clear enemies and everyone is on the front lines. In a few short months, my husband will be, too.

A dozen progressively frightening scenarios run through my mind during the short drive home from work, the day we get the news. By the time I'm in the house, I'm frantic, on the verge of tears. Lorin's on the phone, talking about war with his dad, Hardie, a retired military man. Lorin's grandpa was a soldier, too. He fought in World War II, something Lorin told me a while back, but I conveniently forgot.

Recalling it now, I realize I've been trying to deny his family's history of militarism, to erase it from Lorin's genetic pool. It's not who I want him to be, so I selfishly wiped it out.

But it's not like there aren't plenty of soldiers hanging off of my family tree; after generations of warriors, my dad was the first to break with tradition.

My dad, Russ, is a silly, skinny, deeply thoughtful man, and when I was growing up, he'd take my siblings and me on nature hikes and to wildlife preservations where I learned to love the life in all things. I've got to call him tonight, and I have a pretty good idea of what he's going to say.

When my little brother Steve was seven, my dad had a lawyer draw up a conscientious objector form for him to sign in front of a notary public. Steve did this twice more over the next decade, intentionally building a case history in the event that he was drafted. Having had a brother fight in the Korean War, my father wanted to make sure none of his kids went to war, wanted to prevent any future grandchildren from going through what he did when he was ten, when his job was to collect the mail. Each walk to the mailbox was met with trepidation, hoping for a letter from his brother Jack—on the front lines in Korea—and not one from the war department.

It used to be that the postman delivered death, but fifty years later, technology has changed the way and the speed with which we get our news and our mail, and the Army does things differently, too.

If something happens to Lorin, the method of my notification will come down to a race between the person driving the official United States Government sedan, my Internet provider and access to my e-mail inbox, and the major television networks.

"Well," says Lorin, hanging up the phone, "that was Hardie. I told him, and my mom. I think they took it okay. How're you doing?"

"How does it look like I'm doing?" I snap, trembling from the effort of trying to hold back the tears. "How am I supposed to be doing after finding out I won't see you for over a year, and maybe never again?" I could tiptoe around this, but I'm not going to. If he's going to put us through this, then I feel no need to mince words, or be *nice*. There's no nice here, not in any of it.

"You'll see me again. Don't even think that."

"Is it worth it?" I demand, knowing I shouldn't go here but unwilling to stop myself. Shaky with fear and anger, horror and sorrow, I keep at him.

"Is it worth it now? What's the point in having retirement benefits if you're not here to enjoy them?"

"Tell me, just exactly how much will those benefits add up to, do you think?"

"I'm not sure, I never really sat down and figured it out."

"Well, we're going to. Right now."

On my insistence, he gets an old beat-up calculator out of his desk and we do some quick math, coming up with a total of about a hundred grand.

"So that's the price of your life? Is that it? If I write you a check for one hundred thousand dollars, then will you stay home?"

Who is this harpy in my living room and what is she doing in my body? Coming together in the middle of our lives—my thirty-five to his forty— Lorin and I have been very careful to carry our love lightly, gently. We don't put down or intentionally provoke, we seldom raise our voices, hardly ever fight. So who is this shrew, and why does this assault on my husband seem to be the only way that I can even begin to skim the pain off my heart? As quickly as it comes, it goes, leaving me feeling somewhat ashamed, and even sadder than before.

His face blurs before me when I look at him and whisper, "What will I do without my Scooby?"

There's something in the way he picks up his feet that reminds me of the cartoon dog. Lorin's nearly six-two, and he's got close-cropped black hair and brown skin with undertones of red and gold, the result of Caucasian and African American parentage and an infusion of Native American blood several generations back. Extremely stubborn and, at times, rather clumsy; he's also unbelievably loyal and steady; quick to please and slow to anger.

He's the only person I've ever met that everyone seems to love. I understand why that is, but frankly, it's a little annoying at times, because I simply do not get the same response. "Nice" has never been the first word that people use to describe me; I'm too opinionated, or too intense, always too much of something. But I'm usually better than this at maintaining my composure, and am a little disappointed that I'm unable to hold it together.

"What is this going to do to you? What will it do to us? What if something happens to you? Huh? What then? What in the hell am I supposed to do then?" I demand, angry again.

"Nothing's going to happen to me, okay? I'll be fine," he says. "I'll just be gone for a while, but I'm coming back."

I don't think he *begins* to realize what he's going into. How can he not? He's acting like this is simply an extended campout.

"And who will you be when you come back? You can't tell me that you won't be different. No way can you spend a year or more at war, and do what you're going to have to do, and be the same person that you are right now. No way."

"Well, yeah, but you'll change, too. I won't change that much."

"Don't pretend it's the same thing when it's not. I'm not going into a war zone, and I won't be carrying a gun. I most definitely won't have to be making a decision about whether or not to use it, and I won't be spending the next year or more living in the middle of a combat zone. So don't you make promises to me that you can't keep."

Suddenly, all of my anger evaporates once more, leaving me sad and weak. Leaning into him, I mumble, "I'm sorry I got angry, I'm just so afraid."

"I know. Me, too, but we'll get through this."

After dinner, he goes to his office and I climb the short stairway up to mine. Checking my e-mail one last time before going to bed, I find a message from my dad:

It is almost impossible for me to comprehend the fact that someone I know and love is being put in harm's way due to some misguided, evil politicians. If someone had told me that this would happen some years past, I wouldn't have believed them. The only way that I'll be able to handle this is to keep myself very busy and understand, in my heart of hearts, that he will return to us safe and sound. I know this is true, yet I feel real fear. Mankind fails me too often. Be sure and impress on Lorin just how much we love him and how much he means to all of us.

I sleep deeply, and it's not until I'm halfway through my first cup of coffee the next morning that I remember he's been called to active duty. When it pops into my mind, I have the curious feeling that my heart is imploding. Already I'm trying to distance myself from this, to be the observer rather than the participant. Over the next few days, hours will go by without any thought of war, or what's happening with Lorin and our life together as I've known it. Then it comes to me, sometimes out of the blue, other times triggered by a conversation or a headline.

More often than not, it slips to the forefront during a quiet moment when there's nothing to occupy my mind or distract my heart. Then it sneaks up on me and attacks, like a huge, dark figure appearing out of nowhere. I am grateful then that the job I've got is a series of simple tasks, requiring minimal thought and repetitive movement.

Another five hundred flyers have to be prepared for mailing, and once again, I'm creasing sheet after sheet into a tri-folded piece, the same motions I've used thousands of times before. But I'm feeling it now like I haven't before, and I pray for peace with each page. If I just do enough of these, then maybe, somehow, the war will be over and he won't have to go. The letters that will be received by junior high and high school students throughout the greater Seattle area have become my paper cranes.

The paper crane became an icon for world peace in the aftermath of World War II. Shortly after the U.S. dropped an atomic bomb on her home city of Hiroshima, Japan, Sadako Sasaki contracted leukemia. Determined to fold one thousand paper cranes, believing it would grant her a wish—a wish for peace—she completed six hundred and sixty four before she died at the age of twelve. Her friends folded the rest. I glance at a postcard with Sadako's story that I keep at my desk, and for a moment, wonder why I even bother.

Her efforts didn't stop war; nor did her death, or the subsequent deaths of millions of others around the world. People have become more, not less, violent, and there hasn't been a single year since World War II that some countries, somewhere, weren't at war. Does it really make any difference what I do?

Even if it does, does not the fact that my husband is going to war effectively cancel out my efforts? If one person is actively promoting peace while the other's waging war, hasn't it become a zero-sum game? I shake my head to clear away the darkness, and continue with my work.

I don't talk to Lorin about my internal dialogues, the moments of despair, or the depths of my fear. I'm sure he knows in his way, but I cry on my own time. For the most part, I've been successful, but when I slip and fall weeping in his arms, I feel guilty. Even though he doesn't show it, I know Lorin's emotional cup is filled to overflowing and I don't want to add to it. Once he's over there, I don't want him to be concerned about me when even a moment or two of inattention might mean he gets wounded or worse. I've heard the military mantra: A distracted soldier is a dead soldier.

Hardie called one evening when Lorin wasn't around and asked how I was.

"Not so good. I'm really scared, and I can't believe this is happening," I say, unable to control the tremor in my voice. "What if something happens to him?"

"Stacy, you've got to be strong. It won't do him any good to have to worry about you. He needs to be able to focus on what he's doing and getting ready for what's ahead. He cannot afford to be preoccupied," Hardie replies sternly, and I hear shades of the military man he once was.

I pull the phone away from my ear for a split second, looking at it as though it's the receiver that is responsible for the change in my normally easygoing father-in-law. We talk for a few more minutes, and I tell him I'll make sure to have Lorin call him when he gets home from yet another briefing. A Sergeant First Class in a Mortar Platoon, Lorin's a noncommissioned officer, and his duty began several weeks before most of the other soldiers.

Lorin told his employers he was being mobilized within hours of getting the call, and a few days later, he was off the company payroll. Two weeks after that, we got a notice in the mail informing us we'd been dropped from the company's employee medical policy. This left us without any medical coverage until his military health insurance kicked in, thirty days after he reported for active duty.

A report just released by the General Accounting Office estimated that at least twenty percent of stateside Guard members don't have health insurance. The lack of medical coverage is most concentrated in Guard and Reservists between the ages of nineteen and thirty-five, forty percent of whom have no medical coverage. Up until June of 2003, families of active duty Guardsmen had no military health benefits at all.

The Senate recently approved a plan to give non-active duty Guardsmen and Reservists access to the Pentagon's Tricare health insurance system, attaching it to the $87 billion being requested to pay for fighting and reconstruction in Iraq. The Bush administration is formally opposing the proposal, claiming it's too expensive. Families of activated Guard and Reserves are currently covered for a period of twelve months, although many of the soldiers have had their deployments extended an additional three, six, and sometimes even twelve months. Unless something changes, there's a good chance our coverage will run out months before our husbands are able to return to their regular jobs.

Although Lorin is not going to have to take a pay cut, many families are, particularly the ones with young children and husbands just beginning careers. For many in the Guard, whether single or married, deployment equals financial disaster. Rent or house payments, credit card debt, car loans, and childcare expenses that were calculated according to civilian salaries cannot be covered when their pay plummets to that of a private. The families they leave behind will have to cope with bankruptcy, hunger, substandard housing conditions, apartment evictions, or the loss of homes. No one speaks of what else we stand to lose.

2

Home for the Holidays

NOVEMBER–DECEMBER 2003

I NEVER THOUGHT of myself as a soldier's wife, but then, I didn't really think of Lorin as a soldier. I considered his Guard service a hobby, a leisurely pursuit that dovetailed nicely with Lorin's interest in military novels and war movies. He got to wear a uniform and be outdoors, get some exercise, and have a little male bonding time in the bargain. But he's in uniform all the time now, and in the weeks leading up to his deployment, his interest has become an obsession.

When he puts the DVD into the machine for the third time in as many weeks, I tell him I just can't watch *Black Hawk Down* again. But there's no escape from the war on TV or in the paper. Operation Iraqi Freedom has come into my home, and it sticks to the walls.

Lorin's gone most of the time, in training at Fort Lewis, forty-five miles south of here. His Guard unit has been put on lockdown, so they can't leave the base at night. The active duty units don't have the same restriction, which annoys the Guardsmen to no end. Lorin shares living quarters with Richard, whose wife, Lydia, is also in the Guard and at Fort Lewis, preparing for deployment to Iraq. Richard's folks will take care of their pets while they're gone, but one of Lorin's men has had to give his dog away. At least none of us has children to account for.

Lorin's shown me a few photos of their room, which resemble those in college dorms. Lorin and Richard, both sergeants, have it better than their charges. The snapshots of the barracks where the grunts are staying are some of the oldest in the country, and look like stills from *Full Metal Jacket*.

Lorin calls me on his cell phone nearly every night, and he gets a twenty-four hour leave most weekends. But it's already begun. His loyalties are slowly, subtly, shifting, and I feel myself sliding into second place. In the pockets of time we have together, there are parts of him that I can't get to, parts he will no longer let me see. Hurt and confused by his distance, I confront him.

"Why won't you talk to me about what's going on for you? I feel like a part of you is already gone."

Frustration creeps into his response. "I know, and I'm sorry, but it's what I've got to do. The only way I can get ready for this is to shut down in a way. I don't know what to expect over there, and there's so much I don't know."

I'm sure that's true, although I haven't a clue as to how one can really, truly prepare for war. What, exactly, are the requisite psychological steps that will enable him to make what was only yesterday an unethical, illegal, and morally reprehensible way of being acceptable?

"There are some things I may have to do over there that I don't really want to."

"Like what?" I'm determined to make him say it.

He's silent.

"Like if you have to kill someone? How are you possibly going to go from forty-two years of civilian living, decades without even so much as a fistfight, to carrying a rapid-fire rifle and being willing to use it? How're you going to do that? And why would you want to?"

I think I feel something in his soul slamming shut.

Raising his voice a bit, he responds tersely, "Don't you think I've thought about that, too? Do you just want me to be shot at and not fight back? We've got rules of engagement, and they're very clear, but if it comes down to me or the other guy, I'm going to defend myself. You would do the same."

"No. No, I wouldn't put myself in a situation where I had to make that choice." I cringe a little at my tone, hearing the arrogance, the sense of being morally superior. That kind of attitude isn't going to help anyone.

Quietly, in a resigned voice, he replies, "Yeah, well, it's too late for that."

We let it drop, but it's on my mind almost constantly. I think it's making me ill, literally. I'm weak and shaky, and my whole body hurts. I can't remember the last time I was this sick. When Lorin's mother, Helen, wants to spend time with us while she's in town for the annual Washington State School Directors Conference, I try to dissuade her from coming. I tell her that now's not a great time, but she comes to the house anyway.

I am supposed to present several workshops at the conference, but I cancel at the last minute. It would have been my first time as a presenter at this particular conference, and I'd put in hours of preparation, but I lost all enthusiasm for talking about preventing bullying and harassment in our schools. It seems so pointless, now that we're a nation at war. Now that I'm married to the military myself.

On Sunday, in a quiet moment at the house with her, I question Helen about her thoughts on Lorin's deployment. "So," I begin, "how are you doing with all of this? It's got to be different from when Hardie was away. He never was in combat."

"It is. It's very different. Hardie was gone, but he wasn't in harm's way. He didn't go into war zones. And it is one thing when it's your husband; it is another thing altogether when it's your child."

I study her face, waiting for her to continue. I can see that this is difficult for her.

"I can't believe my little boy is going to war. I've been remembering a lot from when he was growing up, thinking of all the things about him that I love. I'm so worried about him now."

I can make out the beginning of tears in her eyes, and suddenly I see Helen not as my mother-in-law, but as a mother, a scared one.

About six months after Lorin and I got together, we went to his mom's for Thanksgiving. After the slightest bit of prompting from me, Helen carted out some of his high school yearbooks and boxes full of pictures. My favorite photo was one of a deliriously happy four-year-old Lorin standing naked in a wading pool, wearing an oversized pair of dark shades, hands covering his equipment.

I want to hear what Helen has to say, but I've got the cold sweats again and am barely able to hold myself up in the dining room chair. I try to pay attention as Helen vents.

"I can't believe our government is sending soldiers to Iraq without the proper protective gear. What are my tax dollars paying for? Bush wanted this war, and he got the money for it, yet now he can't even see to it that the soldiers have the equipment they need."

This gets her too worked up to talk for a few minutes, but then she continues. "I e-mailed the Washington State Military Department, asking when Lorin's Brigade would be getting their protective vests, and whether the vehicles they had were armored. I sent copies to KHQ television, and several state senators and congressmen. The TV guy was interested in the response and story, but I haven't heard back yet from anyone else."

I've never known her to be particularly politically active, but I guess I shouldn't be surprised. *Everyone's* political when it's personal.

⠶⠶⠶

Lorin's deployment has been a crash course in what the military is—and is not—providing for their soldiers. For decades, the Tiered Resourcing System has ensured that new equipment went to the active Army, and the Reserve and the Guard got the hand-me-downs. This is a huge problem for our soldiers. They are holding the front lines with Vietnam-era guns, falling-apart flak vests in bright orange, and radios that don't work. But the scope of the problem isn't limited to supplies; the government has tried to address training issues for years.

Recognizing the need for better peacetime training and preparation for combat readiness, and more effective integration of the Guard and Reserves into the regular military, the Army implemented the "Bold Shift" strategy in 1991. The congressionally mandated program assigned active Army advisers to Reserve and Guard Brigades in order to correct the pre- and post-mobilization training problems that were occurring at soldier, leader, and unit levels.

Bold Shift methods included reorganizing the command structure of the U.S. Army Reserve and Army National Guard, and using the active Army's Operational Readiness Evaluation for soldier assessments. The program also designated a number of National Guard units as "Enhanced Brigades," making them a top priority for training and resources. In the event of two major and nearly concurrent conflicts, these National Guard Brigades would be some of the first to be mobilized, and it was expected that they would best exemplify the success of the Bold Shift training.

However, the findings of a 1995 review[1] conducted by the General Accounting Office (GAO) at the request of Congress were not impressive. Few of the Enhanced Brigades came anywhere close to meeting the training goals in 1992 through 1994. Even when the Brigades demonstrated progress in individual training, the twenty-three percent staff turnover promptly nullified them.

The Army revised the Bold Shift strategy and goals in January 1995, but the effectiveness of the revisions is yet to be determined. The GAO report identified the problematic working relationships between the Army and the state-run Guard, stipulating that the problems were long-standing and would be difficult to improve. Finding that internal proficiency reviews had grossly exaggerated the true level of combat readiness of the National

---

1. "Army National Guard: Combat Brigades' Ability to Be Ready for War in 90 Days Is Uncertain" (Chapter Report, 06/02/95, GAO/NSIAD-95-91).

Guard Brigades, the report also questioned whether the brigades could be ready to deploy ninety days after mobilization.

Ninety days is the average length of pre-deployment training for National Guard and Reservists heading to Iraq, although some have been deployed in less than thirty days. However well trained the Guard and Reserves are, they're still nowhere near as ready as the regular Army, and even the Active Army soldiers in Iraq are terribly unprepared for the counterinsurgency.

Under-funded and under-trained, treated like second-class soldiers for the past thirty years, the National Guard and Reserve, which typically train for only thirty-nine days a year, must serve side by side with the active duty military, who receive a *minimum* of two hundred eighty days of training, and are expected to perform to the same standards with substandard equipment.

Most Army Guard units are not equipped properly. Some of their radios are so outdated that communication with newer radios, such as those held by the regular military the Guard is stationed alongside, is impossible. Many of the trucks given to the Guard are so old that the Army simply cannot supply spare parts for them. One of their models of tanks isn't even treaded, but rubber-wheeled—a crippling disaster in the Iraq war zone. The soldiers have been told by commanding officers and troops already stationed in Iraq that Global Positioning Systems are extremely helpful, if not absolutely necessary, to maintain contact and bearing in the frequent sandstorms of the Iraqi deserts, but few receive them.

The October 6, 2003, edition of *Nation* magazine revealed that Guardsmen in Iraq were given Vietnam-era M16s that had been retooled, and soldiers were complaining of inadequate food rations. Wearing up to fifty pounds of equipment in desert temperatures of 130 degrees or more, at times they were forced to subsist on a single bottle of water a day.

Treated as cannon fodder by an administration that seems to have little regard for the lives of the soldiers and the realities of the new front line, Guardsmen and Reservists have had to buy their own flashlights, night-vision goggles, radios and boots, protective gear, and armored plates.

Prior to deploying for a one-year tour in Iraq, Army Reservist, Major Jeff Cushman, forty-two, a father of three, was informed that if he and the men in his unit wanted night-vision goggles, they'd each have to ante up at least $2,000 per pair. The unit bought their own Global Positioning Systems, which are vital navigating tools. None of these Reservists were issued side arms, but some of them were given the older M16s.

They've spent their own money purchasing grease and cleaning supplies to keep their outdated weapons operational in the persistent sandstorms that clog their M16 rifles with grit, jamming the firing mechanism. Active duty servicemen first started using the guns—nicknamed "the Widow-maker"—during Vietnam, where they quickly discovered that it misfired if it wasn't microscopically clean.

A letter written by a Marine Corp Reservist who fought in Vietnam about an ambush that occurred on July 2, 1967, says:

> The M-16s would fire once or twice—maybe more—then jam. The only way to clear the chamber and resume firing was to lock open the bolt, run a cleaning rod down the barrel, and knock the casing loose. Soon it would jam again.
>
> This was the rifle supplied to her troops by the richest nation on earth . . .
>
> Sixty-four men in Bravo were killed that afternoon. Altogether, the Battalion lost around a hundred of the Nation's finest men. The next morning, we bagged them like groceries . . .
>
> Today, people are still debating the issue: Was it the fault of the ammo? The fault of the rifle? Neither. It was the fault of the politicians and contractors and generals. People in high places knew the rifles and ammo wouldn't work together. The military didn't want to buy the rifle when Armalite was manufacturing it. But when Colt was licensed as the manufacturer, they suddenly discovered it was a marvelous example of Yankee ingenuity.
>
> Sgt. Brown told them it was garbage. Col. Hackworth told them it was garbage. And every real Grunt knew it was garbage. It was unsuited for combat.

Some forty years later, the weapon is issued to citizen soldiers who are sent into combat and given duties such as driving convoys or manning checkpoints. In previous wars, these activities were considered less dangerous than combat missions.

Iraq is a different war. There, with a mounting resistance that uses guerrilla tactics like car bombs, street kids with explosives strapped to their backs, suicide missions, and Improvised Explosive Devices (IEDs) planted anywhere, the front line is everywhere. But the majority of protective body armor (Kevlar vests and flak jackets) is distributed to active duty soldiers.

Guardsmen and Reservists are the last to get the new Interceptor body armor, the best protective gear on the market. While they wait, approximately forty thousand U.S. soldiers in Iraq have had to beg, buy, borrow, or do without sufficient protection. Made of layered sheets of Kevlar, with pockets in front and back for ceramic or steel plates to protect vital organs, flak jackets can stop a point-blank 7.62 millimeter small-arms fire. That's the size of AK-47 rounds—the weapon commonly used by the Iraqis.

The newest body armor has throat and groin protectors, removable plates in the front and back, and weighs nearly sixteen and a half pounds. The outer tactical vest is another eight pounds plus, made of a high-grade Kevlar weave capable of stopping nine-millimeter bullets.

The United States provided some of these vests to Coalition forces during the invasion, but left U.S. soldiers to fasten ceramic or steel plates to outdated vests that lacked the pockets for protective shields. Some of the Guardsmen and Reserves have been outfitted with older, British-made Tetranike vests, while others have been issued bright orange Vietnam-era flak jackets—similar to hunting vests—held together with duct tape and dental floss.

Police departments across the country have donated their cast-off bulletproof vests to U.S. Army reserve units headed for Iraq. More Kevlar vests and armored plates for vehicles were ordered in September of 2003, but they won't be ready before Lorin gets there, not for months. In the meantime, some soldiers are pulling the Kevlar panels from the old vests and using them to line the insides of their Humvees and other vehicles in combat zones.

Congress approved $310 million dollars for the acquisition of new vests, but the bulk of that was spent elsewhere or siphoned off for non-combat-related materials. The severity of the shortages have been brought to light by the overwhelming number of calls made to local members of Congress by National Guardsmen and their families, pleading for body armor and other equipment. The vests won't prevent the loss of limbs, but they could prevent the loss of my husband. I hate the thought of him going to war; I despise that he will do so without the finest protective gear on the market.

Layered sheets of the fabric have been used as lightweight vehicle armor along the sides and the rear of HMMVs (the military's all-purpose vehicle). The administration has known since 1986 that Kevlar "blankets" offer HMMVs better protection against IED and mortar attacks. Yet many of the vehicles used for patrols don't even have metal protective plates—a minimal step toward protection. After repeated requests, our soldiers were informed that there was no money available for the blankets or protective plates. Those assigned to convoys that are slow-moving targets in treacherous territory have retrofitted their trucks themselves, strapping on scrap metal and sandbags in any manner possible. When that's not available, soldiers spray-paint the sides of the trucks gray, "so that they look like metal." They call their vehicles "cardboard coffins," and Lorin could end up driving one.

There's an underground railroad that runs through the families of the military serving in Iraq, Kuwait, and Afghanistan. I've tapped into it and heard about wives and parents who have sent protective gear in care packages, along with candy, cookies, and the powdered Gatorade drink mix that's in such high demand in the desert. Lorin doesn't have his vest yet, and I'm freaking out about it.

His folks and I put it at the top of the list and start shopping. I ask my neighbor, a DEA agent who is also in the Guard, but his flak jacket is way too small. I keep putting out feelers, and eventually learn about sources and supplies online, in gun magazines, and from other military families. Military-issue jackets, starting at $375, can be ordered over the phone, and gear is up for bid on eBay. I cannot believe I'm doing this.

In the past few weeks, we've spent hundreds of dollars on desert boots, various tools, and a pair of WileyX sunglasses that are supposed to block the furnacelike wind and pelting sand of Iraq. Lorin's folks bought him a Global Positioning System (GPS) with a walkie-talkie feature to navigate unfamiliar terrain. We start searching for the chemical compound that can be added to the wash to coat uniforms with a type of repellant that will offer a first line of defense from the desert bugs and ticks and sand fleas, and we look into buying a satellite phone.

How does the richest nation on the planet justify sending its soldiers to war without proper equipment and supplies? In 2002, while Lorin's unit was driving to Yakima, Washington, for a weekend drill, I got a call at the house. One of the trucks in the convoy was trying to reach him, but the phones weren't working, and the radios installed in the vehicles weren't either. They asked me if I would call him on his cell phone and tell him to contact the base.

At the time it was funny, albeit a tad appalling. I asked the young soldier, "So, this is the best the United States military can do? All of those taxpayer dollars the government's spending, all the technology that's available, and you've got to call me, while my husband's with *your* guys, and ask me to get a hold of him for you? What're you going to do if you're in an actual combat situation? Are you going to call me then, too? Here's his cell phone number. You call him."

My early, vague disgruntlement has a clear, sharp focus now, exacerbated by the news that tours of duty are being extended more frequently, and most often for the Guard and Reserves. For the soldiers and their families, already unprepared for the psychological realities of war, the news of longer than expected deployments hits hard. Some units have had their return date moved back three times, and there have been instances where the soldiers have been sitting in a plane on the tarmac in Kuwait, waiting to come home, when they are instructed to get their gear and get off. They won't be leaving for six months, at minimum.

Trying to boost morale while keeping as many boots on the ground as possible, the military implemented a lottery system for a two-week rest and relaxation (R&R) leave. It's set up to allow R & R for 1,000 to 1,500 soldiers per month, but with at least 30,000 soldiers to process, more than half of them won't get it.

Morale problems have plagued the mission from the start, and thousands of troops have written to the *Stars and Stripes,* a daily newspaper distributed overseas for the U.S. military community. The paper is authorized by the Department of Defense, and was first published as a weekly during the Civil War. It went out of print after the war, but was reintroduced during World War II. *Stars and Stripes* has printed two hundred of the letters received from soldiers fighting the war on terror. Complaints about conditions and poor troop morale were so prevalent that the paper conducted a survey of nearly two thousand soldiers in Iraq, and published the findings in the "Ground Truth" special series (October 2003).

Forty-eight percent of Reserve and National Guard respondents said that their own morale was "low" or "very low." Scores of Reservists said that what they were doing was not anywhere near what they had been prepared to do. Troop concerns about a lack of clarity extends to the mission itself, and over one-third of those surveyed said their mission was "mostly not clear" or "not clear at all."

One National Guardsman penned on his survey: "Our mission has changed more than the president changes his underwear." Army reserve Staff Sgt. Carla Williams, thirty-nine, of the 353rd Transportation Company wrote that she is "not exactly sure what her unit is supposed to be doing." Sixty-three percent of Reservists rated the chain of command's ability to provide them with the supplies they required as "not good" or "poor," compared to the twenty-seven percent of the Army respondents.[2]

About fifty-five percent of the Reservists and Guardsmen surveyed "said they were either 'unlikely' or 'very unlikely' to re-enlist. . . . National Guard units say at times during the recent deployment to Iraq, they have been regulated to different bathrooms and medical care. One unit was so poorly supplied it asked hospitals in the United States to donate medical supplies.

---

2. "Is the Iraq mission clear?" *Stars and Stripes*, October 19, 2003.

Other units said they were asked to get by on two bottles of water a day so regular Army units could have more bottles."[3]

Reservists also registered most of the complaints about having to remain in Iraq longer than they had been led to expect. While active duty units are told that they will serve a one-year tour, Guard and Reserve units have been instructed to plan on spending two years of service.

According to military sociologist Charles Moskos, "Seeing the children of the nation's elite also serving" is one of the key factors that influences troop morale, along with "unit cohesion [and] belief in a cause."[4]

With the exception of eleven members of Congress and three Senators, none of the members of the current administration, Congressmen, and Senators who voted—or voiced—support for the invasion, currently have children in the military. What's more, the vast majority of the pro-war politicians, including Paul Wolfowitz, Karl Rove, Kenneth Starr, Bill Frist, and Tom DeLay, didn't serve. Dick Cheney, John Ashcroft, and others used every avenue available to dodge the draft or avoid enlisting, obtaining multiple deferments to evade serving their country. Sean Hannity, Rush Limbaugh, Bill O'Reilly, Michael Savage, and most of the other warmongering pundits have never worn a uniform.

The cumulative impact of avoidance of military service by the politically and financially privileged, poor planning, inadequate training, a mercurial mission, insufficient weapons, equipment, and supplies, along with extended tours of duty and diminished morale can be calculated in the rapidly rising proportion of casualties suffered by the Guard and Reserve. An article in the *Boston Globe* revealed that as of October 29, 2003, the Guard and Reserve, with 35,000 troops stationed in Iraq at the time, had sustained a staggering 2,600 injuries outside the line of combat; out of 95,000 active duty soldiers, 3,897 were injured.

Rates of Reserve fatalities are also much higher than those of active duty Army. There were few Reservists directly involved in the initial invasion, and they've only recently become about a quarter of the fighting force, but they already represent sixty of the 360 soldiers killed in action, and 2004 is sure to bring more deaths. Department of Defense officials continue to maintain that the Pentagon doesn't differentiate casualty rates between Reservists and regular Army, but it doesn't take much sleuthing to uncover the numbers.

---

3. "From weekend warrior to full-time fighter." October 18, 2003.

4. "Esprit de corps higher when mission defined." *Stars and Stripes*, October 16, 2003.

I do some online research, trying to get a handle on how other families are dealing with this, and come across dozens of blogs written by mothers of soldiers in Iraq. Their fear for their children leaps off the screen, and they sound off about the rise in soldier suicides, not knowing when their kids are coming home, and their anger at the decision makers that send the sons and daughters of others to Iraq, but rarely, if ever, send their own.

Lorin's mom is more afraid than angry right now, but I know she's had some of the same thoughts. In an effort to protect her, I censor the information I share with her. Shortly after her visit with us, Lorin goes too, leaving me alone for a few days. It's a short week for both of us. The Thanksgiving holiday gives him a few days off, and he's back home Wednesday night. We're driving to Spokane to visit his father and mine, and we take off the next morning.

Lorin's parents met while Hardie was stationed in England, and Lorin was born a few years later. They were transferred back to the States when Lorin was seven, and from 1968 until 1970, Lorin was living on a military base in Minot, North Dakota, the same time I was in Bismarck, its capital. At that time, had the state chosen to secede from the nation, it had an arsenal of nuclear warheads sufficient to make it the third most powerful military force in the world. The government put the warheads in the middle of pastures and in the flat, barren prairie of one of the country's most sparsely populated states.

When I first got my driver's license, I would deliver parts for my dad's International Harvester dealership in Mott, always making sure the gas tank never went below the halfway mark. I'd drive for miles in the dry, dusty heat, my left arm burning brownish-red, listening to Christopher Cross on the radio until the signal from Dickinson faded and all I could get was the crop reports. Traveling along straight stretches of highway without ever seeing a town, a tree, another car, or a gas station, I learned how to be by myself.

Hardie, Helen, and their three young kids left North Dakota after a couple of years and eventually landed at Fairchild Air Force Base about twenty miles west of Spokane. Lorin's parents divorced years ago, but they both still live in the area. Coeur d'Alene, Idaho, lies thirty miles east of the Spokane Valley, where my father and step mom have been since 1993. This will be our final visit "home" until his return from Iraq. We never actually say it, but we're both intensely aware of the passage of time, counting the days we have left. Every now and then, it cracks through the wall that I've built around my heart that these are the last days I will have with him. Period. That hole is as deep as forever and I run from the edge.

As we make the slight descent into the Spokane River Valley, I ask Lorin if there's anything he misses about the town he lived in for most of his life.

"No, not really. I guess maybe the weather, because at least there are four seasons over here, not just rain and a little less rain. Oh, and I miss not being able to get wherever it is I'm going in less than twenty minutes. It's cheaper to live here, too. I miss that. But otherwise, no, there isn't anything I miss."

My time in this city was so brutal that, were it not for my family, I'd never return. But since Lorin got called up, I've longed for my folks like a child away from home. I tear up slightly with relief and happiness when we park in front of their white one-story house in Coeur d'Alene. We've got a long afternoon ahead, so pulling myself together, I open the door, and Crimson leaps out of the car. She trots up the driveway to see Pooh Bear, my dad's black chow dog. Pooh is so old that the fur on her muzzle has turned a whitish gray, but she summons enough energy to bark from the safety of the front porch before going back inside.

We join the dozen or so friends and family members already gathered; the women are mostly in the kitchen, moving between there and the table, setting things up for the Thanksgiving meal. As is typical, the men have formed a loose knot by the wood-burning stove in the living room. When Lorin and I arrive, their talk turns from sports to war, a subject they will not let go of for the rest of the day.

Finally, after everyone leaves and Lorin is asleep, I sit down with my Dad and his wife, Jean. They got married when I was in my late twenties, so she and I never went through the usual mother-daughter stuff. Without a long history of hurt trailing behind us, I became the daughter she never had; she's the surrogate mom I always wanted.

Sitting next to me on the loveseat, Russ, my dad, says, "Well, kiddo, it's good to see you. I'm glad you both could be here." He studies me for a moment, "So, tell me, how are you *really?* What's all this doing to you?"

With that, my whole heart breaks wide open. For the first time since all of this started, I talk freely, without worrying about Lorin, without feeling like I have to watch my words.

"I'm sad, and angry, and scared to death. This is all so wrong, and I don't want him to do this. A big part of me is angry at him for joining the Guard. I don't want him to get hurt, and I don't want to be without him for the next year or more."

Jean pulls closer the heavy patchwork quilt she's draped around her shoulders, nodding at me to keep talking.

"I never thought this would happen. He's only in the National Guard, for God's sake. I didn't think they were supposed to go to war. What if something happens to Lorin? I waited so long for him, and it's just not fair. I'm so worried about him getting hurt, and I'm even more worried about what this is going to do to him on the inside."

In a quiet, hoarse voice, my dad says, "I'm scared for him, too. I never thought one of you kids would have to go through this."

"I think one of the things that scares me the most is knowing that there's no way he'll be the same person when he comes home. Even if he isn't hurt physically, it's going to affect him mentally, and emotionally. I love him so much for who he is right now, and I don't want to lose that, but I know I'm already starting to."

They listen for a while longer and let me cry, and when it's time, send me off to bed. The next day, we go to a movie, while Lorin runs out to the Post Exchange at Fairchild to pick up a pair of heavy rubberized boots. In a remarkable military maneuver that my civilian mind cannot comprehend, the Army has Lorin's Brigade training for a desert war in winter conditions.

Exiting the theater, we find Lorin in the mall, and then Russ and Jean take off. Lorin and I walk two blocks down Main Street to meet his dad and Gerry, Hardie's girlfriend of eight months, at a pub called Cyrus O'Leary's. Along the way, we pass store windows with flamboyantly decorated trees and deep red bows made of velvet and satin. Lampposts hung with gold garland stars illuminate the falling snow, and I put my arm through Lorin's and tuck myself tightly against his side, wishing I could freeze frame life.

As usual, Lorin and his dad don't say much during dinner, leaving Gerry and me to talk about the computer classes she's taking at the local Community College, Christmas lists, and the latest fashions. Once we've exhausted these topics, she pulls out a little white jewelry box and hands it to Lorin.

"I hope you don't think I'm silly for doing this, but I really want you to have this."

Lorin sets his fork on his plate and opens the box, pulling out a tiny silver angel.

"I've had this for years. It's seen me through some awfully tough times, times when I didn't think I could go on. I know how worried your dad is about you, and I am too."

Her voice gets shakier with each word. "It's protected me for a very long time. I didn't think I'd ever be giving it away, but I want you to take this with you. It will keep you safe."

Taking Kleenex from her purse, she hands me one, and we use them on our tears. Our two men are silent, sitting very, very still, as if the slightest motion will be their undoing. Then the energy of the moment dissipates, and we finish our food, talking about little more than the weather, work, and sports.

I've got a ticket for the Gonzaga Bulldogs game in the morning, and Lorin's driving back to report for duty tomorrow night. It'll be our last time together for a while, so we get a hotel room in downtown Spokane. The next morning, my dad comes to pick me up for the game.

"I'm sorry, Dad, but I've decided to ride back with Lorin. I know you bought a ticket for me, and I'll pay for it, but it's just a game. Six months from now, I won't be missing the Bulldogs, wishing I'd seen them play. I'll be missing Lorin, and I don't want to wish I had spent this time with him."

I adore the Bulldogs. When my career and my life had gone down the toilet, that basketball program gave me something to believe in, and I loved them for it. I feel a pinch of regret at passing up my ticket for a seat at the arena. But it's nothing when compared to passing up the chance of a few more hours with my husband.

My priorities have shifted in a matter of weeks, and what used to seem so important simply isn't any more. Other things, like my time with him and my family, have become priceless. It takes a lot more to rock my boat these days, too, and things that would've set me off just a few months ago barely even register. War has become the great clarifier of my life.

It has also made me unbelievably vulnerable, and I stand there feeling foolish and exposed, crying in the middle of the hotel lobby, apologizing needlessly to my father while Lorin settles our bill at the desk. I suck it up, but start crying again, appalled at my weepiness. When my dad pulls back from our hug, I see the glimmer of tears behind his glasses.

Oh, Daddy, don't you cry, too.

Just then Lorin walks over and my dad, aware of my fragility, gently hands me off to him. There is something in the absolute tenderness of this gesture that reminds me of a similar exchange after my father walked me down the aisle on my wedding day.

The valet has put our bags in the car, and Lorin has to report for duty at eighteen hundred hours. After thirty-five miles of relative silence, I ask Lorin how the boys in his unit are doing.

"Well, they aren't saying too much, but I can tell they're scared."

"How? I mean, how can you tell?"

"I don't know, you just kind of feel it. They're hyper, really hyper, bouncing off the walls, getting into fights. A few of them talk about it, but not much."

"And what about you? Are you afraid?"

"Yeah, sometimes. Of course I am, but there's nothing I can do about it, so I've got to lock it away and focus on the training." His voice deepens, becoming serious and sure, "You know, when I get over there, I'm not just responsible for my own life, I'm responsible for the lives of more than twenty other men."

"Well, that's nice, but frankly, it's you that I'm most concerned about." I find the Gonzaga game on the radio and turn up the volume. The score is tied and going into overtime when the reception gets too poor to make out what the announcer is saying. Lorin clicks off the dial and resumes our conversation, the most he's opened up to me in weeks.

His eyes are focused on the road stretching out before us when he says, "Don't take this the wrong way, but there's a part of me that's almost looking forward to going."

After a quick sideways glance to confirm that my head is still attached to my neck, he explains.

"I hate the thought of leaving you, of not seeing you for a whole year, but sometimes I've wondered what it would be like to actually be in a war. I've spent all these years training, preparing for *something,* and this'll give me the chance to prove myself, to see if that training really pays off."

Jesus Christ. Please tell me I'm not hearing this, tell me those words did not just come out of his mouth. I don't even know where to begin. He knows there's a storm brewing inside me, and quickly tries to say something to avoid it, anything to make me understand.

"I'll have my twenty in soon, and this is the last chance for me to go to war. I've heard some of the other guys talk about their experiences, and I want to see what I can do, how I'll handle it."

I am out of my depth here. I can't believe he's talking about going to war like it's some great opportunity he doesn't want to miss. He'll have completed twenty years in June of 2004, but the stop-loss order issued on September 14, 2001, officially known as the Title 10 Executive Order, and unofficially known as the Back-Door Draft, could force him to put in almost another full year of service. He won't come home until late spring of 2005 at the earliest. In the past, National Guard troops have been deployed for six months, maximum, for "peacekeeping missions," which is what they're calling the ongoing war in Iraq.

"So this is an ego thing for you, a way to prove your masculinity? Please tell me that's not the case," I demand. "You don't have to prove anything to me, Lorin. I already know who you are."

I pause, then add, "Well, I thought I did."

I've got nothing else to say right now, and retrieve the magazines I bought to relieve boredom from the backseat. They've been stepped on by the dog and are torn and creased. I read about quasi-celebrities for the rest of the trip.

We're both dragging by the time we get home, but Lorin has less than an hour to get ready for his upcoming week of training. As we're saying good-bye, he suggests I start to participate in some Family Readiness Groups. I know I should go, if for no other reason than putting on a good show of support as the wife of a sergeant, but I don't want to.

The Family Readiness Group (FRG) is the result of more than a decade of training, analysis, and research conducted by the Department of Defense. All too aware that the soldier's deployment readiness depends on the family's readiness, and that wives have a significant impact on their husband's decision to reenlist, a comprehensive study conducted by the Army Research Institute for the Behavioral and Social Sciences recommended that supervisors and unit commanders "create soldier perceptions that you care about their families." And voilà, the Family Readiness Group was born, although it's come to the National Guard only after tens of thousands had already been called to active duty.

Each National Guard unit has a Family Services Coordinator (FSC) who organizes the Family Readiness Group, and it's typically one of the soldier's wives. As well as being a resource for spouses with questions about benefits, leave, and other concerns, the purpose is to facilitate a sense of community between the wives. Some of the other functions include setting up a phone tree, sending out regular e-mail newsletters, and putting together socials and activities, mostly fundraisers. They had a rummage sale recently and I donated a bunch of things, including an espresso maker we'd never used, and towels and pillows and clothing.

It triggered something in me, and each night that week I walked from room to room, pink terrycloth slippers chuffing on the hardwood floors, pulling out things we don't use, wear or love. I discarded bags and boxes of stuff, making repeated trips to Goodwill, filling the recycling bin to overflowing. I was preparing for the upcoming months, clearing space for whatever is to come, making a bargain with God that if I only keep the things I cherish, I can keep Lorin, too.

Maybe some of the other wives are doing this psychic clearing, but I don't know. The few social events that have happened were all scheduled on weekends when Lorin had leave, and I won't sacrifice time with him for anything. Besides, the only thing I have in common with the other wives is that our husbands are being deployed. I doubt that's going to make us best friends. It's not a group I want to join, anyway.

I don't want to be one of those women whose husbands are going away and might not return, and avoiding these meetings gives me a tiny degree of defense, a feeling of false safety, and I'm going to use it for as long as I can.

I have the TV on at night now, just for the sound, something I never did in all my years of living alone. The evening news is reporting on yet more casualties in Iraq. I don't bother to sit down. I already know more about this war than I ever wanted to, more about what's really happening to the men and women stationed in Iraq than I can process.

While trying to find out the human cost of the occupation, one of the things the government often files under the heading of "collateral damage," I stumble across a casualty counter on the Internet. It's a free download from Antiwar.com that gives instantaneous access to the most recently updated reports of American soldiers killed or wounded.

The tally also tracks the Iraqi body count and that of other coalition troops. It's meant to be an educational piece that serves as a deterrent, in your face proof of the price of war. But it just makes me hurt and swear and want to lash out. I check it every week.

A friend told me he'd seen the same sort of thing on the nightly news during the Vietnam War. He recalled his horrified fascination with the little box in a corner of the television screen. Night after night, he'd listen to the evening broadcast, watching the figures tick higher, rolling over like a speedometer when the hundred and thousand marks were reached. I suppose it's easier to accept the mounting casualties when it's just a number.

Lorin's going to turn forty-three in February, but he'll be gone before his birthday. He'll miss mine, too, along with next Thanksgiving and Christmas, and our anniversary. Lately, all I can think about is that at least thirteen months of my life will happen without him. A whole year or more will be missing from the photo album of our marriage, and I imagine looking through pictures decades from now. Flipping through pages covered by plastic sheets, will we stop and ask ourselves, "What happened here? There's a big gap between pictures." Only to remember, *Oh, yes, that's when you were at war.*

Who will he be when he comes home? Who will I be? Who will *we* be, together, and what will this do to our marriage? On his last twenty-four-hour leave, we'd skirted the issue.

"Do the guys talk at all about the possibility of their girlfriends, or wives, moving on while they were away?" I asked.

"Why? Are you thinking about divorcing me?"

"No, of course not. But I imagine that the number of relationships that break up escalates during active duty. If there were problems in the marriage, or if the girlfriend had already been thinking about ending things, a long separation is going to force the issue. It'd sure make it a lot easier to tell someone it's over when they're a couple thousand miles away."

Is it possible that I'm a sadist? I'm curious about this, and genuinely want to know, but am I avoiding some deeper truth about myself that I haven't considered? The stress of his impending deployment is bringing out dimensions of my personality that I didn't know were there.

I can tell he doesn't like where this conversation is going, but he grudgingly replies, "Well, yeah, I'm sure everybody's thought about it, or at least it's crossed their mind. But nobody's going to talk about that. No one wants to get a *Dear John* letter."

"I read that some of the guys over there have already gotten them, and there are even wives who're threatening their husbands, telling them that if they don't come home soon, not to bother coming home at all. What do you think about that?" I wait for his reply, but it doesn't come.

This is a sore spot for him, so I let it drop. Although he's got no reason to worry, and I've never done anything to make him believe otherwise, I suspect he will now harbor a shadow of a doubt for the next fourteen months. My shadows are of a darker nature.

I've been scouring the bookstores for firsthand accounts of women whose husbands went to war. There are precious few, especially those pertaining to the most recent U.S. military actions. I purchase *A Mighty Heart,* written by the wife of Danny Pearl, the journalist kidnapped and murdered in Pakistan. I devour it in one sitting, telling myself repeatedly that our story will be different.

It's similar to a shameful practice I've started wherein I keep track of the number of soldiers from the Pacific Northwest who have died in Iraq. Each time I hear of another death—three more today—I figure it improves the chances of Lorin coming home alive and in one piece. In a morbid application of the law of averages, I speculate that only a certain number of soldiers from this region will be killed, and therefore, each loss of life increases the odds that my husband will keep his. I hate myself for doing this, but I can't seem to stop.

It's my dirty little secret, and I don't speak of it at work, or anywhere else. Ever since Lorin was activated, Karen, the cofounder of the Institute, has been especially solicitous, asking about Lorin, letting me know she's there if I need to talk. I pop into her office Monday morning with some papers for her to sign. She's reading something online, and although she hurries to click on another window, I see the headline announcing two more soldiers killed in Iraq.

Our eyes meet briefly, but we don't say a word. She hands me an article along with the signed documents.

"I thought you might find this interesting. It's about a local woman whose son is fighting in Iraq. She's been speaking out against the war."

Still stuck on the announcement I'd seen on her computer screen, I thank her for the article, telling her I'll read it later. I tuck it into a drawer and get back to work making follow-up phone calls to the parents of the kids that got the letters for the peace workshop the month before. That weekend, my dad, my brother Steve, and his girlfriend, Monique, arrive for the Gonzaga/Missouri game, billed as the "Battle in Seattle."

On Saturday morning, Lorin's released just in time to join us. My family hasn't seen him in uniform before, and when he comes through the front door, it's like they're looking at a familiar stranger. Then he starts barking at everybody to get in the car, and it sounds like he's giving orders. I follow him into his office.

"What's wrong with you? Why are you so crabby?"

"I just got home, walk in, and there's people here, and I've got to hurry up and change so we can go to the game. There's nothing wrong." He replies tersely.

"Yeah, right. If you don't want to go, just say so. I'd rather have you stay here than come with, if you're going to be like this."

"Go see if they're ready, and tell them to get in the car," he snaps. "And make sure you've got the tickets."

Getting aggravated myself, I snap back, "Don't order me around, buddy, I'm not one of your soldiers."

"Look, just let me change my clothes so we can leave, alright?"

Throwing my hands up in defeat, I back out of the room. By the time we find our seats, the Key Arena is almost filled to capacity for the 11:00 a.m. tip. Lorin's on one side of me, chowing down on pizza and popcorn, and my dad stands to my left, wearing the beat-up brown leather driving cap he's had for as long as I can remember. Steve and Monique are a few places to the right, getting situated in the slat-backed stadium seats. I catch Steve's eye and grin.

We're on our feet when the Bulldogs hit the floor, and I scan the crowd, coming back to my three favorite men in the world. The game is hard, fast, and intense. The Zags pull it out after a couple of overtimes that leave me so breathless I have to sit down.

On the way home, we stop for coffee, and pick up a tree at Ikea. I'd half-heartedly begun decorating for Christmas earlier in the week, but gave it up quickly.

All of our neighbor's houses have plastic reindeer and snowmen, Santas on rooftops with hundreds of yards of blinking lights. Our little yellow house looks naked; it has no lights, and there aren't any decorations on the lawn. When we first moved in, we were told there was an unofficial contest in the cul-de-sac to see who had the best (meaning *most)* Christmas decorations. We are clearly the losers. One of my neighbors says they called our place the Scrooge house.

Well, by God, we're decorating tonight. With three Christmas CDs in the stereo, a fire blazing in the fireplace, and the results of the first wave of a cookie-baking extravaganza covering the kitchen counters, we spend the next few hours hanging ornaments, positioning stockings, and stringing lights.

We call it a night shortly after Lorin comes in from stringing lights outside. Between the game and our manic burst of holiday cheer, we're wiped out. Lorin gets up at some ungodly hour when it's still too dark to be considered morning. I dream there's a kiss on my forehead, and when I wake, he's gone. A few hours later, so is everyone else.

During the weeks that Lorin's away, I come up with small tasks for him to do when he's home. I want to reassure him that I need him now, and I'll need him when he gets back. I think he's afraid that, after being gone for more than a year, he'll return to find he's become obsolete. Christmas is the longest period of leave he's going to get, and December twenty-third is our third wedding anniversary.

He walks in that day around four, bearing silly little gifts and a beautiful card. Crimson goes crazy, as usual, licking his face, nibbling at the knees of his camouflage pants. She misses him too. I give him his presents and we run out for a pizza and a video.

After we eat, I put the movie in, and he's snoring on the couch before it's over. I watch the rest of the tape by myself, then shake him gently and lead him to bed, which he somehow manages to get into before he falls asleep again. Nine o'clock and the lights are out. Happy Anniversary.

My dad and Jean get in the next afternoon, and Lorin's dad arrives with his girlfriend and her three kids later that night. Helen and her husband, Paul, catch an early Christmas morning flight. For a few days, there's no talk of war, until I have the brilliant idea to go see *Cold Mountain.*

For me, watching how the Civil War affected the lives of the women left behind, while tracing one soldier's efforts to return home, the movie's story-line is a little too close for comfort. When Renee Zellweger's character, Ruby, says something about "sending men off to war with a flag and a lie," I elbow Lorin. Hard.

He keeps trying to convince me—or himself—that the government's rationale for this war was legitimate. It's not working. I'm appalled by the misinformation and outright lies about weapons of mass destruction, and add my name to thousands of others in a petition forwarded by MoveOn .org calling for an investigation and censure of President Bush.

I send letters to Senator Murray, and her responses are so specific and personalized that I'm convinced she's read them. I write to Washington State Congressman Adam Smith, and his reply states, "The nine-person panel commissioned to examine U.S. intelligence-gathering wouldn't report back with its findings until March 2005." Great. And until then?

Like a number of the other men in his company, Lorin has questions about the accuracy of the intelligence and how it's being presented. But he's given up trying to make sense of it. Instead, he focuses on the good they can do, the schools they can build, the people they can help. That's what he tells me, and sometimes it sounds like he believes it.

A few weeks earlier, Saddam Hussein was captured, and for a while the guys thought it might mean something. Lorin's cell phone rang persistently, soldiers speculating that perhaps they wouldn't be going now that one of the stated objectives of the occupation has been achieved. *Yeah, sure, and President Bush said the war was over, too,* I thought. Sure enough, the next morning it was confirmed they're still going, and his phone is silent.

I haven't been working since the middle of December, and I'm starting to get a little antsy about it. Karen's got my proposal to do some fundraising for the Institute, and I'm talking with a few other organizations, but everybody says the same thing: wait until after the holidays. Luckily, I can afford to.

Unlike many soldiers, Lorin's military pay isn't a cut from what he was getting paid at his regular job, so at least we don't have the financial pressure to contend with right now. Although I'm antsy, I'm glad to have this period to myself—no work demands, and I'm always available to be with Lorin when he's got time off.

Since we live in such close proximity to Fort Lewis, Lorin's managed to sleep at home occasionally, and he got another couple of "free" days when a few inches of snow shut down the whole Puget Sound, a region unaccustomed to anything besides rain. Except for the uniform, it hasn't been all that different lately from when he was traveling a lot for work. I've begun to think, "Well, this isn't so bad. I can do this."

At my desk in the upstairs nook that serves as my office, I click on my Outlook Express and find another message from Connie, the Family Services Coordinator. It contains the minutes from a meeting she had the day before with the Colonel of the 303rd. Lorin's unit. I scan it quickly, getting the gist of it right away, but I reread it several times before it really sinks in.

I get up from my computer and run downstairs. Flipping the page of the angel calendar I tacked on the kitchen wall last week, I begin counting backward. He will be gone in less than three weeks.

3

Countdown to D-Day

JANUARY 2004

CONNIE, THE FAMILY RESOURCES COORDINATOR for the 303rd Company, is outlining the afternoon's agenda to thirty plus women when I show up at the Armory for my first wives' meeting. I pick my way through the kids that are running around or playing on the floor and park myself on a bench. There are two rows of folding picnic style cafeteria tables set up in the gymnasium, and I nod hello to my tablemates. Most of them look so worn out and bedraggled that I cannot imagine what resources they'll be able to summon in the upcoming months.

Turning my attention to the front of the room, I try to make out what's being said. All I can hear are the scrapes and screeches of several dozen pairs of kids' tennis shoes echoing off of the hard, flat surfaces, and the nonstop yakking of the five heavyset women closest to me. I shoot them a dirty look, and then kick myself for it mentally.

They drop their voices enough for me to hear Connie shout.

"After a few brief announcements, we'll be doing an icebreaker, and you'll have a chance to get to know each other. Once we're finished, there are materials for making posters and you're all welcome to use them. Before we get started, I want to introduce you to someone."

She motions toward a guy with carefully barbered immobile gray hair standing off to the side with his arms crossed. He gives a stiff little wave that looks like a salute as he walks briskly to the front of the room.

"This is Dan, the new Family Services Support person," Connie says, and there's a light spattering of applause. "He's here to help you, and answer any questions you might have. He's an ex-Marine, and recently retired after thirty years in the active military, so he's got a lot of experience and he knows what you're going through." She takes a few steps back, gesturing for Dan to speak.

"Hello. I want to let you know I'm here for you. My office is right out in the hallway, and I'm here Monday through Friday. If you're having any problems, or need a support group or anything, just give me a call," he says in a clipped monotone, and then bellows, "Any questions?"

Sir, no sir! Nobody speaks.

"Well, if you think of something, I'll be right over there." Then he marches off to his post at the side of the room.

Another woman is introduced, but I can't hear a word of what she's saying. She pulls out the Family Readiness Handbook, which I got several weeks ago at the Family Support Briefing. It contains a predeployment checklist, information about employment rights, legal and financial issues, and a list of emergency and contact phone numbers. The pamphlet includes a thumbnail description of the history and purpose of the National Guard:

> The real mission of the Army and Air National Guard is to preserve peace and protect the people of our country, our state, and our hometowns.

The speaker begins walking us through the handbook page by page. I've already read it, and I tune out immediately, debating whether or not I should leave.

"Sshhhh. Quiet, everybody. Quiet! C'mon, let's hear what she has to say."

I can't tell who yelled, but at least the noise level drops enough for me to hear Connie say, "Now we're going to do the icebreaker. Everybody got a number when you first sat down, and I want you to find the other person with the same number. You have five minutes to get to know a little bit about them, and then you have to introduce each other to the group. Okay? Go!"

Extricating myself from the table, hoping I don't wind up being paired with one of the women I'd glared at earlier, I start asking around.

"Are you eleven?"

"No, I'm twenty-six." My patience for this game runs out after about a minute, and I step up to a woman with shoulder length straight blonde hair. She looks to be in her mid to late thirties, with a pleasant, open expression, and a spark in her eyes that I've come to recognize as a sign of innate intelligence. This one's got something to say, and I want to find out what it is.

"Did you get your number yet?"

"No, how about you?"

"No, me neither. Why don't we just do this?"

"Works for me. I'm Jen." She blurts, thrusting out her hand. Grasping her hand for a quick shake, I barely get the chance to introduce myself before she starts talking.

"What do you think about this? I'll just tell you right now that I'm not on board with this. I know a lot of the wives are kind of going along with it, or agree with it, or whatever, but I'm not on the war bandwagon. I'm really having a hard time with this." She inhales deeply, then it's off to the races again.

"I just don't agree with it. I don't agree with what our government is saying, or doing, and I don't think it's right that they're sending all of these National Guard guys away for so long. It's gotten so my husband is almost afraid to take me to any of the military events, because he never knows what I'm going to say."

Relieved to have found someone I can relate to, I reply, "Lorin's said that, too, but I try to watch myself, because I don't want to get him into trouble."

By now, the two women sitting next to us have quit talking, and are blatantly eavesdropping.

Jen explains, "Well, *I* never signed up for this. We just had a baby about a year and half ago, and I'm not working anymore. I sold my consignment business so I could be at home for her first few years. My husband's military pay is a lot less than he was making at his regular job, and we're just barely going to be able to get by. I never thought I'd be a single parent, which is what I'll be for the next year and a half, and this really interferes with some of our plans."

The other gals nod in agreement.

"We want to have at least two kids, and I'm in my late thirties. So now, I'll be over forty by the time we can even try to get pregnant again. And you know what the odds are as you get older. I've even thought about having my husband go to a sperm bank, and having them freeze it. You know, just in case."

Unbeknownst to us, thousands of soldiers are already doing this, having heard about the overwhelming number of birth defects in babies born to veterans of the first Gulf War.

"Oh my God, I thought I was the only one who'd thought about that, and Lorin and I don't even want kids."

The sweet-faced young woman next to me clears her throat, and I recognize her from the barbeque. Her husband is one of Lorin's men, and she's a doctoral student in biochemistry or physics or something like that.

"I thought about it, too," she says, and then, more tentatively, "Especially since I miscarried a while ago." Glancing around the table, she bursts into tears, mumbling, "I'm sorry, I don't mean to cry."

Jen says, "Oh, honey, it's okay, you can cry," reaching over, cupping her hand gently.

I look at Amy, the other woman in the little foursome that's formed at the end of the row of tables, somewhat taken aback by the instant intimacy. I'm not sure what to do with it, so I just sit there. Amy's eyes meet mine briefly, as she, too, reaches out in sympathy with one hand, the other cradling her full, round belly.

"Okay, who's next? How about you guys back there?" Connie asks, looking right at us.

"Jen, let's go, let's get it over with." I bound out of my seat, pulling her along with me. Once I'm up front, the lethargy of the group becomes apparent, and I feel as though I'm caught in some sort of human low-pressure system. It probably looks like I'm on the upswing of a manic-depressive episode by comparison, but just because our husbands are going to war doesn't mean we've got to stop living.

After quick introductions, we start back to our seats, but Jen detours to talk with Dan. She returns to the table less than five minutes later, shaking her head in exasperation as she says, "Uuhhhh, you probably don't want to talk to him. He's not going to be any help at all."

I'd figured as much. I'd dated a Marine once years ago, and while he had a lot of great qualities, compassion and empathy weren't among them. Addressing our little group, I ask, "What were they even thinking, putting him in that position? He's got the emotional depth of cardboard, not a great resource for a bunch of women with their husbands gone. It's typical military mentality."

I stall slightly before I continue, afraid of seeming too needy. "I know I, for one, am going to need someone to talk to, and I can tell you, it won't be Dan. Of course, I've tried talking to my husband, too, but he hasn't been that great, either."

"I know! I've even given my husband some brochures about communication. He says he reads them, but when I try to get him to open up to me, I can barely connect with him anymore," Jen says, and the rest of us murmur in agreement. "He won't talk to me about how he's feeling, or anything."

"Lorin's the same way, but I am really, really tired of being the only one who's showing any emotion about it." I resent him intentionally pulling away, leaving me before he's actually gone.

Our conversation is interrupted when Connie announces that it's time to make posters; the materials are on the tables in the corner. Nobody in our little group is especially interested in drawing and coloring right now, but I'm trying to be a sport about it. I'm pretty sure a poster for peace will not be well received, but I roll the dice.

"Say, Connie, would it be okay if I did one with a peace sign, or something about putting an end to war?"

Her face scrunches up as she peers at me, attempting to figure out if I'm trying to be funny. Once she sees that I'm serious, her expression becomes one of trying to talk sense to an idiot. A harmless one, but an idiot nonetheless.

Speaking in the tone of voice usually reserved for children (or, in my case, idiots), she replies, "No, these posters are really to encourage the troops, and let our soldiers know we stand behind them."

"Okey dokey then."

Before I leave, I give one of my cards to each of the wives in our little group, and grab a two-page flyer on my way out.

According to "The Seven Emotional Cycles of Deployment" handout, Lorin and I have already moved through stage one, "The Anticipation of Loss," which is summarized as: "Whether you're a man or a woman, it is PMS multiplied by a factor of deployment." If the information is reliable, we're smack dab in the middle of stage two, "Detachment and Withdrawal." We aren't really arguing, but we sure aren't intimate. He's in his corner, and I'm in mine.

Hoping to meet in the middle, I show him the information when he gets home, and tell him about the meeting.

"I saw Oman's wife again, and I met these two other women. Amy, and Jen, you might know her husband. I gave her my number and I really hope she calls, because she doesn't agree with this war, either. She's got a baby now, well, actually, the baby's about two, but before that Jen worked fulltime. She was the coowner of a store, and she's pretty sharp. I'd sure like to get to know her better."

Lorin's distracted, and not really listening, but I press on.

"Then, this guy, Dan, the Family Support guy, is an ex-Marine, just about the last person they should have hired for the job. Nobody's going to talk to him, nobody feels like they can. I went up to him on the way out, and it was like talking to a wall."

I rush forward, begging for attention.

"We were talking about how none of you guys are at all emotional. The other wives told me that their husbands are hardly communicating, and it sounded like there's been a lot of fighting. I know we haven't really been fighting, but I'm the only one who ever cries, and I'm not going to do it anymore, at least not when you're around."

Trying to get a response, I continue. "I can act like this isn't bothering me, too. After all, it's working for you. What do you think about that?" I pause expectantly. "Say something!"

"I will, if you'll let me," he replies, agitation making him louder than usual.

"I haven't cried because I'm not you. It's not that I'm not feeling anything, I just don't cry like you do. I'm sure I will, when the time comes, because I'll have to leave you. This is going to be the hardest thing I've ever had to do in my life. Not just going away, I mean, this whole next year. It will be the hardest thing I will probably ever have to do."

"So why don't you talk to me about?"

"Because I *can't*!" He barks, cementing himself into the corner of the couch. "I know this isn't right, but I've got to dehumanize the enemy. I can't see them as human beings, so in a way, I've got to dehumanize myself as well. I can't allow myself to feel things, and I've got to get ready for situations that I never thought I'd be in."

Holding myself very still, I wait for him to go where I think he's going.

Staring at something I can't see, he says, "There may come a time when I've got someone at gunpoint, and I'll have to make a decision. I'll have to follow orders. I don't know how I'm going to be able to look someone in the face and shoot. It's something I hope I never have to find out. But I might, and if and when that happens, I can't be thinking of the enemy as human."

He doesn't reply when I softly ask, "Did you ever stop to think that maybe *that's* the problem? Has it occurred to you that perhaps if we quit dehumanizing people, if we would allow ourselves to see them as human, just like us, that maybe we wouldn't be going to war in the first place?"

I don't want to make this any harder for him than it already is, don't want to compound the damage. I don't want to make his already impossible dilemma even more untenable, and I regret my words even as they come off my tongue.

Looking him squarely in the eyes, speaking in a calm, measured cadence, I say, "If that time comes, and you're standing there, looking into that person's face, I want you to imagine that it's me."

I cringe with remorse, wishing I could take it back. I didn't mean to be *mean*, and an overwhelming rush of fear and remorse sweeps through me. *How could I have said that? Aren't things bad enough already? Have I just, somehow, inadvertently, signed his death warrant? Will my words cause him to hesitate, and will that hesitation cost him his life? God forgive me. Lorin, forgive me, I'm sorry.*

There's enough guilt for both of us tonight, and we talk no more of war. But I am increasingly concerned about what the next year will do to him, and how long it will take to restore his soul.

I broach the issue of what's being done to help the soldiers after they return when I get together with Vicky a few days later. Her son is stationed in Iraq, and is a member of Military Families Speak Out, a group that's protesting the war and that instigated the "Bring Them Home Now" campaign. We got in touch through Military Families Speak Out (MFSO), cofounded in 2002 by Nancy Lessin and Charley Richardson. Their son is a Marine, and they joined with another military family in an attempt to highlight the need to prevent a U.S. invasion of Iraq. They sent out e-mails to everyone in their address books, and word of the organization continues to spread on the Internet.

Charley and Nancy receive messages daily from people wanting to join—family members with loved ones in Iraq, who feel a special need and have a unique role to play in speaking out against the war. Because it is our loved ones who are at risk, who are returning scarred from their experiences. And they're the people who will have to endure the injuries and deaths—their own, their comrades', and the thousands of innocent civilians' in Iraq.

We're often asked whether the efforts of the organization are damaging troop morale, but we believe many of the morale problems our troops are having are because they have been lied to. MFSO wasn't the entity that said the Iraqi people would greet U.S. troops as liberators; we didn't send our soldiers to war without sufficient housing, food, training, supplies, and support; we never told them they'd be coming home at a certain time, only to move back the departure date by several months; and MFSO didn't violate the implied contract that the political people who hold our loved ones' lives in their hands would put the good of the nation, and the welfare of its servicemen and women, above business interests and the quest for oil.

In less than two years, the group has grown to more than 1,500 members calling for an end to the war in Iraq and the return of all U.S. troops to their home duty stations. There are more military families speaking out in opposition to the Iraq war than there were during Vietnam. I joined several weeks ago, and they sent me a list of MFSO members in the Puget Sound area. I e-mailed Vicky explaining my situation, and asked if she'd be willing to meet.

Removing the white plastic cover from my little cup of Starbucks, I wait for her at a corner table in the store next to Barnes and Noble. At the small circular table nearby, two college-age girls with a laptop are discussing the numbers for the report they're working on.

I try to recapture what that felt like, being in my early twenties, when my biggest concerns were papers and tests, paying the rent, hanging out with friends, and picking up guys. I want to reach over and shake them gently, tell them to hold on to what they've got, to grab each moment and make it as big as they can. I want to impress upon them that their lives are going to change in ways they can't even begin to imagine.

I want to tell them that adulthood will force them into situations for which they cannot possibly prepare—situations that will define who they really are. Nobody ever told me this. I envy them and want to trade places for a while.

The little bell above the door dings, snapping me out of my reverie. A pleasant looking, middle-aged woman with a fair, strawberry blonde complexion makes eye contact with me, and walks to my table.

"Are you Stacy?"

"Yes, I am. You must be Vicky, thank you so much for agreeing to meet with me."

"Sorry I'm late. I'm going to get some coffee and I'll be right back." She deposits her bland tan coat on the back of the ironwork chair, revealing a smock-top shirt over her jeans. Fiddling with the newspaper I'd found at the table, I try to remember what I'd wanted to ask.

"Has your husband been deployed yet?" Vicky asks, getting settled across from me.

"No, he's leaving for Fort Irwin in California in about a week and a half. They're having a big deployment ceremony at the TacomaDome this weekend, and his folks are coming in for that. How's your son doing? Have you heard from him?"

"Not recently. He can't call very often, and when he does, it's usually for just a few minutes. The last time I talked with him was about three weeks ago."

"How was he? How did he sound?" I ask, wanting clues as to what to expect.

"Okay. He's not hurt, but he's tired of being over there. His year will be up in May, and he's supposed to come home."

"So, he's been there for, what, about ten months? Does it get any easier? For you, I mean?" I ask hopefully, willing myself not to give way to the tears suddenly blurring my vision.

"No," she says flatly, her eyes narrowing just a bit, knowing I wanted a different answer, unwilling to lie so I could have it. "It doesn't get easier, it just gets longer. It seems like he's been gone forever, and I think of him and worry about him every day. That's why I had to get involved, I had to do something. I work in computer programming, and I've never done anything like this, but I just didn't feel like I had a choice."

"I work in the nonprofit sector, and I've always been involved in human rights and peace and nonviolence."

"Well, this is new to me. I'm finding out a lot about the military, and about myself, too. I've spoken to a few groups about the war, and I actually like it. I've even done a few radio and newspaper interviews."

"Yes, I saw the article in the *Seattle PI (Post-Intelligencer)*. That's why I contacted you. I wanted to find out how I could get more involved. And also, I'm going to need people who understand what I'm going through."

"That's for sure," she says, an edge in her voice. "People who haven't experienced having a loved one go to war really have no idea what it's like. I know I didn't."

"So, what are you doing to take care of yourself?" I ask, listening intently for her response.

"Speaking out helps, and having my partner with me does, too. I'm taking care of my son's dog, so in a way it's like I've got a part of him here at home. I've also started learning about voluntary simplicity, and recycling, and other things. It's like there this whole new side of me coming out, and I really like it," she says shyly, eyes sparkling with delight.

Reaching into her battered brown purse, she pulls out a few small sheets of paper, unfolds one, and hands it to me.

"Here, this is for a meeting we're having for a project I'm working on. It's called Operation Soft Landing, and we're trying to pull together resources for the soldiers when they get home. A lot of these guys will be dealing with post-traumatic stress disorder, but the government isn't really doing anything for them. Do you know what PTSD is?"

"Yes," I say, nodding. "I did some research on it when I was diagnosed with it a few years ago. I know how it affects people, and how, if it isn't treated, it will stay with you for a lifetime. I've also heard stories about the Vietnam vets. My dad lived up in Bonner's Ferry, Idaho, for a while, and apparently quite a few vets have gone up there to hide out. Or kill themselves. He told me about vets who would just start walking the train tracks, waiting to get hit. At least once a year, there'd be another guy who committed suicide that way."

To which Vicky replies, "Did you know that when they're asked about PTSD and how to help the returning soldiers, the military is just telling people, 'Don't bother them too much, don't have a whole list of things for them to do when they get back. Just leave them alone for a while, and it will go away.'"

"How can they do that? Why don't they take better care of these guys? You know, Lorin still doesn't have his vest, and there are people over there who haven't gotten the ceramic plates that make the things more effective."

I'd read another article about it in Lorin's monthly issue of *Army Times*. That it's being delivered to my house is one more frame in the comedy of the absurd that I call my life. That, and the half dozen practice shells that are in our garage. Some snafu left them unused and unaccounted for, so Lorin brought them home, where they sit in a cardboard box in the garage. I wanted to return them to the armory, but he said no, it'd just cause all kinds of problems with paperwork. He tells me they're safe, not to worry, but when I suggest handing them out to kids in the neighborhood, he balks.

The Army paper had a spread telling the troops preparing for deployment what they could expect, drawn from the experiences of soldiers currently in Iraq. There was the dubiously titled segment, "Dressing for Combat Success," along with a list of some of the must-have items, such as sunscreen, shower shoes, spray or gel deodorant (otherwise it'll melt), a pair of durable, all-weather gloves, DEET insect repellant, and other gear that the Army doesn't provide.

Tucked toward the bottom of one page was a sidebar about mental health issues, reporting that at least fifteen percent of nonhostile deaths in Operation Iraqi Freedom were the result of soldier suicide. In one case, an Army sergeant from Fort Carson, Colorado, was so traumatized by what he'd seen in Iraq that he couldn't fulfill his duties, and was charged with cowardice. The Army later dropped the charges, their way of dealing with PTSD.

Vicky informs me of the next meeting of Operation Soft Landing, and I promise to be there.

The following Saturday morning, I'm trying to single Helen out from the dozens of people standing on the sidewalk waiting to be picked up at SeaTac airport. When I finally locate her, she looks smaller than I remember. She's fumbling with her cell phone as I pull up to curb, leaning over to open the passenger door of my little Rav 4.

"Good morning! I was just calling you," she says in the vaguely British accent that decades of living in the States has not erased.

"I saw that. I forgot to bring my cell phone. I never use it if I'm not making a long distance call, so I didn't even think to bring it with me. But I found you. How was the flight?" I ask, as we turn onto I-5, heading south toward Kent.

"Not bad, it's such a short trip."

"Good deal. Okay, here's the plan. First of all, I think it's important that we try to stay as upbeat as possible. Lorin said he just wants to be able to enjoy the weekend. He still doesn't know anything about the surprise party tonight, so we're good there. His high school friend, Harold, is definitely coming over from Spokane, and he's bringing Pat. I guess the three of them were roommates after they graduated from high school."

"Oh, good. That'll mean so much to Lorin," she says, her voice slightly wobbly. Glancing over, her eyes seem a little filmy, and the tip of her nose is the slightest bit red.

Oh, no you don't, I think, *not already*. Placing my right hand gently, but firmly, on her shoulder, I say, "C'mon, now, Helen, remember, none of that today. We're going to have a party, not a wake. That's how Lorin wants it."

I ply her with coffee, and then my step mom, Jean, keeps her occupied while I shower and get dressed for the day. Jean and my brother Steve had gotten in the night before. My dad had to work, and he couldn't make it for Lorin's last weekend at home. The four of us pile into Steve's pickup and head to Tacoma for the official sendoff.

An hour before the ceremony, the line of cars backed up at the two exits for the TacomaDome stretches for miles. Traffic cops direct us down a road where we sit in silence, crawling forward in the sluggish caravan. Forty minutes later, we find a parking spot about six blocks from the Dome, and join the hundreds of people trekking up the slight hill.

The crowd becomes more congested the closer we get to the Dome and lines snake around the massive circular building, people waiting to pass through the checkpoints on either side. It takes a moment for my eyes to adjust to the dimness inside. We pass by concession stands and skirt around vendors, making our way to a row of seats, claiming half a dozen. Filled to about two-thirds of its capacity, the cavernous structure can hold more than ten thousand spectators, and is used primarily for concerts, monster truck rallies, and sporting events. The smell of popcorn and fast food, sweat and celebration, hovers in the arena.

People are waving signs for their favorite soldier or unit; others chomp on pizza or hotdogs. Built for sound, the noise level hitches up a few decibels when a disembodied voice announces the procession of the 81st Brigade. Marching in single-file formation on either side of the cement floor that's larger than a football field, the desert-camouflaged soldiers are greeted by a cheering crowd. Go soldiers!

The Brigade was formed in 1968, and it includes armored, infantry, and cavalry battalions. In addition to the 3,400 Washington State members, with ages ranging into the fifties, there are another 1,100 Guardsmen from California and Minnesota. After nearly half an hour, all 4,500 soldiers are in formation. I'm trying to pick Lorin out of the masses, an impossible task given the distance.

Focused on the ceremony, I barely nod in greeting when Hardie and Steve join us. We're seated at the end of the arena opposite the dais. Giving up on finding Lorin, I sit back and watch the endless stream of soldiers, lambs to the slaughter. On and on and on, they march onto the floor, finding their designated spot with their unit, and then turning to face the flag hanging above the stage, next to a video screen of almost theater proportions.

Corporate logos are prominently displayed in the staging area and featured in the programs handed out at the doors. As the last man steps into place, the announcer's voice booms throughout the building, "Ladies and gentlemen, I give you the members of the Washington Army National Guard 81st Armored Brigade."

The crowd surges to its feet, yells and cheers reverberating to the steel rafters. Let the games begin.

"Please remain standing as Chaplain Jerry Pryor gives the Invocation."

After asking for a blessing for the friends, families, and soldiers, he starts talking about God being on our side. I tune out, knowing this is the same rationale used by the Taliban. The speaker snags my attention when he says, "You will encounter snakes and lions on the way. And though others will fall dead around you, you will be protected."

The sermon ends quickly, but not soon enough for me. If Lorin weren't here, I'd leave. I recall something I'd read a few years earlier in James Mulholland's *Praying Like Jesus*: "Greed wrapped in a flag and holding a Bible is still greed."

Then the announcer thanks the corporate sponsors. Governor Gary Locke makes a brief speech, followed by a Major General and a few other officials. Afterward, we catch up with Lorin at the designated spot. He's been in this building for almost eight hours, and is anxious to get out and go home.

As he steers the car onto the freeway, I turn sideways in my seat and ask, "So, how was that for you?"

"Boring. We just stood around the whole time."

"But wasn't it nice to be recognized?"

"We weren't recognized, this wasn't even about us. It was about the corporate sponsors. We didn't even need to be there. I'm surprised they didn't give us shoulder patches from Boeing to wear. What's next? Are they going to put signs on the tanks and humvees like they do at NASCAR? This war brought to you by Pemco?" he says sarcastically.

"I've got to admit, I was surprised by that, too. Even the program has logos, and there's a page in it thanking the corporate contributors. How can people still think there's no such thing as the military-industrial complex?"

"Anyway, what's the plan for tonight?"

"We're going to pick up Liahann and meet your dad and Gerry for dinner somewhere up in Seattle. Tonight is just for family," I say, holding to the premise we'd agreed upon to keep his surprise party a surprise.

We stop by the house so Lorin can change clothes. Steve helps him unload the car, sneaking the appetizers we'd made that morning into the storage compartment in the back. A couple of hours later, we pull up to the curb in front of the three-story pink-and-white-balconied building of Liahann's apartment complex. Since we've never actually seen where she lives, that's my excuse for us to go inside. I want him to be the first one through the door, but the narrow third-floor hallway doesn't leave room for me to slip behind him easily.

Liahann invites us in to her cozy four-room space, and I find a spot near the couch, a few yards from the door. Lorin is right behind me, and as soon as he starts talking, at least a dozen people come from the kitchen around the corner.

"Surprise!" his coworkers, high school buddies, and friends from Spokane yell in unison.

Lorin steps back and does a double-take. Spotting his old roommates, Harold and Pat, his eyes get even wider. They've come almost three hundred miles to be here, after working all day at the Spokane Convention Center. Struggling to find his voice, all he can say is "Wow!"

Toasts are made, and the celebration is underway. We take turns gathering around the computer screen for a PowerPoint presentation of Lorin's life.

Helen's been working on this for weeks, and the first few frames are black-and-white baby pictures, soon replaced by color shots of a lanky teen sporting a huge, fluffy Afro. These give way to our wedding photos, and the montage ends with Lorin in uniform.

He spends most of the night catching up with old friends and coworkers. His sister keeps fixing him exotic drinks made with fruit and rum, and Pat's big on the tequila shooters. My brother drives us home, and I join Lorin as he stumbles off to bed.

By the middle of the next afternoon, the worst of his hangover has passed, and we spend the rest of the day lounging. He reports for duty the following morning, and the week blurs by. Suddenly it's Saturday, Valentine's Day, our last night together.

Alisa asked me to bring Lorin over for a few minutes, and after inviting us into her house, she almost crushes me with her embrace. There'd been a night a few weeks back when I'd come to her, crying so hard it hurt. She watched helplessly, trying to comfort me as I sobbed, seeming not to care about the mess of snot and tears that was saturating her shirt.

"Jordan! Shannon! Come here, you guys. Lorin's here."

Her two little boys run into the large living room, skidding to a halt when they see Lorin standing there in his khaki uniform. Jourdan, the youngest, can never remember Lorin's name, so when the boys come over to visit the dog, or get some candy, or just hang out and play with the toys and Scooby Doo and Cinderella coloring books that I keep around for them, he'll ask me where "the Man" is. Shannon remembers, though, and has something he wants to read for Lorin.

Adjusting his little wire-rim glasses, he opens the family Bible to a bookmarked page, and reads:

The Lord is my Shepherd, I shall not want.
He maketh me lie down in green pastures: he leadeth me beside the still
    waters.
He restoreth my soul: he leadeth me in the paths of righteousness for his
    name's sake.
Though I walk through the valley of the shadow of death, I will fear no evil.

My eyes meet Alisa's over his bowed head, and we both look away quickly as Shannon finishes the verse. Breaking the stillness in the room, Lorin pats his shoulder and says, "Thank you, that was very good. I brought you something that I'd like you to wear, if you want to."

Pinning the chevron bars to the collar of Shannon's red polo shirt, Lorin says, "This pin is my rank, it means that I'm a sergeant."

A wide-eyed Shannon inspects the insignia, and Lorin calls out to Jordan, "Hey, little guy, come here. I've got something for you, too."

Both of the boys are biracial, beautiful children with clean, balanced features, close-cropped curly hair, and golden brown buttery skin. I've imagined that had Lorin and I had kids, they might have looked like this. But only if we were very, very lucky.

Jourdan is ridiculously cute, with an impish grin that tells me he knows it. He approaches Lorin somewhat bashfully. Dipping into a squat, Lorin looks at him, and says, "This one's for you. It's the crest from my unit. You see that right there, that's the arm of a knight, just like the one we have at our house."

Once the pin is in place on his sweatshirt, the two boys say thank you, dashing off to compare their new treasures. Our clock is ticking, so we don't linger for too many minutes more before crossing the twenty or so yards from their door to ours.

After dinner, Lorin spends time straightening his office, doing some last-minute packing and reorganizing. Much as I want his full attention, I know he's got to get this done, so I occupy my time, if not my mind, with paperwork: double-checking wills, life insurance, and other documents that I hope I'll have no use for in the upcoming months.

I'm sitting on the couch watching television when he joins me.

"What time do you need to be there tomorrow?" I ask.

"No later than six or so. We'll have to leave here by five. Sorry," he says, knowing I'm not a morning person.

"What time do you want to go to bed?"

"I don't care if I don't sleep at all tonight. I'll get plenty of sleep on the plane."

"Okay."

After staring at the TV for a while, I nudge down the volume with the remote. "I don't know what to say right now. I don't know what I'm supposed to do. I feel like I've already said everything I needed to say, and I'm not going to spend our last night crying."

"Yeah, I know, it's kind of weird. Right now, all I want is to be here with you. I just want you next to me."

He cradles me in his arms, and we stay that way for hours. When I can no longer keep my eyes open, I go to our bedroom and lay down, not bothering to undress. Less than four hours later, I feel the weight of him pressing into the edge of the bed as he whispers, "Stacy, honey, get up. It's time."

I can barely make out his shape in the still dark room. Smelling the clean, astringent scent of his Irish Spring shower soap, I reach up to rub the sandpaper of his shaved head, brushing the stiffly starched sleeve of his uniform.

"Coffee's ready, there's a cup waiting for you."

I'm just starting on my second cup when he tells me we have to get going.

"How soon?"

"Maybe five minutes."

"Come here, then. I want you to listen to this."

He takes a seat on the couch while I cue up the Josh Groban CD I'd loaded in the stereo the day before. Waiting for "The Prayer" to begin, I join him and say, "I'm going to tell you this once, and then I don't want to talk about it again, because we both need to believe that you're coming home. But, just in case something should happen, I want you to know that you are the love of my life. You are the only man I *could* have married, and I would do these last three years with you again in a heartbeat. You are my perfect husband, my only husband, and if there is one word I would use to describe being married to you, it's grace."

I shush him before he can speak, saying, "Now listen, sweet bear, I want you to hear this song." Then I memorize every single feature of his face, the way he looks and feels and smells and moves as the music soars and swings from the speakers:

> *I pray you'll be all right*
> *And watch us where we go*
> *And tell us to be wise*

In times when we don't know
Let this be our prayer
As we go away
Lead us to a place
Guide us with your grace
To a place where we'll be safe

For the first time since this all began, my big, strong, precious man in his camouflage uniform allows me to hold him. I kiss the top of his head as his tears drop on my lap. I've not been exposed to the raw truth of his vulnerability, his fear, sadness, and need for me, until now.

Much too quickly, we're showing our IDs at the Fort Lewis gate. There are no other cars in the predawn darkness, and it's not until we turn the corner near the old barracks that I see any sign of life.

Dozens of soldiers are crowding the sidewalk and spilling into the dead-end street. Shuttling from the doors of the ancient white barracks where they've spent the last of almost ninety nights, they're hunched forward slightly in an attempt to counterbalance the hundreds of pounds of clothing, guns, and gear that they carry in their rucksacks. Staggering from the weight, I watch them move into a loose group at the edge of an open parking lot, standing on cement, grass, and Washington State soil for the last time in months.

Lorin gets out to gather up his men, disappearing briefly into the barracks, returning with a heavy black gun slung across his torso. I am both appalled and vaguely fascinated by my first sight of him with a weapon.

I once shot a gun, a .22 I believe. My father took me to an outdoor range when I was nine or ten. I pulled the trigger a few times, and handed the gun back as I told him, "I will never do this again."

Everyone here's got a high-powered automatic military rifle, and the firepower is sufficient to take out a small community. Slung low in an over the shoulder carrier, they point to the ground. Stupidly, I wonder what cause all of these young men have for carrying all of these guns.

A "Hoo-ah!" breaks the early morning silence. I can almost smell the testosterone filtering through the air and into the vents of the car. I want to pull Lorin out of there, get him into the vehicle and drive, screaming off of this base, never looking back. What can I say or do that will suddenly break through his consciousness, touch his heart, and move his spirit in such a way that he says "NO"? There is nothing.

"Well, I guess this is it," he says, opening the door for me to get out of the car.

Crying silently, wrapped in his arms—I will not be hugged like this, or even really touched, for many, many months.

I smother him in kisses until he reluctantly pulls away. I ask, one last time, "Are you sure you want to do this?" which quickly turns into the plea, "Don't go." But he does.

Sitting in the driver's seat of his Sorento, struggling fiercely to smile, I say, "See ya in a couple."

Watching as the question mark in his mind turns to understanding, then relief, and then finally, approval, I throw the truck in reverse, and pull out of the dirt lot, looking at my husband and his soldiers. It's still dark, so I can't really make out the features of the men, but I recognize Lorin's frame and gait. I glance over my shoulder one last time, catching a glimpse of him, surrounded by his unit.

I have to drive, now, or I will never leave. I turn right at the corner, fighting the overwhelming urge to make a sharp left that will take me back to him. Staring straight ahead, I point the car toward home. Less than an hour later, I crawl into the still-warm bed. Just before dropping off to sleep, I recall the note I slipped into one of his pockets, wondering how long it'll be before he finds it.

Dear Lorin:
In the midst of all that's going on, I wanted to make sure you knew how grateful I am to you for the following:

Being my husband, my lover, my love, and my friend.
Being patient.
Being willing to talk about things that aren't always easy to discuss.
Being able to forgive me when I do stupid things or say words that I don't really mean.
Being able to believe in me, even when I can't believe in myself.
Being able to recognize that marriage is sometimes about compromise, and if I have sacrificed time and put some things on hold—in the past and now—for you to realize your goals and do what you need to do, I recognize that you have sacrificed also, often carrying more than your share of the financial burden.
Being wiser than I am in some ways.
Being willing to not announce it repeatedly.
Knowing more about parts of me than I seem to myself.
Respecting the courage of my convictions, even when they are different from yours.
Agreeing to move out of Spokane.

Finding a safe place for the pets and me for the next twelve months.

Going to the store to "pick up a few things," even if I don't really need them.

Standing in line with a box of tampons and the *National Enquirer* (both of which actually *are* things I need).

Being the answer to every prayer I have ever prayed for love.

4

A Flag and a Prayer

MARCH 2004

THE HOUSE FEELS DIFFERENT when I wake up, like it knows he's gone for real. Needing the distraction, I make a list of projects, and start painting the heavily textured Pepto-Bismol pink walls in the living room and hall. I pull out a couple of half-used cans of white paint, and open a pack of foam rubber brushes, one, two, and three inches wide. I'm not in a hurry.

Later in the week, I go to a market research focus group for members of the military and their immediate family. After checking in at the front desk, I park myself on a low table and browse through magazines until we're ushered into a small conference room.

I end up sitting next to a man in his mid thirties, wearing tan trousers with a razor crease and a flight jacket. On my other side is an elderly gentleman in jeans and a red plaid shirt. Of the thirty or so people, there are eight women, ranging in age from their mid twenties to somewhere in their forties. A handful of men are wearing uniforms from various branches of the military, and the rest of the guys appear to be veterans.

The facilitator stands, and welcomes the group, saying, "I want to hear whatever comes to your mind. There's no right or wrong, and everybody's entitled to their opinion." His first question is, "I want you to imagine that I'm from another planet, and don't know anything about this country. What can you tell me about it, what's going on right now?"

Several of the men start talking at once, volunteering things about the war in Iraq, the 2004 Presidential election, and other current events. The facilitator asks for more information about American culture, and people comment on the media, big cars, fast food, and computers and technology.

I add, "There's one thing you need to understand about this country: *Everything's* for sale."

A few heads turn, and the group leader raises one eyebrow, glancing at me and then nodding his head slightly as he looks into the three-by-five-foot one-way mirrored glass window on the wall nearest me. I think of Kafka and wonder if they'll be coming for me in my home. We move into a discussion about the war in Iraq, and again, the men in the room do all the talking. They're loud and louder, interrupting each other aggressively, although they're all saying pretty much the same thing.

After informing us that he recently returned from serving near Baghdad, and that he'd go again in a heartbeat, a young soldier concludes with, "I fully support the war. We need to kick their asses."

Hard-edged chuckles are emitted from the others in uniform, and most of the men and women around me seem to have caught the scent of blood.

I ask, "Is it really necessary, though? I mean, surely, if we've got the kind of creativity that produced the Internet, for example, we should be intelligent enough to resolve conflicts without violence."

The air force guy next to me shakes his head and says with a smirk, "God save me from peace protesters."

A retired military man follows with, "Those people scare me. Look at how violent they got at the World Trade Organization protest."

All of a sudden, everybody's talking at once, and we're told to take a ten-minute break. Once we're back, the facilitator asks,

"Since you're all connected to the military, what could be done to make your lives better?"

A mousy woman who's done her best to disappear until now finds her voice and says, "For starters, they could provide medical benefits to family members for the whole eighteen-month activation period, instead of just twelve."

A handsome, dark-haired woman sitting almost directly across from me says, "What I'd like is more support for the families of Reservists and Guard members. We don't have access to the established support resources that families of fulltime soldiers have, partly because we don't live on base."

"Well, I do, and let me tell you, one of the things that would help us is better pay." After a second of hesitation, the tired-looking blonde continues, her voice tight with anger, "Even though we shop on base, my husband's pay is so little that sometimes, by the end of the month, me and the kids are just barely scraping by."

The elderly man in the plaid shirt who's been sitting next to me, watching, speaks up for the first time, "I'm retired military, and I go to the V.A. hospital about once a week. What I'm most concerned about is that the government doesn't provide benefits to soldiers wounded in action unless they've got twenty years of service."

I ask, "Wait a minute, are you telling me that someone who's got more than nineteen years in the service could get wounded in action, and not receive benefits or long-term medical care?"

"Yes," he replies, "that's exactly what I'm saying."

That could be Lorin, I think, wondering why none of the men in uniform are saying a word.

I speak next, "I'll tell you what the government, and the military, could do to make my life better: realize that war, like, slavery, is morally abhorrent, fundamentally unsustainable, and ultimately dehumanizing for us all."

The temperature in the room drops a few degrees, and I notice the few African Americans are lowering their heads. The black soldier who'd spoken up earlier with such enthusiasm for war slumps in his chair, busying himself with an examination of the industrial-grade carpet.

In the silence, I can feel thoughts of "traitor" and "betrayal" and "Un-American" rocket through the air, aimed at me. I'm used to it. Suggesting that war isn't a good idea has never won me any popularity contests. My proposal that violence meets the definition of insanity—that is, doing the same thing over and over, hoping for different results—has never been well received. I've found that, at least in certain circles, advocating for peace pisses people off.

The facilitator steps in and thanks us for our time. I'm the first one out of the room, pocketing a crisp hundred-dollar bill, the first money I've made in months. When I talk with Lorin that night, I mention the focus group briefly before asking how he's doing.

"I'm okay, just really tired. They've got us in what's basically a circus tent, and the lights are on all night, which makes it really hard to sleep. Plus, I had to move Padgett to the other side of the tent because he was snoring so bad."

"Worse than you?" I ask teasingly.

"Way worse than me. There are a couple hundred guys in the tent, and our cots are right next to each other, so you can hear everything. And believe me, I do mean *everything*. Better yet, different units get up at different times, so alarm clocks start going off at around three or four in the morning. I'll hear a bunch of buzzers, and then it's quiet for a little while, until the next round. It's goes on like this for hours. Every time I start to fall back to sleep, a dozen more alarms ring. It drives me crazy. I don't sleep, I just lay there."

"How's everything else? How's your training going?"

"Part of it's bad, it's a lot of crap," he replies, frustration churning up his voice.

"Could you be a little more specific than that?"

"We did a practice drill, and my guys were searching a truck to make sure there weren't any explosives planted on it. They missed a bomb, so if it were a real-life scenario, two of my men are dead, and five more wounded."

Several long seconds later he adds, "I was talking to one of the guys afterward, one of the ones who would've been dead. He told me that when he was lying there on the ground, all he could think about was his daughter's voice. It was a reality check for a lot of us, and it really got me thinking about where we're going."

"Well, are you ready? You've got to have your head together on this."

"I'm ready, and I do have my head together, most of the time."

"Most of the time isn't going to cut it, honey. I don't think you get a lot of do-overs in Iraq."

We talk for a few minutes more, until he tells me he's got to go. He hasn't eaten yet today, and if he doesn't get in line soon, he won't. The soldiers have to queue up for everything, sometimes for several hours, the row of uniforms stretching for more than a quarter of a mile.

Over the next few days, the news is focused on the reasons that the Bush administration presented to justify the invasion. Everybody's talking as if violent conflict is rational, which it never is, at least, not completely. So that whole premise just doesn't make sense to me from a couple of different angles.

If war is sane and lucid, then why not just run the numbers, do a cost-benefit ratio of human lives lost, billions of dollars spent, and everything else that goes into the bottom line of war? As far as I can tell, it's a financial and moral white elephant. And I've never ever been in an argument that was purely rational; it's always at least partly emotional. That's the nature of the beast.

But the media, and the public debate, is fixated on President Bush's statement that the United States "must not ignore the threat gathering against us. Facing clear evidence of peril, we cannot wait for the final proof—the smoking gun—that could come in the form of a mushroom cloud. . . . We have every reason to assume the worst, and we have an urgent duty to prevent the worst from occurring."[5]

Nothing I've read or heard has ever confirmed there was an imminent threat. As I pick up the phone to call my father, I wonder how a country can go to war on such vagueness.

"I talked with Lorin last night."

"Yeah, how's he doing? We've been thinking about him a lot recently. Damn that George Bush."

With a *what in the hell was he thinking?* coloring my voice, I say, "Lorin told me he put in for early leave. He'll be going five days from now, first to Kuwait, and then to some camp just north of Baghdad."

Russ listens intently as I tell him about the drill where they missed the bomb.

"He sounded really tired, and depressed. I think it's finally starting to sink in, just what they're going into. He's realizing that the war games are over. Now it's the real deal."

I tell Russ about the sad, lonely letter that I got from Lorin.

"Those letters and packages are going to be his lifeline. As soon as I have the mailing address, I will forward it. Poppa, I've got to tell you, this is not my best day. I can't say anymore right now."

Lorin's advance team is part of the biggest rotation of Army National Guard soldiers ever, and when it's over, forty percent of troops serving in Iraq will be citizen soldiers. The troop replacement has been extensively publicized, increasing the potential for ambush, and a recent article about the "Big Swap in Iraq" described the confusion in the chain of command as a "speed bump."

Speed bump? It involves thousands of people, potentially their lives, and millions of dollars of equipment, and they call it a speed bump?

I'm itching to do something, so I attend my first meeting of Operation Soft Landing at the Bothell branch of the King County Library. Vicky's there, along with a few members of Veterans for Peace, and everybody asks about Lorin. The meeting opens with the old business. A few minutes later, a slender man with a long graying ponytail tiptoes into the room, as if the four of us won't notice him in the eight-by-twelve-foot space so long as he doesn't walk flatfooted.

We exchange greetings before resuming our talk, and moments later, ponytail man says to me, "You must be an officer's wife."

---

5. *Washington Post*, January 28, 2002.

I reply, "Well, I don't know about that. My husband is a Sergeant First Class but he's not a commissioned officer," giving him an exasperated smile. He's got no way of knowing that I have heard this before, and am baffled by what it is about me that would make people assume this.

The rest of the time is spent talking about a new name for the group, and I leave feeling frustrated and a little disappointed. The only thing they'd actually decided to do was participate in the Global Day of Protest on the one-year anniversary of the war in Iraq. I'm already on the program, which takes place about a week after Lorin lands in Kuwait.

Lorin calls from a hangar somewhere in California where he and the rest of the advance team from the 81st Brigade are waiting for their flight. After a bus ride to a small private airport, they've been trying to keep themselves occupied, watching *The Passion of Christ,* followed by *Saving Private Ryan.*

I sarcastically ask, "What's lined up for the inflight movies? How about *Born on the Fourth of July,* or maybe *Full Metal Jacket,* and then, right before you land, you could all watch the unedited version of *Platoon.* You know, just a little something to get you in the mood."

I am a very bad person. He calls again late in the afternoon, right before he's airborne, just as I go into an interview for a management position at the Hate Free Zone. I lose my focus once or twice during the next sixty minutes, but overall, I think it goes well, and leave feeling cautiously optimistic.

Lorin calls early the next morning from an airport in Maine, waiting to board the flight to Germany, and then Kuwait. I'm keenly aware that this is our last conversation while he's standing on American ground. I tell him repeatedly that I love him, and then, sniffling, I place the handset of my princess phone back in its cradle.

I start to sob; it's not a pretty cry. Crimson lifts her head at my distress, pawing my knee. Since Lorin's been gone, she follows me everywhere, and has taken to lying under my desk, making it hard for me to move my chair without the wheels rolling over her tail. I continue to cry, gripping the wooden railing as the dog licks my tears from the floor.

After what feels like an hour, but is probably less than ten minutes, I dry my eyes and grab the dog's leash from the cupboard. This sends her into frenzied laps around the living room, hurdling the coffee table and leaping onto the couch.

The little neighbor boys are playing outside, and they run toward us, dropping their plastic swords and helmets.

"Stacy, can I go for a walk with you?" Shannon asks.

I say yes, and then Jourdan, Hayden, and Jacob want to know if they can go, too.

"That's fine with me, but we'll need to check with your parents," I reply, feeling lighter already.

Crimson is straining at the leash, so once they've all got permission, we take off at a run out of the cul-de-sac. I'm jogging about ten steps behind Crimson, and the boys are riding their beginner bikes, little legs pumping to keep up. They weave around one another, circling me and the dog as we make our way down the street. We're just a few fezzes short of a Shriner parade.

We spend some time playing at the park and I begin to feel better. But I spend a restless night dreaming of planes full of soldiers falling out of the sky, then of myself in a classic fifties-style convertible with the top up. I'm racing down a nearly empty rain-slick street in the middle of the night, trying to outrun the vehicle next to me. At a stoplight, I roll down the window and peer out across the passenger seat to look at the driver of the other car. I am racing with myself. I wake feeling groggy and vaguely nauseated, unable to shake the remnants of my night visions.

The last vapors burn off in the clear morning light as I drive to Lake Forest Park for the weekly Saturday peace vigil. I see a couple dozen people with banners and signs walking back and forth at the intersection of Ballinger and Bothell Way. I slip into the jacket of one of Lorin's uniforms, making my way toward the corner. There are four lanes of traffic, and people wave and honk from their cars as they pass by.

A twenty-something white guy, wearing a kilt and a black leather jacket, silver chains and metal studs, stands at the corner of the sidewalk. He nods tentatively as I approach, unsure if I mean trouble in my camouflage jacket. I duck my head slightly in response, trying to convey that I'm one of them, but he still follows me with his eyes. There are a few men with shaved heads and orange robes, but most of the people here are crunchy granola types.

I move purposefully toward the center island where the streets converge, and a car speeds around the corner as the driver screams, "F***ing hippies!" Settling in a lotus position next to a tree with a yellow ribbon tied around its base, I sit in the middle of the graveyard. The verse I memorized in the third grade floods my mind:

In Flanders Fields the poppies blow

There are nearly six hundred thin white plywood crosses and makeshift tombstones punctuating the triangular island, each standing about a foot and a half above the green grass carpet.

Between the crosses, row on row

Put there earlier that morning by members of Lake Forest Park for Peace and Sound Nonviolent Opponents of War, they represent the number of American soldiers killed in Operation Iraqi Freedom. So far.

That mark our place

I thought I had steeled myself for this, but now, sitting here, crosslegged in the grass, my heart is rent.

And in the sky, the larks

I think of the men and women gone, of the children without parents, of the mothers without sons. I think of the overwhelming grief of the wives left behind, of the millions of women widowed by war over the centuries, of mothers birthing, and later burying, their children.

Still bravely singing, fly

I think of sisters losing their beloved little brothers, of the hundreds of Iraqi women who have vanished since the war began. When will this world have had its fill of women's tears?

Scarce heard amid the guns below

I weep for the thousands of people in Iraq who have already died, and those who will surely die today.

We are the dead. Short days ago we lived, felt dawn, saw sunset glow.

I cry at the ceaselessness of war, and at the certain knowledge that my husband's boots are now on the ground.

Loved, and were loved, and now we lie in Flanders fields.[6]

Eventually, I turn toward the sun. The group of peaceful protesters has grown to perhaps fifty people standing or walking along the boulevard.

---

6. "In Flanders Fields," John McCrae, 1915.

They're talking to one another or swapping slogans with the people driving by. But this is a time for peace, so I say nothing. I hold this space on the damp, cool earth that has hollowed a bit, and cups me where I sit.

After one hour, I stand, brush off my jeans, and walk to my car. That night, I read about the bombing of a Baghdad hotel that kills Iraqi civilians. The headlines report the deaths of dozens more, mostly Marines, some U.S. contractors, all human beings. The following days bring news of an escalation of violence, particularly in northern Iraq, near my husband's base.

I draw shut the hanging vertical blinds in our living room, imagining this will protect me. In the same batch of mail that contained Lorin's latest pay stub was the Department of the Army's Casualty Reporting Process. I figure if I can't see the Casualty Notification Officer and Chaplain, and they can't see me, they can't make a report.

Several long days go by before Lorin calls, and I'm giddy with relief when I hear his voice. Sounding just the tiniest bit disappointed, he tells me he's still in Kuwait, and he's bored. His Mortar Unit packed two dozen Conexes with tanks, HMMVs, guns, shells, ammo, and other supplies before they left Fort Lewis, but the ships carrying the gear still haven't been allowed to dock. Once they can unload, the convoy will drive five hundred miles to Camp Anaconda at about forty miles an hour, a very slowly moving target.

The phone keeps cutting out, but before we hang up, I tell him that I've been asked to read some of the names of the American soldiers, allies, and civilians who've been killed in Iraq at the Global Day of Protest on March 20th, the one-year mark.

I-5 heading into Seattle is even more congested than usual for a Saturday morning, and I'm a few minutes late. I hurry over to the cluster of volunteers at the First Baptist Church, and we do a quick practice run as the semicircular sanctuary begins to fill. By the time we start the program, there are probably three hundred people in the pews, and dozens more in the hallways and on the balcony. A local children's choir performs, and then I join two other readers at the front of the church, taking my place behind a microphone.

Sunlight streams through the red, yellow, and blue stained glass windows; an amber-colored haze hangs in the air. There is a solemn sense of purpose, a gravitas that even the nest of reporters in the back and creeping along the sides cannot disturb. I begin a litany of death. After each name, the trumpet sounds. About halfway through, a flutist begins to play, and the music seems to soothe the crowd, smoothing out the edges.

I set aside the thoughts of my husband that threaten to bring my house down, and take my turn reading the names of people I'll never meet, my voice cracking only twice: first, when declaring the demolition of a whole family, and second, when a Jewish woman begins chanting "Shalom, shalom, shalom." Her sweet, pure voice seems grounded in the heart of the earth. I feel the flash of all of those lives leaving the planet. It's almost as if we had called their spirits when we read their names, and I cannot shake the sense that they are gathered in the rafters high above the room.

After one hour, I offer a benediction to the crowd, the living and the dead. For a moment, no one moves, like we're all waiting for God to go first. The spell is broken and people file out onto the street, where a crowd has already gathered for the march to the pier. I descend the three steps and take a seat in the corner of a wooden pew in the front row, lowering my head so that my tears fall directly on the floor. I had hoped to be able to wait until I had the privacy of my car or home.

On the street, an animated crowd is milling about, responding to directives blasted through bullhorns. As I'm searching for the MFSO banner, a woman about my age approaches. Clasping my hands in hers, she says simply, "Thank you so much. Bless you for your courage," before she melts back into the crowd.

My first letter from Lorin comes later that week.

> My Wife, My Love:
>
> This is a sad time. I know now that for the next twelve-plus months I will be thousands of miles from you. I am so very sad and lonely as I write this letter to you. It is light out now, morning here.
>
> As for my thoughts of going to war—I am ready. I have more training to do, but I am ready. Don't get me wrong, I am not liking this, am not relishing this, but I'm ready. I am here with two goals. My first is to ensure that I come home to my wife in one piece, alive and well. The second is to bring home with me all the soldiers I brought over. I will be home, and we need to start counting the days until I return. I have my golf ball, and will color in a dimple a day.
>
> Life here is just dirty and dusty. The food is barely adequate, the coffee is horrible. The only good thing right now is that I get about eight hours of sleep a night, but I'm tired of sleeping with a bunch of other people.
>
> I miss hearing you sing the Scooby song. I love you and I miss you. I know that I'll be safe. Kisses to you and the pets.

He's been at a military base just north of Iraq for about a week. His platoon is still sleeping in tents, but they've been told they will move into trailers soon. Not all of the Guard is so lucky, and citizen soldiers are sometimes relegated to sleeping in canvas tents, while regular Army soldiers are housed in fortified accommodations, such as hangars, bunkers, or Conexes.

"No *conscious decision* has been made in this unit to put the interests of Active Duty Soldiers ahead of National Guard soldiers' lives," read an e-mail message from Captain Ian Palmer, public affairs officer for the 1st Squadron, 4th U.S. Cavalry, the unit to which B Battery is attached. But e-mail messages from Staff Sergeant Roosevelt McPherson, stationed at Forward Operating Base McKenzie, near Samarra, said that the National Guard soldiers have nowhere to seek shelter from almost daily mortar attacks.[7]

Lorin told me that his camp got nineteen mortar attacks in one day. I can barely process the fact that someone is trying to kill my husband, and I wonder whether or not he should return fire. Doing so could save his life, but it contradicts everything I believe.

---

7. May 26, 2004, *The News & Observer.*

5

Collateral Damage

APRIL–MAY 2004

THERE WERE SEVEN FUNERALS this week for soldiers killed in Sadr City on the first day of the Shiite riots, and the mid-month casualty rate is the highest of the invasion so far. Stepping outside to get the paper, I wonder what the news will hold today.

I almost stumble over an Easter lily in full bloom, next to a basket full of candy and a pink stuffed bunny. I'm still holding the basket when I get a call to come outside for an Easter egg hunt. Joining the knot of half a dozen parents, I trail after four little boys, and one sweet six-month-old baby girl, cradled in her grandpa's arms, going from yard to yard, hunting for neon and pastel colored eggs.

Done with the search, the boys sit on the ground, sorting through their buckets and baskets. The adults are standing in a loose circle around them, making small talk. When Jacob is finished picking through his pile of treats, he waves me over. I crouch down next to him, and he very seriously hands me all of his chocolate. He doesn't like it, but he knows I do.

Minutes later, the boys have shed their shirts and are tearing through the sunshine in my backyard, running around and around, jumping over the tractor sprinkler that reminds me of growing up in North Dakota. I think about Lorin, half a world away, and wonder, surrounded as I am by peace and light and joy and life, how this world can possibly be big enough to hold so much violence and anger and pain and death on the very same day.

A few hours later, Crimson barks when the doorbell rings. It's one of my neighbors, holding a feast on a plate in one hand and his baby girl hugged tight to his chest. In the e-mail I write to my husband that night, I say, "Yes, Lorin, there is an Easter bunny."

He calls the following day to let me know he's all right, but he's returning the high-tech GPS gadget we bought for him before he left. He's not sure why, but the things seldom work over there.

"Is there anything else you need, or want?" I ask.

"No, not right now. I got Easter baskets from my mom, and your dad and Jean, but by the time they were distributed, the candy had melted, and the jellybeans were a gummy mess."

I ask Lorin what he's been doing over there, but our fifteen minutes are up, and he promises he'll call as soon as he can before we're disconnected.

I wasn't able to ask him what he thought about the photo of the flag-draped coffins that made the front page of newspapers worldwide, so I put the question in an e-mail.

He wants to know, "What picture? I haven't seen anything about that over here. I don't know what you're talking about."

I write him about the photo of twenty caskets being loaded into a military transport aircraft that was published in the *Seattle Times,* and then picked up by the international media and circulated widely on the Internet. Tami Sicilio, a Maytag aircraft employee working in Iraq, had taken the shot, and given permission for its printing, in the hope that "The publication of the photo would help families of fallen soldiers understand the care and devotion that civilians and military crews dedicate to the task of returning the soldiers home."

Tami and her husband, also a Maytag employee, were fired one week after the picture was made public, because the Pentagon had issued a veritable lockdown preventing the publication of such photos. In previous wars, media footage of flag-draped coffins was standard, and generally viewed as a way to honor the dead for their sacrifice while showing the public the human cost of war.

The Pentagon has broken with that tradition, going so far as to discourage, and at times even prevent, bereaved families from receiving the bodies of their loved ones when they are returned to Dover Air Force Base and other military posts. The picture and ensuing debate have made headlines around the world, and I can't imagine that it hasn't found its way into the mess halls in Iraq. But I don't hear from Lorin for days.

By the second voice mail, I know something is wrong. I'd been to a movie, and made a quick stop at the store for coffee, chocolate, chili cheese Fritos, and several packs of AA batteries to send to Lorin. Rummaging in the shallow kitchen drawer by the phone for a pen to complete the customs form, I notice the blinking red light. An electronic voice tells me that I have three new messages. I grab a Post-It note, anticipating requests for interviews, maybe even a job offer. Not a week has gone by that I haven't sent out at least one resumé, and I feel frustrated by the lack of response.

I spoke with Lorin a few days ago, so I'm surprised to hear his voice. "It's me, I just wanted to call and see how you are. I miss you. I'll try again later."

Pen poised, I erase it and go on to the next one. Again, it's my husband. He sounds tired, and lonely, but there's something else that I can't quite put my finger on.

"I was hoping you'd be home by now. I just wanted to talk to you. I miss you. I love you . . . I miss you so much."

It's the space between the words that gets my attention. Whatever has happened, it's shaken him badly. There's something in his voice—vulnerability, fear?—that I haven't heard before. I dismiss the worst-case scenario because obviously, he's alive, but what in God's name is going on over there? Then I hear him speak for the third time.

"It's me again. I really wish you were there. My heart is feeling really heavy, and I'm very, very sad. These last few days have been pretty hard. I just want you to know I'm so sorry. I didn't want this to happen. It was an accident."

Carried over thousands of miles, kept in an electronic storeroom, I feel the sorrow in his words. Wherever he is right now, he desperately wants, even needs, to cry. But I doubt he will. What could've happened to make him sound this way?

I run through a handful of possibilities, recalling one of our conversations when he was trying to convince me that he was going to Iraq as part of a peacekeeping mission.

"Then why do you need the heavy artillery? I've yet to take an M-16 to a peace rally."

His response was, "They're for protection, in case we get fired on."

April was the deadliest month of the occupation, with 126 reported casualties, and his base has been under heavy mortar attacks. Maybe they were just returning fire, and there'd been a minor mishap. Maybe that was it.

The phone rings as I'm putting the eggs in the fridge.

Nudging the door shut with my foot, I stretch across the counter to grab it. "This is Stacy."

"It's me, I've been trying to call you," he says with relief and a smidge of rebuke. He hates it when he can't reach me right away, and I've still not gotten used to having my cell phone on all the time, much less carrying it with me everywhere I go.

"I know, honey, I just got home. I heard your messages. What's going on? Are you all right?" I ask, climbing the stairs to my office, taking a seat at my desk.

"Yeah, I'm fine, well, I mean, I'm not hurt or anything."

It dawns on me that although he's probably been trying to frame his next words for a while, he's still struggling with it, and needs me to draw him out.

"How about your men? Are they okay?"

"Yeah, they're basically okay."

"What do you mean, basically? Did somebody get hurt?"

After a beat or two of crinkly, static silence, he says, "No, nobody got hurt. At least, none of my guys."

Oh, Christ, honey, spit it out! I want to reach through the phone and shake the story from him.

"Tell me what happened," I ask as calmly as possible.

"It was an accident, you have to know that. They weren't supposed to be there. It's bothered me so much, and I feel so bad about it, but there's nothing I can do. Nothing I could have done. It wasn't our fault. It wasn't my fault."

"I know, sweet bear, I know. It's okay." I hear how much this is hurting him, and wish I could ease the pain.

"You can't say anything about this right now, because they're still wrapping up the investigation. But they told me that we didn't do anything wrong, it was just an accident."

After another deep exhalation, he continues, "We were firing a couple of practice rounds. We finally got all of our equipment up here, since it took so long for the ships to dock."

"Yes, dear, I know."

Rumbling, tumbling, the words come pouring out, carried in a river of remorse, bumping up against and then parting around the stones of his conscience. "The Forward Observers [FO] were out there, and they didn't see anybody. Nobody was supposed to be there. The area was empty. They said it was empty. So we fired a couple of rounds, just like we were supposed to, and the next thing I know the FOs are yelling, "Check fire! *CHECK FIRE!*"

I flinch, awaiting his next words.

"I'm not sure what happened next, because I wasn't right out there, so I didn't actually see it, thank God. Somehow two people had gotten out into the practice area."

Stupefied, I can only say, "What?"

"Apparently, between the time when the Observers were out there and when we gave the order to fire, a carload of Iraqis wandered into the firing area." Something has shifted and closed in his voice, and it sounds like he's reading from a report.

"Were they soldiers?"

"No."

"Well, do you know anything about them? I take it they were civilians, right?"

"Yeah, they were civilians. They were thirteen and twenty, on their way to school and work."

I fumble the phone. It buys me a few seconds to figure out what I'm going to say, knowing my next words are critical.

"I am so sorry, I wish I could be with you right now. How are you doing with this?"

"The first couple of days were awful, and I still struggle with it, but they said I didn't—that none of us—did anything wrong. They said those kids came out of nowhere, and it just couldn't be helped. I've prayed about it a lot, and I feel really bad about it, but at least I didn't see the bodies. It's harder for the guys who did."

Before I can say, "I suspect that it is," Lorin tells me that his calling card is almost out of time. We hang up after a volley of I love you's.

I glance around the room, staggered that nothing's changed. It doesn't make sense. I know we've just turned some kind of corner that we'll never go back around, and it seems ridiculous that it doesn't show in my surroundings.

I flash back to the briefing at the armory, and everything that was said by the speakers, thinking they left this part out. They never said what we should do if our loved ones inadvertently killed innocent civilians, children, really. We weren't given the protocol for that, and I recall no instruction offered in my high school civics class or our premarital counseling.

So what am I to make of this, my husband's hand in the ending of two young lives? How is he going to live with himself, knowing what he's done? How will I? And why do I feel a faint flicker of guilt?

Somewhat detached, over the next couple of days I pray a lot, and think too much. God's not talking. Maybe I'm just not listening. All I can think about, besides the poor families of the boys that were killed, is that, if this happened in the States, Lorin would be convicted of manslaughter, at the very least. Am I married to a murderer?

He never would've done something like this on his own, but now he has to: he's in the military. After determining the approximate point of origin of an enemy attack, using high-tech sensors and scouts, it's up to Lorin's superior officers to approve a retaliatory strike. Once approved, Lorin relays the target information to the guns in the field.

Am I guilty by association? If so, do I continue to associate, or do I walk away now, alone but smug, bloated with moral authority and the cold comfort of my convictions? Wrestling with my "Sophie's Choice," I begin to think maybe there really are no moral absolutes. Or perhaps I'm just looking for an easy way out.

I envision myself as an athlete in a sort of Moral Olympics, two announcers providing color commentary from a booth high above the floor.

Anchor One says, "Well Bob, our next competitor got off to a slow start, but it seems that after working her way through the double axel of the MLK Center, she's going to attempt the triple toe loop of her husband at war. This back-to-back sequence is one of the more difficult maneuvers, and something she's never tried before."

Anchor Two adds, "That's right, Frank, she's got a lot riding on this one. Let's see how she does."

I hate that I have to deal with this. I'm angry that the troops were sent to Iraq, and that Lorin signed up for the Guard in the first place. I want to be the kind of person that can accept this with equanimity, casually dismissing death as part of the cost of war. I wish I could move through this like it just doesn't matter. I would like to be able to handle it as if I were in the military.

After World War II, it became clear that soldiers were reluctant to open fire on adversaries. In order to overcome the troops' seemingly innate resistance to killing another human being, the military replaced bull's-eye targets with objects shaped like humans, recreated battlefield conditions more accurately, began using computer games to hone sharpshooting skills, and essentially programmed soldiers to become automatic killing machines.

Taught to shoot without thinking, much less feeling, the revamped training was incredibly effective, raising the number of soldiers who opened fire on the enemy from a low of fifteen percent in World War II to ninety-five percent in Vietnam. Not coincidentally, almost half of all Vietnam War veterans displayed some sort of psychological damage. Troops returning from

Iraq aren't exhibiting the same frequency of post-traumatic stress disorder, but the numbers are rising, as are the suicides. And it's not over yet.

When the investigation's complete and I'm finally ready to talk about it, I broach the subject with one of my neighbors. They've all said repeatedly, "If there's anything you need, anything at all, don't hesitate to ask." I tell them what's going on, and they shrug their shoulders and say, "Well, that's war." Then they ask whether or not I think they should trim their rose bushes back a bit.

Talking with Lorin's mom one night, I share my angst, expressing my concern for the families in Iraq.

"I'm going to be selfish, because all I care about is that Lorin's okay."

When I press the issue, I have the distinct sense that she's implying that my grief and moral dilemma around the murder of two children somehow subverts my love for her son. As if it's a mathematical equation, easily diagrammed, that people and feelings, the "accidents" of war, and the moral and ethical code of a lifetime, are readily reduced to discrete quantities.

Strangely, this hasn't fundamentally changed how I feel about him. I'd have thought for sure it would. I have a tiny worry that when I first see him, I will shrink from his touch. But after grappling with this for days, I come to the realization that my love for him transcends my beliefs, and there are few things for which I would not forgive him.

By the time I hear from him again, the Abu Ghraib prison abuse scandal has been made public. I ask if they've heard about it over there.

"Oh, yeah, we've heard about it all right. I can't believe they did that. I don't know any guys who are doing that. It's just stupid, and it makes everybody look bad. It creates a whole lot of problems for us, including retaliation."

"I suspected it might. It's all over the news here, but this is war, so I don't know what people expected. Besides, I'm not sure why prisoner abuse is a bigger deal than killing, but it seems to be. Is there anything you guys are doing in response?" I have no idea what this might be.

"Oh, no!" he replies, with a hard, humorless laugh. "Now it's all about winning hearts and minds, so we can't even fire back. I don't want to hurt anyone, but I'm very tired of having rockets and mortars shot at us every day. I want to shoot back. I don't understand the point of being here and not really being able to defend ourselves against the few who want to kill us. When I checked our equipment yesterday, there were bird's nests on some of the mortar rounds."

I listen as he continues to vent.

"This place makes no sense. The alarms don't go off until five or ten minutes *after* we're bombed. Here's another example: they sell rugs with a picture of a mosque on them in the PX. Word came down today that we can't put them in front of our doors. It'll offend the Iraqis who are working on the base if we step on them, and we need to be sensitive to their culture."

Speaking faster, louder, he continues, "Since when is the U.S. so concerned about offending a culture it declared war on and invaded? I could go on, but I want you to know you don't have to worry. When I get back home, I am *done*. This place is as close to hell as I want to get. Too bad it's taken this to open my eyes and my mind."

Thank you. I've felt this coming but it's a relief to hear him actually say it. And though it's probably not politically correct, I can appreciate his aggravation about the rug policy. What I don't understand is why a country, and a culture, seems to value its beliefs more than the lives of its people. I ask him gently how he's dealing with the deaths of the boys.

"It's tough. I try not to think about it too much. I've been told that a lot of Iraqis just say *Inshallah,* and accept it as being God's will."

That sounds a little too pat. How convenient to use their cultural beliefs to rationalize the loss. But then, what do I know? Maybe that is how the Iraqis feel; although I would think their children are as precious to them as ours are to us.

"I feel bad about it, though, and wish I could find the families and apologize. I want to tell them how sorry I am, that it was an accident."

I've also thought about finding the families and expressing my profound regret. That we seem to be communicating on some other level while he's half a world away no longer seems unusual. I've gotten used to things like getting an e-mail from him recommending I read a particular book, one that neither of us had ever mentioned before, which just happened to be the book I'd finished that very day.

My next e-mail from him reads:

Good morning. I was rudely awakened by rockets landing this morning. This has just got to stop. Yesterday, I was sitting around with some of the guys, and we were so bored we came up with some ideas for ways to make money out here.

Mobile helicopter cleaning and detailing service.

Mess Hall valets.

Tactical Center concierge.

At least he's managing to keep his sense of humor. I get cranky from time to time, like when I went to pick up my military ID. I had the urge to interrogate every person in uniform, demanding, "Why aren't you over there?"

Instead, I sat in the waiting room for nearly two hours, watching a cartoon video called *Our Friend Martin*. It's all about Dr. King's life, and his work for peace and civil rights, so I can see why they'd have it playing at Camp Murray.

The monthly Veterans for Peace meeting is at Ben Sherman's house on Mercer Island. It's a lovely, stately home, with a terraced lawn in the back, and lots of wood, windows, and open space inside. Nearly fifty people are crowded into the living room and dining area, and like most of the other men here, Ben served in Vietnam.

Drafted even though he'd established himself as a conscientious objector, he served as a medic. I spy his book of the same name lying on the dining room credenza and sneak a look. It opens with him putting bodies into heavy black plastic bags. When the business portion of the meeting is over, we talk briefly, and I'm appalled to learn that cadavers were used as mules to ship drugs to the States.

Some of the guys in Vietnam packed drugs into the body bags, at times sewing them into the body cavities or large gaping wounds of the deceased. When the corpses got to the States, there'd be someone in the receiving room waiting to retrieve the drugs and sell them.

I sit next to Vicky at the meeting and ask her about her son. "You must be pretty excited, he's coming home in a couple of weeks, right?"

Her face closes up a little when she replies, "No. I found out last week that they're keeping him longer, maybe until September."

I say I'm sorry, but I don't think it means much. She's a tired, frustrated, worried mommy, and she needs more than words. She needs her boy back home now.

I cut out early to get back to Kent for another Family Support meeting.

The Family Support staff and some volunteers have collected a couple of video cameras, and each family gets three minutes to tape a message to their soldier. The segments will be put on individual CDs, shipped to either Camp Anaconda or Victory, where most of the 81st is based, and given to the soldiers.

A few announcements are made before the taping begins, including a brief mention of the Brigade's first casualty. Sergeant Jeffrey Shaver was twenty-six when a roadside bomb in Baghdad killed him, but the military personnel at the front of the room don't come right out and say "dead," or "killed," or "bomb"; it's referred to as "an incident." They don't even say his name.

None of Shaver's family is here, but I doubt they think of this in terms anywhere near as neat and sterile and dismissive as "the incident." I bet it doesn't feel like just an incident to them, and frankly, it demeans Shaver, his family, and all of us to call it that. Shaver's name has been added to the lengthening list of dead U.S. soldiers, 856 to date, not a single one of them casual. I want to say so to the group, but I'm tired, and a chicken, and I don't have the energy to handle the animosity that will assuredly come my way if I do.

I've been here before, back when I was the first white executive director of the MLK Center and my very presence seemed to irritate, sometimes enrage, both blacks and whites. Although the particulars have changed, it's basically the same thing.

Unless they're in Veterans for Peace or Military Families Speak Out, many of the wives and military families of the National Guard unit resent the handful of remarks I've made questioning the wisdom of American forces being in Iraq. And just the other day, I got a lovely little anonymous note. He—or she—obviously knew my husband was in Iraq, and that I was an active pacifist. Or is that passively aggressive?

It read, "The concept of a peace activist being married to a military husband doesn't work for me, too much of a dichotomy. National Guard = Military = War = Death."

It's not working for me too well, either, but it is what it is, and I'm doing the best I can to keep my balance on the wire.

There are at least five more deaths in the following week, all of them on or around Camp Anaconda, Lorin's base near Balad, fifty miles north of Baghdad. After the initial twenty-four- to forty-eight-hour communication blackout that's imposed whenever there are casualties, the soldiers' access to phone lines and the Internet is restored.

Dear Wife:
    In case you haven't heard, we had a big rocket attack. three died and about twenty-six were injured. The ones who died and were wounded made a grave mistake. The alarm had been given and we had been in condition red for twenty minutes when the rocket that killed them hit. They weren't wearing the IBA and helmets, and were sitting outside of the PX when the rocket hit right in front of them.

They might not have died if they were inside the building like they should've been, or if they were wearing their IBA like they're supposed. The unit I am in hasn't allowed us to take the IBA off, and when the rockets start to hit, I find a place to be. I want to hold you in my arms. I am thinking of you and want to let you know I am safe and very much in love with you.

6

The Long Summer Season

JUNE–JULY 2004

THE 579TH ENGINEER BATTALION, 81st Brigade, has been tasked with training members of the Iraqi National Guard, preparing them to take over the policing of their nation. After spending the day working with the Iraqi men, Second Lieutenant Andre Tyson sat down for dinner in the mess hall, where he and Lorin spent the better part of an hour shooting the breeze.

After dinner, 2LT Tyson gathered up his gear and prepared for evening duty on ground patrol. Several hours later he was killed in action, along with Specialist Patrick McCaffrey, when the Iraqi soldiers that *they had trained* ambushed them. Tyson was probably still digesting when the bullet hit him in the head, ricocheted around in his helmet, and exited through his eye.

I'm growing increasingly numb to the regular news of guns and bombs and the deaths of soldiers, 135 in April alone. Without my intention or invitation, it has begun to weave itself subtly into the fabric of my life, an unusual thread, but no longer startling, not terribly out of place anymore in the pattern. Is this how it happens? How quickly, and unwittingly, we become inured to war.

Resisting the easy, tempting slide into complacency, I write another slew of letters to the editor and to congressmen. I get a four-pager from Representative Adam Smith, outlining his concerns about the increasing lengths of deployment, the abuse of Iraqi prisoners, and his call for Rumsfeld to step down.

I slither into the muck of feelings I have about this war and my husband's involvement in it. I haven't been able to muster the words when we talk on the phone, and I debate whether or not I should let him know now. Maybe I should wait until this is all over, maybe there's such a thing as too much truth in love. My index finger hovers over the send button for a long time, but finally, it descends.

My Dear Husband:

Tell me, how is it now with your boots on the ground?
With guns and grenades and children's cries as the sound?
Do you take to the sand and the heat very well?
Tell me, how is it now, your khaki circle of hell?
How is it now, a million light years from home?
Are you peaceful at war camp, do you get time alone?
Do you remember the life and the wife that you left?
Do you think of the women that your work leaves bereft?
Tell me, how is it now as you stand on foreign soil?
Has it dawned on you yet that your blood goes for oil?
Do you sweat and hope and curse in your tent?
Do you wonder what happened to the prayers that you sent?
Do you wish for escape when the bombs start to fall?
Do you ask for deliverance from anything at all?
Does war softly sit in your mind and your soul?
And what are the odds you'll return to me whole?

I'm afraid for him, and sometimes fear turns to fury. But if we're going to survive fourteen or more months apart, our ability to connect emotionally is going to have to do double duty, and compensate for our inability to be together physically. I need to let him know how I'm feeling, and not pretend that he doesn't hold some tiny measure of the weight of this war.

You're not supposed to ask soldiers who've been in combat how many people they've killed. It's considered rude, I guess, and nobody wants to admit to taking another person's life, even if it is patriotic. Waiting for his response to my little poem, I worry that I've been too harsh, but the feeling dissipates. I don't want my much-removed experience of the horrors of war to become normal. I don't *want* to get acclimated to this.

The prospect of eight or more months of this makes me feel both incredibly powerless and intensely angry—especially since Lorin has now completed the twenty years he thought he signed up for. But he still hasn't received the letter that will qualify him for retirement benefits, which is issued to National Guard soldiers who've completed two decades of "good" service.

In the Guard and Reserve, the time actually served isn't as important as what was done during that time, such as the number of trainings and courses they've completed. So although Lorin's records show that he's got twenty, because the Guard is so heavily involved in fighting the war on terror, he's unable to get out. And even the men and women who did get out are now being forced to get back into uniform.

Thousands of former soldiers on the Individual Ready Reserve (IRR) list have been called up in recent months. The standard Army contract covers an eight-year period, so that people who thought they'd enlisted for just one or two years can be held liable for up to seven more. After completing active duty, the soldiers are released from service and resume their civilian jobs. They're placed on IRR even though they are no longer on the military payroll or going to training.

The rule allowing IRR activation has seldom been enforced, but the unanticipated resistance and a growing insurgency has created a desperate need for soldiers in Iraq, and the military has begun resorting to emergency measures. At least thirty-five percent of the nearly 3,900 former soldiers mobilized for yearlong assignments are challenging the IRR call-ups, requesting postponements or exemptions. The military is dragging its feet in prosecuting the resisters, concerned about the political ramifications and the effect on recruitment and troop morale.

Different "stop-loss" (which bars military personnel from retiring or leaving the service at their scheduled time) and "stop-move" (preventing permanent changes of post) programs have been implemented in a piecemeal fashion since the war began. But on June first, the Army's assistant secretary for manpower and Reserve affairs signed a blanket stop-loss order that universally prevents any soldier whose unit is deploying in ninety days or less to Central Asia or the Middle East from leaving the service or transferring units until ninety days after his or her tour of duty is over. Active duty personnel who have completed their contracts are exempted, and allowed to retire, as was the case with General Tommy Franks. National Guard and Reservists are not.

More than 16,000 soldiers have been affected by the stop-loss order, which opponents have dubbed "the backdoor draft," because it's a type of conscription that forces soldiers to stay in uniform. The Pentagon claims it's necessary for troop cohesion, but they're adding an additional twenty-seven years to the contracts of some soldiers, explaining that it's just to give them "wiggle room."[8]

---

8. "Stopping the Stop-Loss," *Seattle Weekly*, March/April 2005.

It's what happened with Oregon National Guard soldier Emiliano Santiago, who was told he couldn't leave the Guard on June 11, two weeks before he'd fulfilled his eight-year contract. When the then seventeen-year-old Santiago was thinking about joining, the recruiter who came to his high school told him that the Guard would only get deployed if World War III began. The recruiter never mentioned the fine print that allows for involuntary extensions.

The contract spells out conditions under which that fine print can be enforced, and one is "A time of war or national emergency declared by Congress." The law says that, "During any period members of a reserve component are serving on active duty . . . the President may suspend any provision of law relating to promotion, retirement, or separation applicable to any member of the armed forces."

Santiago has begun proceedings to take his case to court and challenge the stop-loss order, but until then, he'll be at Fort Sill, Oklahoma, on active duty and training for deployment. Which, according to his new contract, could last until 2031.

Retired U.S. Army Colonel David Hackworth, Chairman of Soldiers for the Truth (SFTT), an organization committed to ensuring that American soldiers, sailors, airmen, and Marines are getting the proper training, leadership, and equipment, shared this comment from a Special Forces noncommissioned officer (NCO): "Stop-loss is not only a breach of contract, it's a form of slavery. There's a tidal wave of folks getting out. . . . The number of senior NCOs leaving is amazing."

Hackworth added, "Despite all the accentuate-the-positive spin coming out of the Pentagon, the anecdotal reports I've received—especially from Reserve and National Guard folks—point to a mass exodus that will reach the hemorrhage point by mid-2005."[9]

The 2004 recruiting year ended earlier this month, and for the first time since 1994, the Army National Guard had a shortfall, missing its target of 56,000 by 7,000. In an attempt to counteract this, the Army has stepped up its Delayed Entry Program for new recruits at the same time that it's breaking its promise to limit the length of combat tours in Iraq and Afghanistan to one year. An Associated Press article reported, "Typically, the Army wants to enter each recruiting cycle with a cushion of incoming volunteers whose entry has been deferred from the previous year—about thirty-five

9. "U.S. Army's expanded 'stop-loss' program prevents thousands from leaving military." David Walsh, June 2004.

percent of the service's overall goal for the year. But several weeks ago the Army projected that it would reach only twenty-five percent, and officials said Thursday that the cushion was eighteen percent."[10]

Internal measures to retain troops are also underway, as evidenced by the following memo from Major General Claude A. Williams of the Army National Guard, dated May 2004: "Effective immediately, I am holding commanders at all levels accountable for controlling manageable losses."

The document also says that commanders must retain at least eighty-five percent of soldiers who are scheduled to end their active duty, ninety percent of soldiers signed up for Initial Entry Training, and "execute the AWOL recovery procedures for every AWOL soldier." According to a study released by the U.S. Army Research Institute for the Behavioral and Social Sciences, entitled *What We Know About AWOL and Desertion(2002)*, this will result in more soldiers going AWOL.

"Although the problem of AWOL/desertion is fairly constant, it tends to increase in magnitude during wartime—when the Army tends to increase its demands for troops and to lower its standards to meet that need. It can also increase during times, such as now, when the Army is attempting to restrict the ways that soldiers can exit service through administrative channels."

The Pentagon listed 1,470 soldiers as absent without leave (AWOL) in the first five months of 2004, twenty-five percent more than documented during the first half of 2003. Calls to the GI Rights Hotline have doubled since 2001. Most of the calls are from soldiers with untreated injuries or pressing family problems, combat veterans who have since become pacifists, National Guardsmen prepared to deal with floods, fires, and hurricanes, but not fighting overseas, and inactive reservists who thought their time was done.

Five of the eleven active duty and Reserve soldiers who submitted petitions for conscientious objector status in 2003 were released from service. But when Florida National Guardsman Camilo Mejia filed his fifty-five-page conscientious objector application, he was charged with desertion. Staff Sergeant Mejia spent nearly eight months in Iraq, and during his two-week leave, he decided that the war is illegal and immoral, and refused to return. When he finally turned himself in to military authorities, carrying his application with him, he was jailed.

Most of the reasons he provided for seeking CO status were ruled inadmissible during his court martial at Fort Stewart, Georgia, and after twenty

---

10. "Iraq War Casualties Mounting for U.S. Citizen Soldiers, With No Letup in Sight," Associated Press, June 26, 2004.

minutes of deliberation, the jury gave him the maximum sentence of one year behind bars, removal of rank, loss of pay, and a bad conduct discharge. Camilo is currently doing time in an Oklahoma military prison—over a thousand miles away from his Florida- and California-based relatives.

Specialist Dana Jensen, a Guardsman from Virginia, was also charged with desertion when he tried the kitchen sink approach to avoiding an eighteen-month deployment. His initial claim was that his real estate business would suffer and his wife's pregnancy should qualify him for a family hardship exemption. Jensen filed, and then quickly retracted, a conscientious objector application before asserting that he was homosexual. When he didn't show up for active duty on March 1, 2004, he was declared AWOL and charged with desertion.

The Army tracked him down and put him in the Fort Knox desertion center, where he was ultimately granted an administrative discharge. Whatever the reasons for Jensen wanting out, they had nothing to do with a stand of conscience. But according to the military's code of justice, Mejia sits and Jensen walks.

Camilo's family belongs to MFSO, which is actively protesting his sentence. I sign petitions and go to meetings, marches and demonstrations, but it doesn't feel like anything near enough. And I question the wisdom of continuing to do work that I'm not getting paid for, wondering what it says about me. I once heard someone say, "Most women do for free what men wouldn't do for money."

There's no amount of spin that can make framing a job search in millennial terms anything other than what it is: ridiculous and depressing. At least I've got health insurance as a military dependent. When I start to feel nausea and intense lower abdominal pain, sharp and relentless, I drive myself to the emergency room. Waiting for the intake nurse to call my name, I am struck with the full force of my aloneness.

I thought maybe it was appendicitis, but it turns out to be nothing more than a large, albeit benign, ovarian cyst. I feel foolish, and apologize to the staff for being a bother. But as I'm lying in the hospital room, intubated, waiting to get a CAT scan, it occurs to me that if something were to happen to me at home, a seizure or life-threatening injury that renders me unconscious, it would be days, perhaps weeks, before anyone found me.

I don't mention that when I write Lorin, letting him know what happened. He calls after getting the message, and the tone of his voice tells me it's crossed his mind, too. I tell him not to worry, that I'm fine; it's no big deal.

I ask if he's still sleeping in a tent, and he replies, "No. We finally moved into trailers. I'm sharing it with another guy, and it's got a small television and a refrigerator. The cot's not so great, but it's a lot better than where we were."

I tentatively ask, "What did you think of my little poem?"

"I liked it," he answers immediately. "I thought it was really good, and it got me thinking about some things." Before we hang up, Lorin wants to know what my plans are for the Fourth of July, and I say I'm not sure.

"How are things over there with the transfer of power coming up?"

The United States is supposed to hand off leadership to an interim Iraqi government in the next couple of weeks, and there've been rumbles of increased violence.

"Okay. A little tense. We're just buckling down and getting ready to return fire if we need to. Actually, it'd be nice to have the chance." Catching himself, he explains, "Well, not nice, exactly, but we're tired of getting hit and not being able to hit back."

None of Lorin's men have been hurt, but almost one hundred and sixty Guardsmen and Reservists have died in Iraq, fifty-seven within the past three months. A comparison graph tracking the fatalities in Vietnam and Iraq shows that the monthly death tolls in Iraq are substantially higher than in Vietnam, which began with a markedly slower death rate. It also started with significantly fewer troops, and it wasn't until the sixth year of fighting that the number of KIA surpassed five hundred.

That grim milestone occurred during the thirteenth month of the war in Iraq. Considered a less conventional war than Vietnam, personnel in supply and support units are getting killed at equal, if not higher, rates than combat specialists and infantrymen. As the number and proportion of citizen soldiers in Iraq continues to rise, so does the average age of casualties. In Vietnam, it was twenty, but the mean in Iraq is almost twenty-seven.

The administration maintains there's no comparison between the two wars, but that doesn't stop the speculation. As I'm driving to the doctor's office for a checkup, the bumper sticker on the midnight blue Volvo in front of me reads, "Iraq Is Arabic for Vietnam."

When Lorin was mobilized, we enrolled in TRI-CARE's active duty standard coverage, offered to Guardsmen and Reservists. Even though we reside approximately forty minutes from Madigan Military Hospital in Washington, when I called to ask about coverage, I was told to find a provider close to home. I wasn't informed that meant I would have a twenty percent copayment. I assumed that because my husband was federalized, and fighting in Iraq, that all of my medical and dental expenses would be paid for, that we'd have the same benefits as active duty families, which is what the government promises.

Active duty families that live on base, or very close by, have immediate access to free health care at military hospitals. The vast majority of National Guard members and Reservists don't live within driving distance of a military base, and the health insurance available to us covers just eighty percent of the costs. I was billed almost a thousand dollars for my emergency room visit, and when I called TRI-CARE's assistance line, I was told, "Well, if you'd gone to one of our network providers, your copay would only have been fifteen percent."

The neighbors are doing the annual Fourth of July block party, but it's becoming increasingly difficult for me to see the families together when I'm feeling so alone. Sometimes it seems like there's an invisible barrier rising up between myself and the rest of the world, the world inhabited by people whose loved ones aren't at war. I talk about how I'm feeling with Alisa, and I think she understands—at least, as much as anyone who hasn't been through it can.

On the morning of the Fourth, I get a quick message from Lorin: "Enjoy the grill and cook up something really good. Damn it, a rocket attack right now and we are at RED ALERT. I will finish this later my love. Kisses to you."

Reading this makes my heart clench. I feel it like a tight, hard little fist in my chest, clubbing against my bones, and nothing can pry it apart. The rest of the day is marked by the incredible tension of not knowing if my husband is dead or alive.

There's an edge of resentment that my neighbors' lives are going on as usual, that this day holds nothing more for them than hot dogs, flags, and fireworks. I want to yell at them, at someone—anyone, I don't really care. I want to find a place to vomit out the fear and anger that festers in my gut. I want to scream at the president, at the people who put him in office, at the world.

Instead, when I am asked about my husband, all I can offer is, "Well, last I heard, he's still alive."

I drink more than I should, wanting to take the edge off the worry and pain. All it does it numb it temporarily, and that night I dream I'm sitting on a bench in a large locker room. Three men in uniform, one with a cleric's collar, walk purposefully through the door, asking for me. The attendant, holding white terrycloth towels, points me out, and they approach. I try to run, but am seated in the corner, trapped by metal lockers. I cannot escape the messengers of my husband's death.

When I wake up the next morning, the worry and the hurt are still there. So I stomp around the house, crabbing at inanimate objects, cleaning vigorously, until I've shaken loose the gunk from the day before, trying to keep myself busy.

Whenever there's an attack, and soldiers are injured or killed, the military shuts down all outgoing communications. All I can do then is pray. It's a peculiar thing, this waiting for word of whether or not your husband is still alive.

My neighbors have taken me into the circle of their lives in way that never would've happened had he not gone off to war, but they still don't understand what it's like, much as they try. Two days stretch into three, then four. Finally, on the fifth day, I get an e-mail, with parts of it rendered unreadable by military censors.

> I tried to send you this several days ago, but it got stopped for content violation. I am fine, and my guys are okay.
>
> 9 July 2004

> My wife:
> SEND MORE BROWNIES!!!! HURRY! I let some people try them, and they raved. They were so good. Thank you for the package, the books are great, but don't send any more gummy bears, they all melted together into one big lump. It's usually 135 degrees here during the day. I keep my head shaved, but I'm sweating all the time, probably lost about thirty pounds so far.
> How are you? I want to hear about everything. How's the doggie? Do you give her belly rubs from me? Kiss yourself for me.

My heart lets loose, and I weep, another cup of tears poured into the ocean I've already cried. Then I pull myself together and try to cheer myself up by rereading a letter from Lorin, which included a list entitled "How to Prepare for a Deployment to Iraq."

1. Three hours after you go to sleep, have your wife or girlfriend whip open the curtain, shine a flashlight in your eyes and mumble, "Sorry, wrong cot."

2. Stop using your bathroom and use a neighbor's. Choose a neighbor who lives at least a quarter mile away.

3. Set your alarm clock to go off at random times during the night. When it goes off, jump out of bed and get to the shower as fast as you can. Simulate there is no hot water by running out into your yard and breaking out the garden hose.

4. Invite at least 185 people you don't really like because of their strange hygiene habits to come and visit for a couple of months. Exchange clothes with them.

5. Announce to your family that they have mail, have them report to you as you stand outside your open garage door after supper and then say, "Sorry, it's for the other Smith."

6. When your five-year-old asks for a stick of gum, have him find the exact stick and flavor he wants on the Internet and print out the web page. Type up an 1149 and staple the web page to the back. Submit the paperwork to your spouse for processing. After two weeks, give your son the gum.

7. Announce to your family that the dog is a vector for disease and shoot it. Throw the dog in a burn pit you dug in your neighbor's back yard.

8. Go to the worst crime-infested place you can find, go heavily armed, wearing a flak jacket and a Kevlar helmet. Set up shop in a tent in a vacant lot. Announce to the residents that you are there to help them. *(Source unknown)*

I consider trying out a few of the suggestions with my neighbors and acquaintances when they tell me that they're not really paying attention to the war in Iraq, or the upcoming Democratic and Republican conventions. It's all I can do not to grab them by the shoulders, and ask, "Pray tell, *what* are you thinking about?"

Instead, I keep my hands to myself, and ask if their lives, and the lives of the people closest to them, have genuinely improved over the past four years. More often than not, they haven't. When I ask if they agree with American troops being in Iraq, they usually say they don't.

This includes several dozen gentlemen wearing veterans' hats, or driving cars with veterans' plates, whom I've accosted in waiting rooms, grocery stores, and parking lots all over south King County. Then I shake their hands and suggest that this year, they vote.

The U.S. transferred political sovereignty to the Iraqi interim government a month ago, officially ending the occupation. In the days that followed the June 28th shift of power, Military Families Speak Out campaigned hard for the return of the troops, arguing that as long as the U.S. military occupies the country, the Iraqis cannot conceivably take control.

Those who disagree with the MFSO position say that withdrawing the troops will lead to civil war, and the U.S. has an obligation to the Iraqi people to rebuild what we've destroyed. But no one seems to be interested in whether or not the destruction was necessary, or if the majority of the people of the country actually want a foreign military presence with no end in sight.

There are presently 160,000 coalition forces in Iraq, and no plan for withdrawal. The handover hasn't diminished the danger for U.S. troops, which sustained fifty-four U.S. deaths in July. Since the March 2003 invasion, the monthly death toll for American soldiers has averaged fifty-five. For older troops, some of those deaths have been the result of age-related medical complications rather than combat.

Of the 275,000 American troops in, or on their way to, Iraq or Afghanistan, 5,570 are fifty or older, and nearly all of them in the Guard or Reserves. Ten U.S. soldiers over the age of fifty have died in Iraq, seven from medical ailments such as heart attacks, which probably would've prevented them from being deployed in earlier wars.

The loss of senior soldiers in Iraq is ten times the percentage of that age group who died in Vietnam. This can be partially attributed to the fact that experienced soldiers with dangerously high blood pressure, cholesterol levels, or other health concerns are being declared fit for deployment if it's judged that they can be treated with medications. New recruits with the same conditions are barred from enlisting.

Military regulations require five-year physicals for Guardsmen and Reservists, but medical assessments are highly subjective. I've heard from MFSO members who've had kids twice pronounced undeployable, and then sent overseas anyway. Another case involved a twenty-five-year veteran who was sent to Iraq too soon after a hysterectomy. After a few weeks, she was flown out under emergency status.

A number of soldiers have been forced back into service after up to eight years of being out of the Reserves, and then sent to Iraq with blood pressure levels that are almost off the charts.

The Guard maintains that all soldiers are given comprehensive physicals prior to deployments, but all that David Lloyd, a forty-four-year-old mechanic with the Tennessee National Guard, got was a series of vaccinations. Lloyd died of a heart attack in Iraq, the result of three blockages in his arteries, as revealed by an autopsy. His wife, Pamela Lloyd, said her husband wasn't aware he had a problem.

Documents obtained by United Press International reveal that hundreds, perhaps thousands, of soldiers with mental health problems were "inappropriately" deployed to Iraq. The after-action report generated by the Army Medical Department implies that the Army sent some soldiers to war even though they had been diagnosed as mentally unfit.

"Variability in predeployment screening guidelines for mental health issues may have resulted in some soldiers with mental health diagnoses being inappropriately deployed," the report said. That could "create the impression that some soldiers develop problems in theater, when, in some cases, they actually have preexisting conditions."

More than two dozen U.S. troops have committed suicide in Iraq, and there have been hundreds of medical evacuations on the basis of psychiatric problems.

Dental problems are also interfering with Reserve readiness, and at least twenty percent of citizen soldiers have shown up at mobilization sites with conditions severe enough to be given a dental classification three. About thirty percent of the 81st Brigade was deemed level three, meaning that the soldiers would likely experience problems within a year, and were therefore undeployable.

Most of the Brigade's twelve hundred soldiers who were diagnosed class three were shipped to Iraq after receiving corrective dental care. But at least a dozen were eventually released from active duty when doctors were unable to fix their problems, which were so severe that they were documented for future use as worst-case examples for Army dentists.

The Army first began tracking the situation during the Persian Gulf War mobilizations, when large numbers of Reservists couldn't be deployed due to extremely poor oral health. Active duty personnel receive dental care at little or no cost, but there's none available for Reservists, and dental insurance is a luxury that most can't afford.

According to an article in the *National Guard & Defense Review Magazine,* forty percent of Guard members have no dental insurance. They're able to enroll in a government plan that costs about $120 a year, plus fees and deductibles, but it's an exorbitant expense for the National Guard soldiers whose only income is the monthly military paycheck of $125-$500. For the handful of soldiers in the 81st who are living in their cars, that money is all that's keeping them from the streets.

Guardsmen and Reservists are also grappling with a higher incidence of physical and psychological health problems when they come home. An analysis of Operation Iraqi Freedom veterans who have received Veterans Administration health care reveals that fifty-seven percent of the 27,571 Iraqi Freedom veterans seeking treatment are members of the Reserve or National Guard. Over forty percent of the citizen soldiers sought treatment for stress-related symptoms, and the report cautions, "Veterans may not develop mental health problems for months to years following wartime trauma." Combat: the gift that keeps on giving.

7

Conflict of Interest

AUGUST 2004

A MASSIVE WINNEBAGO pulls into the cul-de-sac shortly after 11:00 a.m., and two men in their late forties tumble out of the cab. Mark Manning, the founder of Conception Media, and his cameraman have been traveling around the country for weeks, asking people what they think about the war in Iraq. I've got a one o'clock flight to Los Angeles, where I'll be speaking at the National Fellowship of Reconciliation Conference, but I've agreed to be interviewed for the *American Voices* documentary on my way to the airport.

They load my suitcase in the back, and we drive down Military Road and then set up in the football-sized field next to the Kent National Guard Armory.

Mark asks a couple of general questions about me, my husband's rank, branch of military, length of service, all the necessary background information. Then he asks me what this war is about.

"I'm not sure anymore what it's about, but I can tell you what it's not about. This war is not about freedom; it's not about weapons of mass destruction, September 11th, or homeland security."

After five minutes, give or take, we're wrapping up. Out of the corner of my eye, I see two cars, and then a third, coming out of the gate. Each vehicle carries at least two uniformed soldiers, and they drive alongside the perimeter of the fence, heading our way. The lead car stops a few yards from where I'm standing, and a young man in his early twenties approaches.

I step forward and introduce myself, offering my hand. He takes it, glancing at Bob and Mark as they finish packing equipment.

"You're Sergeant Bannerman's wife? I'm in his unit. What're you doing here?"

If you're in his unit, I think, *what are* you *doing here*?

"Oh, we were just doing a little taping for a video they're putting together. He wanted to talk to me, as the wife of a soldier. He just had a couple of questions about my perspective on some things, but we're done now."

"Well, you can't tape any of the buildings."

"We didn't. We're done, and they're taking me to the airport right now."

I have the sense he wants to confiscate the tape. Debating what to say or do next, he looks at the other Guardsmen, who just shrug their shoulders.

He turns back to me and asks, "So, have you heard from Sergeant Bannerman? I hear from the other guys, but never from him."

Dodged that bullet.

"Actually, he just called this morning. He's doing okay, but, as I'm sure you know, there was an incident the other day. How's Connie doing?" I ask.

"Who?"

"Connie Ozmer, the Family Services Coordinator. I just wondered how she was doing, since her husband got hurt. It sounds like he'll be okay, but I was concerned about her."

"Uhhhh, we don't know anything about that," he replies, looking at the soldiers gathered around him, all shaking their heads. "We're always the last ones to find out."

"Really? They got hit by a roadside bomb at least twenty-four hours ago. Are you telling me that she hasn't even been notified yet? Well, please don't say anything. I figured since so much time had passed, and the phone lines were back up again, that she for sure must've been told by now."

Hoping I haven't said too much already, I beg off, telling him I've got a flight to catch.

The plane lands at LAX during rush hour, and it takes nearly two and a half hours to travel thirty miles to my hotel. I have dinner around the corner, and try to settle in, but I can't sleep. I'm wide awake when the phone rings shortly after midnight, with my very irate husband on the line.

"Hey. I just got out of a meeting with a Lieutenant Colonel, and he's not real happy with me. What did you tell that film crew?" Lorin demands.

"What?" I haven't had the chance to tell him about the interview. "Well, they asked what I thought the war was about, and I said I was no longer sure, so I talked about what it wasn't about. I talked about all of the different kinds of collateral damage, the costs of war that most people never see, and what this has been like for me. Why?"

"Well, apparently you talked to one of my guys, and he sent an e-mail report saying Sergeant Bannerman's wife was yelling and screaming, and had told the camera crew about some of the guys being hurt."

"What? No, no way. At no point in time did I yell or scream. I asked your soldier how Connie was doing, but I never said anything on tape. I wouldn't do that. That kid, your soldier, is just making things up. He didn't even see the interview. By the time he got there, they'd turned the camera off and were packing up."

"Well, did you say anything about needing replacements?"

"Not on tape. I asked your soldier why *he* wasn't over there, since I know you're short-staffed, working twelve hours days, especially since that one guy got sent home for the million-dollar injury, as you called it. But, that was it. What's going on?" I ask nervously.

"There's a shit-storm coming down on my head, is what. Because of the report this guy sent, they're talking about giving me some shit duty, maybe pulling a stripe so I'd be demoted. They're even talking about sending me home."

That's the Army's idea of punishment? Sending my husband home? But it would be a dishonorable discharge, and he doesn't want that, nor do I want it for him. I also know he would hate to leave his men there, and that for him to be sent home now would be humiliating.

I apologize repeatedly, and he says he's going to go back to the Lieutenant Colonel with my account of events, and try to get things straightened out. I lay in bed feeling guilty and afraid, worried about the mess I have made for my husband.

He calls just before noon, sounding much better. He tells me it's been taken care of, not to worry.

"Are you sure?" I ask anxiously.

"Yeah, I'm sure. I explained to the Lieutenant Colonel a little bit about you, and that you'd ask some questions, but you're not the type to yell and scream. I told him you didn't say anything about Ozmer to the film crew, and that there's tape available to prove it."

"But are you *really* sure? I feel so bad about this, and I really don't want you to be in trouble."

"I'm not. It's okay, and here's how I know: one of the Senior NCOs pulled me aside, and he was kind of laughing when he said, 'Good for her, asking about replacements.' The Brigade Commander said the same thing, so don't worry, and good luck today."

"Thank you, honey, and again, I'm sorry. I'd never do anything to jeopardize you. But, I've got a question: isn't it illegal to knowingly provide false information to a superior officer?"

"Well, yeah, but I'll deal with that later. I've got to go."

I hang up, greatly relieved, and grab my notes for my presentation. I've got nearly an hour before my talk, so I wander around the Occidental College campus, checking out displays and enjoying the sunshine on the mall. The Fellowship of Reconciliation (FOR) is the oldest interfaith peace organization in the country, and this conference marks their ninetieth year.

The Fellowship is the result of a conversation between two men who were at an international ecumenical conference in Switzerland, which was cut short when World War I began. Upon learning that their respective homelands were now at war, the two men made a pact to work for peace. FOR is committed to resolving human conflicts by engaging soul force, the power of love, and truth. Modeled after Gandhi's teachings, soul force is the combined capacity of emotional and spiritual intelligence, the heart of Dr. King's Dream, and the topic of my presentation.[11]

Once everybody's settled in the small classroom, and we've introduced ourselves, I talk about what these last five years have taught me about soul force. Then I sit with the small group and discuss how we lost the soul force of the sixties and how it can be restored. Afterward, one of the audience members joins my friend Christina and me for dinner.

Christina drove up from Laguna Niguel to provide a little moral support, and just hang out. I've known her for about eight years, and she's one of the best friends I've ever had. Even in my funkiest of moments, she loves me, and forgives me, and can usually get me to join her when she laughs.

We didn't have much contact while she was transitioning from male to female (she was Ed when we met), but she's been back in my life for several years now. She's a tall redhead with remarkably piercing blue eyes, and more than a few heads turn as we make our way toward the front of the auditorium for the evening's keynote.

Before Mike Farrell steps up to the podium, those who have been members of the Fellowship of Reconciliation for at least fifty years are asked to identify themselves. The crowd of about three hundred becomes silent as

---

11. "Soul force" refers to an unwavering commitment to the principles of nonviolent resistance. Both Gandhi and King thought that we were created to do justice and that any action in that direction restores our spirit (liberates our own "soul force") while it transforms society.

twenty or so gray-haired or bald people slowly raise their hands. A young woman carries a microphone from person to person, amplifying the aged voices as they tell their stories.

The atmosphere in the room, which is large enough to seat a thousand, has become a sanctuary. The old ones have made this mundane space a church; their lives have hallowed the world.

Many of these people have been members through both World Wars, Vietnam, Korea, the first invasion of Iraq, the conflict in Kosovo, then Afghanistan, and now, again, Iraq. When a tiny old woman in a wheelchair whispers into the microphone, held for her by her daughter, that she joined almost seventy years ago, I realize I've barely begun.

These are my grandparents in peace; some of these people worked side by side with Dr. King. To be in their presence is enough for this night. I settle back in my seat and listen to Mike Farrell, inevitably comparing the person on the stage with his character, B. J. Hunnicutt, on M.A.S.H. I doubt my parents missed an episode, and I saw most of them myself. He looks pretty much like he did back then, and there is something of B. J. in his persona.

He's a thoughtful, deliberate speaker, but witty, with the kind of insight that comes from a combination of intelligence and considerable contemplation. He shares a quote he's picked up in one of the many books he's read, and the instant I hear it, I know it will be with me forever: "The duty of privilege is absolute integrity."

I'm the first in a crush of people wanting to talk with him when he's done, and I introduce myself and briefly remind him of the e-mail I'd sent a few weeks ago to Artists United Win Without War, asking them to endorse some of the volunteer projects I've been doing. He remembers, and says he's interested in learning more.

"Great! Thank you so much. I'll send some information when I get home."

Alisa and the boys pick me up at the airport Sunday night, and I read the *Seattle Times* before going to bed. There's a thumbnail article about the death of a Scout from the 81st. Twenty-year-old Specialist McCune was riding in the gunner's hatch on the roof when his truck detonated a homemade bomb buried in the road. He was in the patrol with Ozmer, who sustained serious injuries to his spine.

Sergeant Robert Johnson, a sniper who was riding in the seat behind West, was the only one to escape without major wounds, although he suffered a back injury. Johnson dug West out of the rig with his bare hands, and was awarded the Bronze Star for his response.

It's not the Brigade's first casualty, and I wonder how many more there will be. I pray for the soldiers and for their families, and then I pray for my own. *Dear God, please keep him safe.*

August is shaping up to be one of the deadliest months of the invasion, with 1,100 injuries, the highest number of wounded soldiers on record. Many of the injuries are the result of Improvised Explosive Devices (IED), the Iraq war's donation to the catalog of low-tech but highly effective weaponry. The explosives are usually factorymade 155-millimeter artillery shells that are hidden in roadside debris. Upon detonation, shrapnel is propelled through the air, causing record rates of head and neck wounds in U.S. troops, and more than double the number of amputations than in any previous war. Thousands of soldiers have paid an arm or a leg to keep this country in oil, which crosses my mind every time I see an SUV.

The U.S. military death toll is averaging approximately fifty-five soldiers a month, but in this, the seventeenth month of the invasion, that figure rises to sixty-six, bringing the total number of dead close to the one thousand mark.

The media is anticipating this milestone, and every time I turn on the news, there's a report of another bombing or attack. The *Tacoma News Tribune,* a paper published for a city about fifteen miles south of Kent, has an embedded reporter on Lorin's base. One of the articles says that Camp Anaconda is the most attacked coalition post in Iraq, something Lorin has failed to mention.

I ask him about it the next time he calls.

"Well, yeah, that's probably true, but I didn't want you to worry."

How can I not? Worry and fear have become a constant river that runs through my life, pushing aside so many other things that I used to think were important. I'm not bothered anymore by the sorry-looking lawn, or how my hair is, or if I've got the right purse. The only thing I worry about now is that I will look out the window and see a late-model Ford sedan with government plates pulling up in front of my home.

In my brief conversations with other military wives, I learn their drapes are drawn, too. When the Brigade went on active duty, I thought the women left behind would form a tight little group, but instead, we've retreated from each other, and maybe a little from life.

When Lorin calls again, I ask him how things are going.

"Fine. Everything got worked out, and there haven't been any more questions about your little incident at the armory."

"Thank God for that. How's everything else?"

"Okay, I guess. I can't really talk about it. There's a lot that never makes the news. You have no idea what's really happening here. You don't seem to understand that most of what's going on won't ever be made public."

I've suspected as much, and global non-U.S. military reports have tracked much higher U.S. troop and Iraqi civilian loss than the Pentagon has revealed. When I check online with international news sources, everything I read backs that up. What's being reported in other countries about dead and injured Iraqi civilians, and wounded and killed American soldiers, is significantly more than what's been presented here in the States.

All too soon, a prerecorded voice lets us know that our fifteen minutes are up. A short time later, I get an e-mail from him, saying:

> You really need to understand that American people are not welcome in war zones in many places on this planet . . . take it from me and what I have seen.

Attached to the document are photos of soldiers' corpses, horrible pictures of broken, gutted bodies with charcoal limbs and glassine eyes that will never make the news. Over the course of the week, Lorin and I go back and forth, arguing via the Internet about the American presence in Iraq.

But I weary quickly of fighting, and after the first couple of exchanges, it's virtually impossible to keep an argument going on the Internet anyway. I lose track of who wrote what and why, and it just gets ridiculous.

And then it's Wednesday, middle of the week, middle of the month. How I've grown to hate this day. Everyone I know has people to be with, things to do: jobs, husbands, kids. Whatever it is, it doesn't include me, and I refuse to beg for inclusion. I've checked the local community colleges for classes or activities scheduled on Wednesdays, but have yet to find anything I'm even remotely interested in attending. There aren't any women's groups meeting regularly, so I'm becoming accustomed to a whole different level of being alone. A few people have asked if I've thought about volunteering. What the hell do they think I'm doing?

Greenlake Way is a main arterial in north Seattle, near the University of Washington. It's the site of one of the longest-running peace vigils in the country. I'm a little bit late for today's gathering, and am surprised to find a parking place without too much difficulty. I scamper across the boulevard where several hundred people are standing, holding signs or banners. Vicky's already here, along with a few other members of Military Families

Speak Out or Veterans for Peace. I stop by before heading toward the mock graveyard.

The crosses are out. The same crosses and headstones that were there the day Lorin landed in Kuwait. I'd been told they'd be there at the VFP meeting I went to yesterday, but I didn't realize there'd be so many. Seeing the rising death toll in print did nothing to prepare me to see it in person. When I saw the crosses this spring, dozens of them were grouped together randomly, a bunch of stakes in the ground. Today, the stretch of grass looks like an actual cemetery, and the nearly one thousand crosses and fake tombstones are arranged in six rows that extend for more than a city block.

Some have names, ages, and dates. A few are marked with bleak, black script, written in wavering lines: KILLED BY A ROADSIDE BOMB; DIED IN MORTAR ATTACK; HELICOPTER SHOT DOWN. I walk slowly through a small white sea of memorials, pausing before the ones with names, saying a prayer for the dead. I trace my steps up and down each row, holding high the laminated sign with Lorin's picture, which reads: MY HUSBAND IS *NOT* AN ACCEPTABLE LOSS.

I pray while my feet are moving, and as I turn to walk the third row, I am hit by a wave of intense grief. It is as if I know these soldiers, as if one of these soldiers could be mine, and God knows, they could. I hide under the low-hanging branches of a nearby tree, waiting for it to pass, caught again without Kleenex, like a Seattleite without an umbrella. I'm vaguely aware of runners running, of daters dating, people walking dogs and strolling babies. All around me, I see life living itself, but this is my life now.

My sign is visible from the jogging path, and I guess my tears are too, because a woman trotting by with her teacup boxer looks, looks again, and then breaks stride. Approaching me with outstretched arms, folding me into her slim, bony chest, she says, "I'm so sorry you have to go through this. I'm sorry."

She feels it so deeply that she starts to cry, too. Even the camera crew that's been sneaking around behind me has the decency to turn away.

PBS's *Lehrer Newshour* has been compiling footage about MFSO for months, starting with a march in New York City. They're taping today, and Lee Hochman is conducting the interviews.

One of his first remarks to me is, "You sure don't look like a peace protester."

What, because I'm not wearing Birkenstocks, tie-dye, and something with fringe? Poor fashion sense is not a requirement for pacifism.

"There are a lot of people who are against this war; millions of people who want peace," I reply. "This is what some of us look like now."

"How do you do this, with your family members in the military?" Lee asks.

"Uhmmmmm, *he's* in the military. I'm not," I say, stating the obvious.

"Yes, but I thought people in the military were kind of brainwashed. I didn't think you were supposed to think for yourselves."

Why is he pandering to these stereotypes?

"Obviously there's a code of conduct, and rules about insubordination, but that doesn't mean they're not capable of thinking for themselves. It doesn't mean they don't have their own questions and concerns, it just means that they can't voice them. I can."

"How does your husband feel about that?" Lee asks the question I've heard dozens of times already.

"He recognizes my ability to speak for myself, and supports me in doing so."

I stand along the roadside with the MFSO contingent, holding my sign as cars pass by. Some of them honk, and people wave or flash peace signs. Occasionally, we're offered other fingers, but it doesn't faze me. People start packing it in after about two hours.

Vicky asks me to join her for an early dinner, and I follow her to a vegetarian restaurant. We make small talk, but once our meals arrive, she looks across the table at me, sighs heavily, and says, "I can't keep doing this. I'm really tired, and my son will be home soon, and I need to take care of him. He was here for a visit about a month ago, and he's definitely got PTSD."

"How can you tell?"

"He's really nervous and jumpy, and loud noises scare him. He reacts to them in a way he never did before. He's also really, really short-tempered, and he wants to sleep a lot."

"Was there a specific event that triggered it?"

Vicky describes the catalyst. A bomb was planted in a pickup-type truck with over a dozen day workers riding in the back. The truck was driven into a restricted area before the guards could search it, and it exploded. Her son saw the whole thing; he watched from a stretcher as medics and emergency workers picked up the body parts that had been blown all over the yard, and spattered over a quarter-mile radius. He could've died, but escaped with minor physical wounds.

"You've got to be available to provide the support he's going to need, and you can't do that if you're not feeling well yourself. I understand, but I'm sorry that you're having to pull back."

Shaking her head, Vicky asks, "How do you do it? I was only involved for a year or so, and I'm beat. I just couldn't believe how hard it was to get people involved, even people you'd think for sure would want to be."

"Well, I'm sorry you had to find out this way, I know it's disappointing. Unfortunately, that's how it is. Not all the time, of course, but more often than not. I know people are busy, but frankly, I think working for peace—and you cannot separate that from human rights—is *the* critical issue of our times." I shrug, spreading my hands, as if this were self-evident, and continue, "I'm not even talking about doing this as a career or anything like that. I'm talking about a little bit of your income, a little bit of your time, a little bit of your vote, and your heart, and a whole lot less apathy."

"But why? *Why* do you keep doing it?" Vicky repeats, a little frustrated, wanting an answer.

I pick up my fork and say, "Because I can't not do it, and don't think I haven't tried. But even when things were really, really bad, and I tried to walk away, I couldn't. Well, actually, I suppose I did for a bit, and let me tell you, it was killing me, I swear, actually *killing* me, not to be doing the work."

I pause, shaking my head, remembering how horrible it had been. "When I said no, I began to die. Literally, physically, I felt it."

Vicky's fading fast, and we clean our plates quickly. We hug outside, standing on the curb, and before she tells me how to get back to the interstate, we talk about going to a movie. Unlike so many of the social niceties that are said, but never meant, I have a feeling we will.

I hibernate for most of the Labor Day holiday, spending my time reading, cooking, gardening, and watching videos. I venture out for a movie with Vicky, and then go to a small family gathering at Julie and Dan's, Lorin's brother. Helen is there with Paul, and we get to talking about why Dan decided to work at Boeing, which consistently receives large contracts from the government for the manufacture of fighter planes.

Helen says, "Dan was trying to decide on a career, and I asked him if he was more interested in people or things. He said things. So I told him that maybe the military wasn't right for him."

"Pardon?" I ask, not knowing the military to be particularly people-oriented.

"Well, we just thought that if the boys weren't sure what to do, we'd encourage them to sign up for the military."

I try to modulate my voice, but the sarcasm seeps in when I ask, "Hmm. How's that working for you now, Helen? Still seem like such a great idea?"

Shamefaced, she shrugs—although cowers might be more accurate—and the topic drops from our conversational radar screen. She already knows, and suffers, enough.

8

Halfway Home

NEWS OF THE WAR IN IRAQ is eclipsed by the horrific siege at a Russian school that ended with the deaths of more than two hundred and fifty people, most of them children. The front-page story features close-up photos of their small, bloody bodies laid out on the ground.

When the *Seattle Times* published pictures of soldiers in flag-draped coffins being loaded onto an aircraft carrier in April, the national outcry cost the photographer, Tammy Silicio, and her husband their jobs. They'd violated the government's moratorium on releasing pictures of dead American G.I.s, and for weeks afterward, every nightly news segment and talk show in the nation dissected the wisdom of printing those relatively benign pictures. I expect a similar debate about the Russian pictures, but it never comes.

How can a whole nation rise up in anger at the printing of relatively sanitary photos of dozens of flag-draped coffins, yet not utter a word about grisly pictures of *hundreds* of torn and lifeless children? Are American lives so much more valuable?

MFSO cofounders Nancy and Charley are in town for their jobs as labor organizers, and we discuss the ban on printing photos of coffins at our first group meeting in Seattle. The consensus is that it's just one more way of hiding the true costs of this war. As of the second week of September, tens of thousands of Iraqis have been killed, almost seven thousand U.S. troops have been injured, and more than a thousand Americans have died in Iraq. Yet President Bush allows no photos and attends no funerals.

Ten times as many Guardsmen and Reservists died in the second quarter of this year than the first, when they were just a small part of the invasion.

They now represent about forty percent of the troops overseas, and their rising death toll reflects that. Eighty-five percent of troop casualties occurred after President Bush declared major combat operations over, fifteen percent in the two-plus months since the transfer of power.

The President is telling the public that things are getting better in Iraq. What isn't being said is that the Army's Reserve Mortuary Affairs Company has been activated for duty, and authorized to create a new company. They have been directed to triple their current capacity to handle and process dead soldiers by mid 2005.

We're hoping to get our soldiers home, alive, before then, and Charley and Nancy facilitate the meeting of a dozen Puget Sound MFSO members. What was intended as a strategy session quickly becomes a support group. Everyone else at the table is there as a parent. There are only a handful of military wives who are active in MFSO, because of fear of repercussions for their soldier. I understand that parents live with a different tenor of worry, but when one mother remarks that it's so much worse to have a child in combat than a spouse, I have to interrupt.

"I understand that the mother-child dynamic is different from husband and wife, but I'll have you know I waited for my husband for nearly thirty-five years. I haven't gotten married and divorced several times. He's *it* for me. So please, let's not pretend we can measure and compare the nature of love, or the depth of our pain."

Worried I've been too harsh, I don't speak again until the group has moved on to action items. Nancy slides a glance at me as she announces, "This week President Bush will speak to thousands of Guard and Reservists at the annual Convention of the National Guard Association in Las Vegas. We're looking at organizing a press conference of our members who've got loved ones in the Guard in Iraq."

When the meeting wraps up a short time later, Nancy asks if I'm interested in going, cautioning me I'll have to leave within twenty-four hours.

I send Lorin a quick note about the conference, and his response is waiting for me when I open my mailbox the next morning:

Well, I hope this trip is worth it. Here are things you cannot say:

Where I am in Iraq, what I am doing and the unit I am with; talk about replacements, our training, or equipment. I know these are questions that need to be asked, but not while I am here. They have the possibility of causing me grief.

What you can ask is why Halliburton is making so much money; some of their employees are making $15,000 a month. Ask questions pertaining to why we are here, and how long we will be here. You can ask if we are here because it was an easy target, and the chance to set up a strategic base in the Middle East. Ask if the people who planned this war thought the insurgents, who hate Americans, wouldn't attack. All we've done is provide a killing ground for these people to get their message across, and a stage for the media.

Ask why the leadership isn't being held accountable for things that happen here, like the prison, for example. Why punish the lower ranks? The top needs to be held accountable, because it is their decisions that led to the effects. A slap on the wrist or a letter isn't enough. Careers need to end.

Ask the smart questions, and remember that the stakes are very high for me. I have to bring my troops home. I'm here in the shit. Ask if they've ever thought about what it's like to go to sleep every night and wonder when the next rocket or mortar will land. Will I wake up in the morning?

How about the soldier that wakes up one morning and can walk, and then several hours later, wakes up again, to find out that he'll never see his legs again, and has only one arm. Ask them to realize what they're doing.

I thank you for doing what you are doing. I thank you for having the courage to speak out. I thank you for believing and praying. I thank you for your love and support. I support you my wife and I know you will do the right thing.

Given what happened on my way to L.A., I'm not surprised by his warning, but much of what he's told me to avoid talking about has already been printed in various articles by reporters embedded at Logistical Support Area (LSA) Anaconda with the 81st. Brigade General Oscar Hilman commands the 81st, and has twice requested an additional five to seven hundred soldiers. Both requests have been denied.

The base is temporary home to about 22,500 soldiers, who live—and die—with the attacks that come twice a day. It's considered too dangerous for the Air Force to station its big cargo plans at Anaconda, so the pilots keep the engines running when delivering supplies, taking off as soon as the last package is unloaded.

Half a dozen soldiers and contractors have been killed at Anaconda since April, and nearly a hundred wounded. There have been twenty-seven attacks on the base in the past two weeks, the most recent costing a soldier three of his limbs. Lorin has seen the guy, and it's clearly shaken him, changing his perception of this war.

The next night, I join seven MFSO members who have flown in from all over the country. The huge, fabulously gaudy Las Vegas Hilton is overrun not by the tipsy, bleary-eyed gamblers one might expect, but rather extremely sober men and women in starched uniforms. For the first time since Lorin's been gone, I catch a glimpse of someone out of the corner of my eye, and for a heart stopping second, think it's him. But he's just completed the first six months of his tour of duty, and I won't see him until he gets his two weeks of leave in November.

After depositing my bag in the room I'm sharing with Karma Kumlin, the new bride of a National Guardsman from Minnesota, I hook up with the other MFSO people in the lobby. They're standing by some slot machines with Parker Blackman and Michelle Mulkey, consultants with Fenton Communications, a public relations firm that specializes in working with progressive groups like Moveon.org and Win Without War.

When I join the little cluster, Dante Zappala and his father, Al, are talking about their brother and son, Sergeant Sherwood Baker, killed in Iraq on April 26, 2004. The last time a Pennsylvania National Guardsman died in combat was 1945, during World War II. In the military's official tally of soldiers killed in Iraq, Sherwood is number 720.

He was part of a contingent that was on a mission providing convoy security for the Iraq Survey Group. Sherwood was a Forward Observer, and it was his job to go out ahead of the tank lines to target missile and shell strikes. On this particular day, his unit was in Baghdad looking for weapons of mass destruction when a building exploded. Sherwood was struck by flying debris, and died of blunt head trauma.

After a brief silence, introductions are made and we go to the hotel restaurant for the ubiquitous buffet dinner. We spend the next hour getting to know each other, sharing horror stories about what the Guardsmen and Reservists have been dealing with.

The September 2004 issue of *National Defense Magazine* quoted retired General Jack Keane, former Army vice chief of staff: "Despite the fact we knew we were going to war in Iraq for seven or eight months, we gave [Guardsmen and Reservists] on average about a week [of notice]. We were not able to prepare their employers properly, not able to prepare their families properly and we were rushing their equipment to the fort—and not in the configuration we would have liked."

More than ten thousand Reservists were given a mere three to five days to get back into uniform, only to arrive at training camps that were less than welcoming. One National Guard unit that was preparing at a base in Texas before leaving for Iraq was served two meals a day, while regular units ate three.

Colonel Mike Caldwell, deputy director of the Oregon National Guard, said his troops had also experienced unequal conditions during training. "There were a lot of problems in their treatment. It was deplorable. They were treated like slaves in some respects."

Reservists in Iraq have been assigned to guard private contractors, like Kellogg, Brown, and Root employees. The soldiers get paid about $24,000 to protect the civilian contractors, who are raking in a base pay of $70,000 tax-free, plus overtime. When the shooting starts, the contractors can—and often do—hop the next flight back to the States, but the soldiers have to stay for as long as the government tells them, regardless of their contracts.

We're discussing how the stop-loss order, extended deployments, and pay differentials are undermining troop morale when Parker and Michelle gently remind us that it's after ten, and we have an early call for interviews the next morning. We move to a table in one of the restaurant's back rooms where we're briefed on tomorrow's agenda.

I join the little group at the front of a hotel conference room the following morning, and we stand in a clutch, whispering, as members of the media stream in, filling up most of the seats and setting up lights and cameras around the perimeter of the room.

Parker welcomes everyone, and introduces the Zappalas. Dante and his father stand behind the podium speaking in calm, measured tones, relaying the story of Sherwood's life, death, and love for the Guard. Dante says tightly, "Sherwood died trying to make an honest man of President Bush."

Dante's father, Al, bows his head, tears dropping onto his plaid shirt as twenty or so reporters scribble in their notepads. Wanting to reach out, but not sure if we should, the rest of us huddle in the background, waiting our turn at the mike.

The cameras focus on our faces, missing what's happening with our hands, which have found their way to one another. We open and close the chain as each of us takes our turn in front, but we don't let go until it's over. Nancy Brown has a son in the Vermont National Guard who's partway through a tour of duty in Iraq, and Dave Durman of the Virginia National Guard just got back. They talk for a few minutes, their discomfort apparent. The bottom-line message of both is: End the occupation. Bring the troops home now.

Adele Kubein of Corvalis, Oregon, talks about her daughter, who was deployed to Iraq in February of 2003 while recovering from surgery for a shattered leg held together by eighteen steel screws and two eight-inch metal plates. Ten months into her deployment, Adele's daughter was in a helicopter shot down over Mosul. The impact of the crash fractured the metal in her leg, and pulverized the bones. Military physicians said that her injury wasn't sufficient to warrant treatment. Two months later she was sent to Fort Collins, Colorado, for an operation, which was postponed due to doctors' concerns about her liver failure a few months previous.

She and thirteen other soldiers in her National Guard unit had been medevaced to Germany after their livers shut down. Four soldiers died as a result, but Army doctors weren't sure if the illness was due to coming into contact with hazardous chemicals while excavating under Saddam Hussein's palace or breathing in the red dust of depleted uranium. Other National Guard units stationed in Iraq have already tested positive for depleted uranium exposure, most likely originating from weapons used by American forces in the initial invasion.[12] Adele is trembling with rage at the conclusion of her speech, and I feel it emanating from her as we trade places at the mike.

"Maybe I've just misunderstood the definition of 'support.' Ever since my husband's National Guard Brigade got deployed to Iraq in March of this year, I've been trying to decipher where some of the President's strategies for winning the war on terror and supporting the troops originated."

After pausing to make sure I've got their attention, I continue. "Apparently, the President's challenge to terrorists to 'bring it on' was drawn from a popular movie of the same name. While it made for a great film about a cheerleading competition, 'bring it on' has proven a somewhat less effective strategy for winning the war on terror and ending the occupation in Iraq.

Now, granted, I'm no military tactician, but I've heard the President, and so many others, talking about the need to support our troops often enough that I've wondered exactly what they meant."

I glance at Parker, who's nodding reassuringly from the front row.

"I thought supporting our troops meant making a decision to send them into harm's way based on accurate intelligence, a compelling need, and a clear objective. I thought supporting our troops meant we didn't send them anywhere without an exit strategy in hand, much less without some level of backing from an international coalition. I thought it meant that the administration wouldn't send other people's kids off to fight a war that they haven't sent their own to."

I feel myself winding up, and try to slow down.

---

12. *New York Daily News*, April 3, 2004.

"I interpreted supporting the troops as making sure all of them had body armor, not just seventy-five percent. Some of the soldiers got Vietnam-era flak jackets, spray-painted bright orange like a hunter's vest and held together with duct tape and dental floss. I thought support meant that Humvees were plated and protected, not that the soldiers would have to retrofit the vehicles themselves—with scrap metal.

"My understanding of support includes the expectation that our government will uphold its moral obligations and legal contracts, and not implement the backdoor draft of the stop-loss order. I've believed support to entail making sure all soldiers and veterans have the very best benefits and medical care available. Support means we're not sending soldiers to fight on crutches, or with undiagnosed cancer raging in their bodies."

After a brief pause, I resume.

"Support *should* mean that if the government can pay fire jumpers an additional $700 or more per month for 'hazardous duty,' then they can certainly pay more than $225 for 'hostile fire.'

"So it seems I've located the source of the misunderstanding. The President has a different dictionary. In *his* dictionary, it's okay to criticize the family members of soldiers currently stationed in Iraq by saying that raising questions isn't supporting the troops."

I'd cleared it with Parker and Michelle the night before, and now I pull out my videotape of the *Bring It On* movie, hold it up for the room, and say, "And one last thing: The head cheerleader who said, 'Bring It On'? Her team lost."

Parker strides to the podium, and opens it up for questions. Reporters swarm around Dante and Al, wanting to know more about Sherwood's death and what it's been like for the family. I hang back until one woman comes up to me with a small tape recorder in her hand, and asks, "Why are you so angry?"

I reply, "Moral outrage can be a good thing, but I am not doing this out of anger. I am doing it out of love: love for my husband, love for the troops, and love for this country."

We do interview after interview with Michelle hovering like a mother hen, coaching and clucking, keeping us fed and on point.

We get word that last-minute arrangements have been made for a live remote on Deborah Norville's show on MSNBC. My overnight case is loaded into the trunk of a limo, and I'm whisked to a small television studio, where I'm miked and told to stare at the screen.

Karma will be on the show, too, but she's been taken to a different studio. We're interviewed at the top of the hour, along with Jessica Hildebrandt, the pro-war wife of a fulltime Army captain, and Congressman Joe Wilson, who has three sons in the military, two of them in the Guard, and one in Iraq.

Congressman Wilson has been in the Reserves for thirty-one years, and he talks about how the government is increasing benefits for Guard members and Reservists, and the "wonderful" extension of health insurance to their families. Once they're federalized, health care is legally mandated, and really, isn't providing medical care for the families of deployed soldiers the very least the government can do?

The Congressman fails to point out that the White House is blocking legislation that would help reduce the medical bills of 670,000 disabled vets. The Pentagon has recommended a presidential veto, saying it cannot afford the $5 billion-a-year expenditure. Republican leadership has forbidden its members from pressing for the passage of the bill that more than a hundred of them cosponsored, perhaps because the money is earmarked for Bush's $87 billion war budget.

When asked about the financial impact of deployment on her family, Jessica says, "Well, for us, we were in the advantage. Prior to my husband being deployed, he worked fulltime with the military anyway. We did not personally suffer much of a change in our income. But, yes, financially, there is hardship for a lot of the families."

Karma and her husband, Brad, are one of those families.

"We're newly married, [and] now that he's gone, and I just started going back to school fulltime, I have had to move back in with my father, both for emotional support and for financial support."

Karma mentions the fundraiser they held for her husband's Guard unit to pay for equipment, and how most of the group he was deployed with didn't receive body armor until after they were in combat.

Congressman Wilson says he appreciates the concerns of the spouses, and that the administration is trying to correct any problems. Ms. Norville refers to a lawsuit filed in August, suggesting that the stop-loss order is a lack of due process and a violation of a signed contract.

Wilson replies, "I'm familiar with the contract that I had committed myself to. But it's more than the contract, Deborah. It's a commitment to serve the American people, to protect the American people, to stop the terrorists overseas, and that's what we're trying to do. And so people can be technical, and they have a right to challenge. But I know that there's a moral and a genuine commitment by Guard members to protect the American people."

I interject, "In addressing the moral issue, I believe that this administration has a moral responsibility to the people of this country, and most certainly to our servicemen and women, to make sure that when we are putting their lives on the line, we are doing that with absolute integrity and with intelligence that can be relied on. This really has got to be a war not of choice, but of necessity. That's our moral responsibility."

Deborah interjects, "You question, Ms. Bannerman, the necessity of the military action in Iraq?"

"Yes, based upon the intelligence reports about whether or not there were weapons of mass destruction. And then the objective shifted to being the capture of Saddam Hussein, well, Saddam Hussein has been captured. Then the war was declared over, and yet our soldiers are still dying. They're still getting wounded, and we don't have an exit strategy yet."

Ms. Norville reads a quote from David Segal, of the University of Maryland's Center for Research on Military Organizations: "This is the first war I can remember in which the nucleus of the antiwar movement was not found on college campuses, but in Reserve households."

And it's a wrap. I rush to make my flight, but when I get home, I don't put away my suitcase; I'm leaving again in less than two weeks.

I tell Lorin I'm going to D.C. at the end of the month, sending him the MFSO itinerary. Twelve hours later, when I go online, I see his scathing reply.

Yeah, well, that's nice, but you better tell those people to stock up on candles. Peace vigils aren't changing anything, and with the elections coming up, both in the States, and then over here in January, it's only going to get worse.

His pessimistic projection matches that of the National Intelligence Estimate's council, which determined that any kind of stability in Iraq would be shaky, at best. The worst-case scenario pointed to a civil war before the end of 2005, and this was the assessment *before* the U.S. invasion and subsequent escalation of violence.

Seventy-one percent of soldiers in Iraq have been involved in an active firefight, as compared to about thirty-one percent of soldiers who served in Afghanistan.[13] President Bush's "grand coalition" consists of ninety percent

13. "Combat Duty in Iraq and Afghanistan, Mental Health problems, and Barriers to Care." *New England Journal of Medicine*, July 1, 2004.

American troops, and a rapidly dwindling number of forces from Britain and Poland, desperately trying to hold their ground in an ever-widening war zone. Last month, the growing insurgency attacked 2,700 times, a four hundred percent increase from March.

The citizens of Iraq are under siege, and basic living conditions are deteriorating. Daily electricity blackouts in Baghdad and other urban areas last up to fourteen hours, raw sewage fills the streets, and children slog through garbage on their way to school.

Unemployment has topped fifty percent, so it's not too hard for insurgents to find people willing to throw grenades at passing U.S. convoys for about a hundred and fifty dollars. Working against overwhelming odds, American troops have succeeded in opening some schools, shops, and hospitals, but the progress is always overshadowed by death and destruction.

My Republican neighbors echo some of President Bush's statements about the invasion of Iraq being a moral war. They won't send *their* children to fight it, but it's a good cause, nonetheless. When I suggest that one of the best ways to measure whether or not something truly is a moral good is that it needs no justification, they balk. Then I'm told that this is a necessary war.

When I ask where they think more soldiers might be coming from, the men stammer and the mothers get as skittish as a racehorse. When I pose a question about whether or not they support the return of the draft, they say no without an iota of hesitation, eyes darting about the cul-de-sac, searching out their offspring, as if worried they've been snatched away by the Draft Board.

Rumors are flying around the country about bringing back the draft, aggravated by a petition that calls for the reinstatement of the draft, which was submitted by Democratic Congressman Charles Rangel (NY). I talk to his office about it, and am told it's a political ploy intended to wake people up to the fact that the poor, working class, and minorities are most often the ones wearing the uniforms.

That's the same thing I'm trying to do with my Republican neighbors, who adamantly profess their support for the troops, and occasionally insinuate that I don't.

"First of all," I reply, "my husband *is* the troops. Without him and thousands of others like him, there wouldn't *be* any troops. Second, this country was founded on dissent; silence is not support. And third, the best way I can support the troops is to make sure that when a decision is made to send them to war, it's not a war based on lies."

My personal stake in this is raised again when my brother's girlfriend, Monique, goes into labor. I tell Steve that as much as I would love to come, I have to fly to D.C. in three days. The drive to Coeur D'Alene takes about six hours, and it's just not practical. But after I hang up the phone, it settles in that my baby brother is having a baby of his own, and any thought of practicality flies out the window.

Russ, Jean, and I spend the night catching catnaps in between quick trips to the hospital. In the early morning hours, Keegan arrives, tiny, pink, and perfect, and I watch my brother as he holds his baby boy with more grace, honesty, and love than I knew him to have. I try to compress a fragment of that and carry it with me when I fly to D.C. forty-eight hours later.

The Institute for Policy Studies in Washington, D.C., is one of the country's oldest multi-issue progressive think tanks. Founded in 1963, the Institute utilizes a combination of advocacy and action to advance national and international efforts addressing peace, justice, and the environment across multiple disciplines.

Orlando Letelier and Ronni Karen Moffitt, employees of the Institute, were killed in 1976 by a car bomb planted by agents of Chilean dictator Augusto Pinochet. Two years later, the Institute announced the Annual Letelier-Moffitt Human Rights Awards as a memorial to its fallen workers. It has since become one of the most prestigious awards in the field, and Military Families Speak Out was selected as the recipient of the 2004 domestic award. MFSO is the first and only organization formed by military families who oppose the war, and it has been credited for leading antiwar efforts and reinvigorating the peace movement.

Breaking with centuries of tradition, members are disavowing the traditional code of silence of military families. It's a hodgepodge of personalities and politics united around a single cause.

Some of us are, or were, Republican, and many families have been in the military for generations. Others are college professors who come down from ivory towers to connect with social workers and labor organizers that never really left the streets of dissent. MFSO ranks include veterans of the Korean, Vietnam, and first Gulf wars, as well as recently returned Iraq veterans who are also involved with Operation Truth. I've marched beside gray-haired parents who protested the Vietnam War, and are stunned to find themselves protesting again, even more so because now it's their children who are at war.

However adamant they are in their opposition to the war in Iraq though, the majority of members fall in line with Mildred McHugh, who has a son in the Army: "We are not radicals or career peace activists. . . . Our sons and daughters are in Iraq, or have died there. It makes it harder to dismiss us as nut-cakes."

By and large, the people in MFSO identify as being pro-military, not pro-peace. Most believe there is such a thing as a moral war, they just don't think Iraq is it. It's a tricky thing to challenge the administration and policy decisions while supporting the troops, and we've all been called traitors, and unpatriotic, and much, much worse. Nancy and Charley have gotten death threats, and some of us have been spit on, had things thrown at us, or been physically challenged. It comes with the territory, but I've been through it before, so it doesn't really bother me.

There are other things that turn my stomach, such as the soldier at a Bush/Cheney rally. Seeing the picture of Specialist Casey Sheehan, KIA, the young Republican said to Casey's bereaved mother Cindy, "Hmmmm. I came back."

To which Sue Niederer, MFSO member, would reply, "My son is home now, too. Six feet under."

All of the MFSO members were invited to D.C., but we had just a few weeks notice, and most people have jobs and kids and other things to contend with, not the least of which is money. Established as a nonprofit, MFSO has gotten some donations, and Charley and Nancy use those funds to help with travel, but we all pay some portion of expenses. My trips to Vegas and D.C. have cost me more than seven hundred dollars out of pocket, and others have declined financial assistance, spending thousands of their hard-earned dollars.

The morning of the awards ceremony, MFSO members start trickling in to the Institute to prepare for the noon press conference. I'd gotten in late last night, and was already in bed when Judy Linehan and Sally Davidson rolled in. Judy's from Olympia, and her son, Colin, is in Iraq.

Sally lives in New York, and as we're riding the morning Metro to get to the Institute, she talks nonstop, which she will do for the next three days. The Institute's offices are on the tenth floor, and the staff greets us as they show us into a meeting room. Nancy, Charley, and a dozen other MFSO people I've never met are deep in conversation, so I grab some coffee and sit down.

Mike Farrell is presenting the award to MFSO at the National Press Club tonight, and he walks in with several people circling around him. Leveraging the celebrity of having a hit television show, and thirty years in the public eye, he's been promoting human rights in the United States and around the world for decades. He served on the California Committee of Human Rights Watch, as a spokesperson for CONCERN/America, and as a Good Will Ambassador for the United Nations High Commissioner for Refugees, before cofounding of Artists United Win Without War.

Feeling rather awkward, I wait until he's got a little breathing room, and say, "Hi, Mike, it's good to see you again."

He hesitates momentarily before recognition glimmers in his eyes, and then replies, "Hello, Stacy, how are you?"

We talk briefly before he excuses himself, and I find a seat next to Sally, who's chattering animatedly to Nancy. The meeting begins and as we're going around the room introducing ourselves, I feel a gentle hand on my shoulder. It's Dante, and he has his mom with him.

I feel like I know him much better than I possibly could after spending such a short amount of time together, and I'm relieved and comforted by his presence. Which is odd, because I should be comforting him.

Dante is a parttime schoolteacher in L.A.; a handsome, lanky man with tightly coiled energy wrapped in a cloud of calm. He's extremely intelligent, quick-witted, and insatiably curious—all great qualities for an educator, but not so good for those who would rather keep the facts about his brother's death, and the circumstances that led up to it, quiet.

Celeste and Al Zappala took in Dante's brother, Sherwood Baker, on Veteran's Day 1974, after he was abused and abandoned by his biological parents. Dante was born a year later, and his little brother, Raphael, a few years after that. Growing up in Philadelphia, the taller, huskier Sherwood was Dante's protector, a boy and later a man devoted to family, friends, and country.

Sherwood's view of the world was shaped by two people who didn't let their kids play with water guns: Celeste is the director of the Philadelphia Council on Aging; Al worked at the Department of Defense for thirty-two years and was a Reservist himself. Their combined sensibilities helped forge three good and generous sons with a deep sense of commitment and service to their country, inquiring minds, spacious hearts, and the ability to laugh often and loud.

Sherwood joined the Guard in 1997, after he saw them helping local communities that were devastated by the heavy spring flooding. He told his mom he wanted to join as "another way of helping out," and reminded her that Guardsmen don't go to war.

The Guard quickly became his family too, in addition to his wife and infant son, James-Dante. When his unit got called up, Sherwood had his own questions about the suspicious evidence used to justify the war in Iraq. But he had a job to do, and he was going to do it and then return to his wife, little boy, and his job as a county caseworker for the mentally handicapped.

Sherwood made Dante the executor of his will, asking him to make sure that, should something happen, he would be buried with full military honors, so his little boy could grow up knowing his daddy died a hero.

Dante was standing in front of his fifth-period class when he got the call. He and his wife, Selma, took the red-eye from L.A. to Philly. When they came through the gate, Al was standing there, alone and helpless, emanating grief and shock in equal measure. It took a while before Dante could hold his father's gaze, because when he did, he had to "Shed my disbelief about what I was doing in Philadelphia on a cold Tuesday morning."

The funeral was in Wilkes-Barre, a blue-collar community in the Wyoming Valley of upstate Pennsylvania, where Sherwood went to college. Dressed in a uniform and medals, Sherwood's body lie in a casket. He was buried with full military honors; his wife got a flag. I glance at his mom, and wonder what she got.

After the press conference, we are headed back to the Institute for a late lunch when I get a call from Washington State Congressman Adam Smith's office.

"A spot just opened up on the Congressman's schedule, can you make here in the next twenty minutes?"

"I'll be there in ten," I say, grabbing Judy on my way out.

We flag a taxi, and move slowly through the heavily barricaded streets to Cannon House. We've just pulled up to the curb, and already several policemen are motioning the driver to keep it moving. I hand over some cash and hop out of the cab. Judy is still sitting in the back seat, counting out change, when the driver speeds off. I see her head pop up in the rear window, and swivel around as if she's worried she's been kidnapped. It strikes me as absolutely hilarious, and I'm laughing so hard as I walk up the broad beige stone steps that people cut a wide swath around me.

I've just taken a seat when a rather flustered Judy bursts into the high-ceilinged reception area. Smith's legislative assistant ushers us into his office, which is beautifully appointed in an understated way, with several family photos scattered about the room.

The Congressman is wearing a dark navy suit that drapes his lean frame perfectly. His persona is buffed, but not overly so, and he comes across as a human being who has taken on the role of politician, rather than the other way around.

When I was living in Spokane, I hosted *Value Added*, a talk radio program about current events and social issues. Guests on the show included local and national leaders, community members, educators, best-selling authors, and activists. And politicians. My producer, a card-carrying Republican and son of a past President of the National Rifle Association, got Senator George Nethercutt to come on the show. The Senator not only ate me for breakfast, he made *me* clean the plate.

Senator Nethercutt has had years of experience dealing with the press. What strikes me, though, is that after sitting two feet away from him talking for nearly thirty minutes, I never once catch even a hint of humanity.

Smith is on the House Armed Services Committee, and he's done a great job of advocating for the troops. Once we're settled in the wingback chairs, I thank him for that before running down my laundry list.

"I'm extremely concerned about what's happening with the soldiers when they get return. I have heard, first hand, all kinds of stories of them being refused treatment for post-traumatic stress disorder. Some soldiers have been billed for their stay in the hospital, even though they were wounded in combat. Others are soldiers being redeployed with broken limbs and torn ligaments. The pay and benefits package for Guard and Reservists is not equal to that of regular enlisted. They have fifteen to twenty percent copays while they're on active duty, and their dental coverage expires thirty days after they come home."

I catch my breath and then continue, "One family, whose son died, got his last paycheck, minus five days of pay. He'd been killed before the end of the pay period, and therefore, didn't work." I let that sink in for a moment, as Mark, the assistant, hastily makes notes.

"I think it's time for the administration to put together an exit strategy, and bring the troops home. It's extremely poor planning to send them in there without one."

"Well, we can't just pull out of there."

"Which is why an exit strategy is needed. And that leads me to my final point. I would very much like you to consider supporting the bill to create a Department of Peace. I don't know if you're familiar with it; it was sponsored in the House of Representatives by Dennis Kucinich."

"No, I really don't know much about it, but I think that's what the State Department is for, so I don't know that we need another layer of bureaucracy."

"Well, I appreciate that, but it seems the State Department could use some assistance. And the Department of Peace would serve several purposes. In regard to the war in Iraq, had a Department of Peace been in place, it could have been called on to possibly prevent the invasion. It could've worked with the people of Iraq to help establish and implement a plan for peace over there, which has been a stated mission of the invasion.

"The Department would also operate domestically, working to prevent and reduce violence in schools and society, and really promote nonviolence as a basic organizing principle in this country."

He nods thoughtfully, and I turn to Judy, who starts talking about the problems with supplies and armor. Like all of the other family members, I'm already painfully aware of the shortages, so I tune out a little, thinking about the horror stories I've heard from others.

After spending a year in the midst of heavy fighting, one young man returned home with PTSD so severe that he's been hospitalized twice for suicidal tendencies. His frequent flashbacks involve the smell of burning flesh, the sounds of battle, the sight of crushed, burning soldiers, dismembered women, and dying children that lie screaming on the road. Rather than treat his PTSD, the military gave him a "less than honorable" discharge.

One soldier in Iraq sustained devastating injuries when his Humvee stopped on an IED. The blast came so quickly that the damage was done before his mind could signal his body to raise its arms and shield the head. Shrapnel tore through his right eye, decimating it on its way to his brain. Body armor can't protect the head and limbs from bullets and bomb fragments that carve chunks of flesh from faces, leaving gaping wounds that no amount of plastic surgery can correct. The sheer force of the impact rocks the body, slamming the brain back and forth against the skull, causing permanent damage.

In a coma since March of 2004, this soldier's mom goes to the hospital daily, his wife is devastated, and their baby girl . . . well, the father she *might* grow up with will never begin to approximate the daddy who was there at her birth. As if he and his family don't have enough to deal with, watching his achingly slow journey to regain consciousness, they've had to beg, and sometimes bully, the military hospital and administration to get him the treatment he needs.

The scorched faces, absent arms, and vacant eyes belong to the wards at Walter Reed Medical Center, an acute-care military hospital with a cannon out front. Although the general in charge of the facility has been asked repeatedly to quit firing the thing every single afternoon, he refuses.

I pull my attention back to the room as Congressman Smith thanks us for coming in. We do the obligatory round of handshakes, and promise to keep him up to date. By the time we get back to the Press Club, there are a couple hundred people milling about the handsomely appointed rooms. We slide our bags and backpacks under a registration table and mingle, quickly gravitating toward the little clusters of MFSO members.

The adjoining ballrooms fill up quickly, and the thirty or so MFSO people rapidly form little social knots. I'm introduced to Elaine Johnson, and her sister from South Carolina. They're two of a handful of MFSO members who have just arrived, and more will be coming over the next few days. Elaine is a handsome woman, perfectly turned out, but the façade breaks at her eyes, dull with grief.

She shows me a picture of her son (we all carry photos of our soldiers), and he's a beautiful, dark-skinned boy that was killed in Iraq last year. She speaks in a monotone voice, betraying nothing. Elaine has repeated these words so many times that she's learned to say them as though they tell someone else's story.

I say, "I'm sorry," and press her hand in mine, wanting to absorb her pain.

Staff members from the Institute direct us into the adjoining ballroom, where the first four rows are reserved for us, with Nancy and Charley directly in front of the podium, between Mike Farrell and Seymour Hersh. I find a seat in the first row, next to a soldier who recently returned from Iraq, and pull Dante into the chair on my right. There's got to be at least three hundred people here, dignitaries in the peace and justice world.

Mike speaks eloquently of the work MFSO has accomplished, of the moral vision of our founders and the courage of our members. Video highlights of MFSO activities are shown, and then Nancy and Charley are introduced. Standing onstage, eyes shiny and wet, they motion for us to join them. We look at one another, shrug our shoulders, and pile onto the platform. It's congested, and we're a little discombobulated, so it's a second or two before I finally get turned around and am facing forward.

Everyone in the room is standing, clapping furiously, an ovation that lasts long enough to sweep away some of the ache of the past year. Then Nancy steps up to the mike, clears her throat, and begins to tell our story.

Who knew, two years ago, that this is where we were heading? What we did know in August of 2002 is that my stepson—Charley's son Joe—a Marine, had deployed for Kosovo. He told us he would be ending up in Iraq, and indeed he did, in spring of 2003.

Fall of 2002 was when the drumbeats for war in this country were getting deafening, and we noticed that all those saying "We gotta go to war!" weren't going anywhere—nor were their loved ones. It was OUR loved ones who would be used as cannon fodder in a war that was about oil markets and dreams of empire—not protecting and defending country and Constitution, which is what our troops signed up for.

In fall 2002 we made our first poster, with Joe's picture on it. It said "Our Son Is a Marine—Don't Send Him to War for Oil." In October 2002 we met Jeff McKenzie at an antiwar demonstration in Washington, D.C. His son, who flew medivac helicopters, would be deploying in January 2003. In a phone conversation in November, 2002, our two families decided to form an organization—Military Families Speak Out—to use our special need to speak out, and the special voice with which we speak, to try to prevent an invasion of Iraq.

It is now two years later, and we have grown to more than 1,700 families. We have families who opposed this war from the beginning; and families who supported the invasion, only to find out it was a war based on lies. We are Democrats, Republicans, and Independents; we are pacifists and we are longtime military families who have never spoken out against any military action taken by the U.S. until this invasion of Iraq.

Tonight we have families here from across the country. We wish you could hear from Elaine Johnson whose son Specialist Darius Jennings, age twenty-two, was one of sixteen soldiers killed on November 2nd 2003 when a Chinook Helicopter was shot down in Iraq. That helicopter, not properly outfitted with an anti-missile system, was piloted by Sergeant Brian Slavenas of the Illinois National Guard.

He too was killed that day; his mother Rosemary Dietz Slavenas is also a member of Military Families Speak Out. Elaine Johnson had the opportunity to meet President Bush a number of months ago. She asked him questions that he could not, or would not, answer. So much for this administration's concerns for bereaved parents, for "Gold Star" families.

We wish you could hear from Maritza Castillo of Miami, Florida, who was supposed to be here tonight, but a hurricane got in the way. Her son, Staff Sergeant Camilo Mejia refused to return to the war after serving in Iraq for seven months.

Camilo wrote a fifty-five-page Conscientious Objector application in which he detailed, among other things, prisoner abuse at a detainee camp in Al Assad. He turned himself in to the military in March 2004, Conscientious Objector application in hand. In May of this year he was convicted of desertion and received the same one-year prison sentence that Jeremy Sivits, photographer of the Abu Ghraib prison abuse photos received.

Here is one small piece of Camilo's Conscientious Objector application: *"I have held a rifle to a man's face, a man on the ground and in front of his mother, children and wife—and not knowing why I did it. I have walked by the headless body of an innocent man right after our machine guns decapitated him. I have seen a soldier broken down inside because he killed a child. . . . It is the war that has changed me forever. By putting my weapon down I choose to reassert myself as a human being."*

Nancy slides over and Charley introduces himself, and addresses the silent crowd.

Today, there is a conspiracy in this country. A conspiracy that destroys good jobs, makes college a distant dream for so many; that attracts young people to the military with promises of college, career, and stability, that calls on people to "stay at home and serve their country"—and then ships them off to a war based on lies. A conspiracy that says there is no draft in this country, but then drafts those who have already volunteered—through stop-loss programs—and drafts the National Guard and Reserves into a war in a foreign land.

These bastards have created a world where we wait for the phone call that will tell us that our loved ones are OK—and dread the ring of the phone that might tell us otherwise. These bastards have created a world where their children are wined and dined, while ours face rocket-propelled grenades, improvised explosive devices (IEDs), and post-traumatic stress disorder. But I am once again standing with a strong and courageous group of people. This war and the reaction of military families—the families you see in front of you—is a study of fear and courage.

The fear that was used by this administration is still being used to drive and drag this country into war. The cowardice that was shown by so many in our Congress when they illegally turned over to the President the right to take the nation to war. And the courage of military families who stood up and said no. Who faced their own fears, their own feelings about the war.

There is nothing harder than knowing that your loved one is at risk or has been killed in a war that should never have been fought. It is easier in many ways to just go along and believe the war is, *has to be,* just.

But our families challenged the code of silence that says that you aren't supposed to speak out—to oppose the war. They stood strong as they were called unpatriotic, treasonous, and unsupportive of the troops. As they were called a disgrace to their loved ones, and worse. They risked the ire and disdain of family, friends, and strangers. To speak truth to power. They have left behind their quiet lives to make their voices heard.

Our families are creating a world where normal people have become heroes. People like Jari Sheese, whose husband was deployed with a Vietnam era flak jacket, and who on March 20th of this year stood up in front of 1.5 million people in Rome to voice her opposition to the war.

And Sue Niederer, who went to a public rally with Laura Bush the other day and asked Mrs. Bush why her son had to die in Iraq and why Laura's daughters aren't over there fighting.

I could go on and on. . . . There are so many acts of courage. We are proud to be standing here tonight. To be with the families who are here with us. And to be, in our hearts, with all of those across the country who have been speaking out against this war. To stand with giants. To be humbled by the courage, the passion, and the dedication of military families who have found their voices and who will continue to speak out, and say:

Not one more DAY
Not one more DIME
Not one more LIFE
Not one more LIE
End the Occupation
Bring the Troops Home Now
And take care of them when they get here.

Charley's words reverberate as the room rises with thunderous applause. We return to our seats, and Seymour Hersh is presented with the special award for his years of investigative journalism. He won a Pulitzer Prize for breaking the story of the My Lai massacre, a revelation that so stunned and horrified the world that it's pointed to as one of the catalysts that heralded the beginning of the end of the Vietnam War.

In the spring of this year, Sy exposed the abuse occurring at the Abu Ghraib prison, torture that White House counsel Alberto Gonzales, among others, condoned as justifiable in fighting the war on terror. In his brief acceptance speech, he said that he continues to receive e-mails, letters, and phone calls from soldiers describing their experiences, and sometimes seeking absolution.

As he is discussing one of his most recent conversations, his voice breaks. Sy had spoken with a soldier who had befriended some Iraqi families and was struggling to make peace with the fact that he stood by and watched when the order was given to kill them all.

———❧———

With the presentations out of the way, two huge screens descend from the ceiling at the front of the room, and for the next hour, people watch the second debate between President Bush and presidential candidate John Kerry. When the debate ends, Judy, Sally, and I find a little sidewalk café and have a glass of wine. We talk about the day, and share stories about ourselves and our loved ones in Iraq, alternately laughing and crying. Finally ready to call it a night, we grab a cab back to the hotel, and fall into bed.

9

The Politics of Peace

OCTOBER 2004

SEVERAL DOZEN MFSO MEMBERS clog the hallway in front of Senator John Warner's office, marked by the Virginia state flag standing sentry at the door.

Warner chairs the Senate Armed Services Committee, which oversees all things military and defense related, including pay, benefits, supplies, and equipment.

None of the Full Committee members have children or spouses in Iraq, so they're not hearing frontline reports from soldiers whose lives are jeopardized or assignments made more difficult by shortages. We do, and we're bringing our stories to the Senator. The meeting was set up weeks ago, and we called yesterday to confirm. We've been waiting about a quarter of an hour while flustered aides try to figure out what to do with us.

Cord Sterling introduces himself as the Senator's military legislative assistant, and says they can't find a meeting room, and the Senator's not available. However, if we'd like to share our concerns with him, he'll pass them along.

I'm one of several people grumbling about the situation as we're herded into the building's rotunda. Cord finds a spot near the wall, and we quickly form a semicircle around him. Hovering on the outer fringe, I catch snippets of what's being said, including a question from Charley about why the Senator's not there, speculating that this wasn't the reception given to Halliburton.

People start throwing out questions about the lack of food, water, and supplies, asking what's being done about it. Cord stumbles as he tries to respond, seemingly unaware that after a dispute with the government about a couple million in overcharges, Halliburton said, "We may withhold all or a portion of the payments to our subcontractors."

The net result of all these issues is that soldiers sometimes have just one meal a day. One of the mothers tells Cord that in the early days of the invasion, she sent water to her son and the guys in his unit.

Raising my voice to be heard, I ask, "Why are some of the National Guardsmen in Iraq getting paid about five bucks an hour, and yet government-paid private contractors are compensated to the tune of upwards of a thousand dollars a day?"

Looking increasingly like a deer in headlights, Cord responds: "We don't have any control over that."

I reply disgustedly, "What do you mean, the government doesn't have any control over that? Who do you think is paying the private contractors in Iraq?"

Cord backpedals, "Well, I can't speak for the Senator."

Charley demands, "Well, where is the Senator, and why isn't he here?"

An increasingly red-faced Cord is jotting down notes, saying he doesn't have much more time. We've pressed in so tightly that his back is literally against the wall. Cord asks if we have any more questions, and several people speak at once.

"Why is the administration telling the American people things are getting better at the same time that our loved ones on the front line are telling us that things are getting worse?"

"Why isn't there an exit strategy?"

"When is this administration going to admit it lied, and bring the troops home?"

Cord is searching for an escape route, but before he can scurry away, Celeste Zappala thrusts a picture of her son, Sherwood, in his face. Several other people step up with pictures of their own dead children.

Cord barely glances at the photos.

His lack of empathy erases much of the pity I'd been feeling for him having been sent as the fall guy for the Senator. I follow Cord back to his tiny little cubicle to get his business card, and as I'm leaving his office, I turn and say, "God be with you."

We regroup for dinner, and I end up sitting next to Bill Mitchell, whose only son, Michael, was killed in Sadr City on April 4, seven days before he was scheduled to come home.

"Bill, if you don't mind, can you tell me a little bit about what happened, and how you found out?"

In ordinary circumstances, I'd never ask, but the ordinary no longer applies.

Looking beyond me, Bill softly says, "Mike volunteered for a rescue mission of twenty soldiers from another company who'd been ambushed. I found out later, from his buddies, that they'd turned in all of their equipment the day before. He took a bullet in the head. They gave him a Bronze Star for it."

"How did you find out he'd been killed?"

Shuddering slightly, Bill replies, "A phone call. I got a phone call at home. They said it was a military representative, and they told me to stay there. They said they were sending some people over. And I knew. But I asked them, 'What for? What are they coming here for?'

"She said, 'Sir, I cannot tell you. Just please stay there. Someone will be at your home shortly.' And I was just yelling, I kept yelling, 'Goddammit! You tell me now! You will tell me now! Is my son dead?' And she said, 'Yes, sir, I'm sorry, sir.' I dropped the phone and fell on the floor."

"Jesus. I'm sorry. I didn't think they were supposed to do it that way."

"They're not. I guess she got in a lot of trouble for it. Remember that picture of the coffins that was in all the papers? I'm sure Mike was in one of them."

Elaine Johnson got the call while she was at work. "My husband phoned, and said to come home. People were looking for me. Nobody would tell me what was going on. So I went home, not really thinking too much about it, I guess. I don't really remember much of what happened afterward, but I remember that I screamed when they told me, and my whole body gave out. I just fell down and sobbed. I stayed there for hours."

Notification of your child's death seems to collapse the body as much as it does the heart. I know of one mother who sold her house in the months after her son's death, when the walls seemed to be imploding with grief. My involvement with too many parents just like her has given me the ability to pick them out of a crowd. They are the ones who've had the first few layers of their energetic skin stripped away, and replaced by a caul of pain.

I tell Elaine that I'm sorry, recognizing just how insignificant a word "sorry" is, but not knowing what else to say. Out of the corner of my eye, I see Sally waving me over to her table.

Crouching next to her chair, I ask, "What's up?"

Sally says animatedly, "This is Jessica, and that's her husband, Chad. They just got married before he was deployed, and she got really depressed, and anxious. She was on the verge of a total meltdown when they discharged her husband so he could come home and be with her for medical reasons. You should listen to her story, because maybe it's something you could do, too."

I didn't know it was possible, so ask, "Really? What happened? How did you do that?"

Jessica and Chad, a Specialist in the Ohio National Guard, are both in their twenties. He's slim and quiet; she's heavyset and has an aura of insecurity that can be felt yards away.

Jessica says, "Right before he left, we lost everything we owned in a flood. We had to move, and then I was all alone, and then things kind of fell apart financially. He was stationed just outside of Baghdad, and I just couldn't stop worrying about him. I would constantly check my e-mail, and watch the news, even when I went to the grocery store, it would be on the sound system. I just couldn't get away from it. I started seeing a counselor, and I was having anxiety attacks all of the time. I couldn't sleep and they put me on some medication."

I settle back on my heels, waiting for her to continue.

"I cried all the time, and was afraid to answer the door. I was terrified when the UPS man came. I spent our first anniversary by myself, and my birthday, waiting for a call from my husband. When he finally called, he told me he that I would not be seeing him within a week, like we'd thought. The leave schedule was rearranged, and he went from being seventh on the list to twenty-second."

Jessica glances at her husband, and he grabs her hand in both of his.

"I had another anxiety attack, and things kept getting worse, until I had a nervous breakdown. I'd been seeing a therapist, but I wasn't getting any better, so I talked to Chad, and we applied for him to be discharged because of my medical situation. We had to file a lot of paperwork, and several doctors had to sign off on it, but thank God he's home. I'm so happy to have him back that I'm doing much better now."

If this is her "better," then thank goodness she got her husband home. I recall hearing something somewhere about being able to apply for a medical discharge if you can prove overwhelming hardship. It's been hard for me, hard for all of us, and I could probably work the system, but that doesn't feel right. I don't think it's the solution for me, and I whisper that to Sally, before returning to my table, still thinking about what I've just heard.

After ordering coffee, I ask the people at my table how they're coping, something we don't often speak of because it opens the gate to fear. Some of the women have gotten prescriptions for Xanax, to hold off the nightmares and make it through the day. Others use the tried and true method of alcohol sedation, and God knows, I've done that myself from time to time. But nothing like the newlywed wife who picks up a bottle of wine every night after work, or the mother who downs almost two cases of beer a week, something she never did before, not even in college.

I've heard that the families of deployed soldiers, especially the soldiers in the Guard and Reserves, who never really imagined they'd ever be in a war zone, are experiencing a type of secondary post-traumatic stress disorder. I've seen nothing to contradict that; we're all struggling to survive in whatever way we can.

There are those who find comfort in denial. I understand it, and wish, at times, I could go there, too.

I have also wished for the comfort of the absolute conviction in the righteousness of this war. Not by a long shot am I the only one whose extended family has tuned out, without turning on. Many of my relatives are staunch Republicans, and when I share with them how I'm feeling, the response is, "Isn't it nice that we live in a country where everyone can voice their opinion?"

Sometimes, when we MFSO members talk about our dead soldiers, absent spouses, and missing children, sent to fight a war that was wrong from the start, the response is, "Well, they volunteered, didn't they?"

More often than not, those words spew from the mouths of people with six-figure incomes and stock dividends. The ones whose wives, husbands, and kids haven't been drafted by poverty. The people for whom the false promises ring true; those who are fearful that it will cost them too much to change.

They don't seem to realize that there is no such thing as security, homeland or otherwise. Go ahead, buy your Hummers and build your gated communities, proceed with your plans, but there is no amount of money that can ever be made that will fully insulate anyone from the instability of the market, or the tenuousness of health, much less the random attack of terrorism. In fact, the United States' decision to invade Iraq as part of the war on terror has been directly tied to an increase in attempted terrorist attacks on this country.

The idea that we are ever truly in control of our safety is laughable. Maybe it's just that I learned that lesson long ago: I don't bank on what should be, or is supposed to be anymore. I live with what is.

On a good day, the days when I know my husband is still alive, and hasn't lost any of the men in his unit, I can deal with the comments from people who support the war. But there are others days when I'm tempted to give their names and addresses to a military recruiter, and see what they do when someone shows up at the door to recruit their child or grandchild.

On my worst days, when I am feeling so much less than charitable, I want to ask how they can respond to my e-mails with so much blood on their hands. I listen to the other women in MFSO and peace groups like Code Pink (there are always so many more women than men in this work), and they speak of the gaping divide in their families, of lost relations, of discarded friendships. We will never be able to measure the real cost of this war.

I see that cost the next morning in black coffins and white crosses at a vigil at the Arlington National Cemetery, where Section 60 is designated for the dead soldiers of Operation Iraqi Freedom. Several hundred MFSO members are in town, along with representatives from Women in Black, Veterans for Peace, and more than fifty-seven other affinity groups. We're all dressed in black, and meet near the reflection pool by the Women's Memorial.

It's ridiculously muggy, and by the time the noon ceremony begins, everybody's a tad bedraggled. Gone is the spark that's been present the past two days; we are here to mourn the dead.

Prayers are said, and some of us speak. When it's my turn on the little square stage, I declare, "I stand near the Capitol of a nation that claims to value life, liberty, freedom, justice, and truth. I call out to the people of America to rise up so that we may become the country we have said that we are. I stand next to the Women's Memorial and see the mothers, daughters, sisters, and wives of dead soldiers."

Waiting for the electronic echo to subside, I conclude, "I stand here as the wife of a National Guard Soldier. President Bush: Do not make me return a widow."

The memorial procession begins moments later, and the crowd carries one hundred cardboard coffins, draped in black cloth. They will join one thousand more when we arrive at the Ellipse.

As we walk, we're escorted by dozens of police, on foot or horseback, in cars and heavily armored trucks. Tour buses come and go, spilling out gray-haired veterans and families from Iowa. Fifty or so counterprotesters are standing on the sidewalk across the street, yelling and cursing, holding up signs. One reads, "Go to Hell, Traitors. You dishonor our dead on Hallowed Ground."

We walk for about thirty minutes, and by the time we get to the front lawn of the White House there are several thousand people on the grass. We file to the front, our procession captured by a phalanx of foreign press. More of our members speak, as well as Arun Gandhi, the grandson of Mahatma, and Michael Berg, whose son Nick was held hostage before being decapitated by insurgents.

After the closing ceremony, twenty-eight protesters try to deliver the names of the Iraq war dead to the White House. They are arrested on the third attempt, cuffed, searched, and tagged by park police, and then taken to small holding cells, where they are released several hours later.

Unable to find a cab or a stop for the public transport system, I ask one of the cops how to get out of here and back to my hotel. He points the way, and then scornfully remarks, "Next time, get a map."

I reply sweetly, "Well, I figured if President Bush could go to war without one, I surely wouldn't need one to visit the Capitol."

The American public was told that this war would be a quick strike, and Secretary of Defense Donald Rumsfeld promised last spring that by now there would be only 30,000 American troops still stationed in Iraq. Instead, there are over 140,000 soldiers in Iraq, with more on the way. Rumsfeld also claimed "We don't plan to function as an occupier." But on a recent visit to Iraq, Richard Lugar, the Republican chairman of the Senate Foreign Relations Committee said, "At least a five-year plan is required."

I relay this to Lorin, but it's not news to him. He's already told me that there's a five-year plan for occupation in order to build and secure bases in Iraq, mostly for the purposes of protecting the American oil supply. But he doesn't much care about politics right now, anyway.

It's Saturday morning, and I am thinking of what I would be doing if I were there, drinking coffee and taking the doggie for a walk, getting ready to watch some football. We'd probably go to a movie later in the afternoon.

I was up all night as I went out on a patrol from 10 p.m. till 6 a.m. It was very uneventful. Almost nothing happens at night here, since the Iraqi insurgents, while determined, have a bad work ethic. At night it is time to stop. Go figure.

I am sorry that you were sad yesterday, I too miss you a lot. You asked about me crying and right now I have not really given it much thought. I do have things to cry about, things that make me sad, you are one of them, my not being able to see you and missing the pets. A lot of the reason is the time and timing. Plus right now my testosterone level is pretty elevated. And I need to keep a straight head and clear mind, my love.

I don't like to keep a hard edge but I do. I would like to be able to just relax and not worry about things but I can't. I need to be on top of things all the time. The one time I am not is when the shit will happen and I will get caught with my pants down . . . and someone could DIE.

So far I am glad that I have not been out on a patrol when someone has been killed, because the worst part would be there is no time to stop and feel sorry, it is Charlie Mike, "continuing mission."

How do I feel about all this? I feel lonely and scared at times. I feel angry at other times. I feel as if I am in prison sometimes, that I did something very bad and was put in a place away from everyone I love and confined to a small area, looking out through a fence.

I hate being here. Every day is filled with noise I can't get away from. I am sick of dust and dirt. I am sick of gravel and having to wear a helmet when I get in a HMMV to go somewhere. I have to take my weapon everywhere I go except the gym and shower. I am tired of smelling other people fart. I am sick of being hot and sweating all the time, I want some rain, but with the rain comes the peanut butter cement mud.

I want some private time to myself. I want to be able to go where I want to go. I don't like having to deal with others all the time; some of them can really get on my nerves. I have to listen to three radios most of the day and also have people talking at the same time.

I am sick of not having you. Of not being able to be there for you. I am sick of not seeing you. I am sick of knowing that you are home alone and you are there cuz I am here and in some way I am somewhat responsible for that.

I would like to not have to worry about having a mortar or rocket land nearby. Not exactly how I want to end my days. I am tired of having to go to meetings, which is what I have to do now.

I just want to love you.

I reassure him that I love him, and pray for him, and support him, but I worry about what this is costing him, and us. I've been home two days when I get a call to tape a thirty-second commercial for Texans for Truth, a grass-roots nonprofit in Texas that is affiliated with DriveDemocracy.org. Founded by Glenn W. Smith, the fledgling organization assists citizens in making their voices heard in politics. Glenn is a longtime journalist, and has been politically active for years, serving as a behind-the-scenes advisor to several U.S. senators and governors.

Glenn's second book, *Unfit Commander,* is coming out next week, and it's an in-depth exploration of Bush's military service, including new documents released by the Pentagon. Texans for Truth has been dogging President Bush about his questionable record in the National Guard, and just announced a $50,000 reward for anyone able to prove President Bush fulfilled his drills and duties in the Alabama Air National Guard.

The ad will air in the swing states, and the focus is on the backdoor draft, enacted by a President who appears not to have completed his own military contract. I fly out the next day. After picking up my bag, I find Glenn outside the Austin airport. He bears a striking resemblance to Billy Bob Thornton, but if the actor is the prototype, Glenn is the upgrade, version 7.1. His Texas drawl reinforces the similarity, and we talk about the election on the way to the hotel. After checking in, we go to a private residence of one of the Drive Democracy members.

I spend the next hour and a half being interviewed by Glenn about the irony of the National Guard being sent to fight a war by a President who appears not to have completed his own commitment to the Guard. What's more, the President has already forced more than twenty thousand soldiers to serve long after their contracts have run out. Glenn and I go to dinner while his partner, Margie, the video director, edits the tape.

We stop by for a preview before Glenn drops me off at the hotel, and six hours later, he's back to take me to the airport. I'm exhausted when I get home, and although it's just after noon, I fall fast asleep, surrounded by my pets.

The next day's breaking story from Iraq is about the 343rd Quartermaster Company, a seventeen-member Army Reserve platoon from the Southeastern United States that has been arrested for refusing a "suicide mission" to deliver fuel. An initial delivery attempt was refused when it was discovered that the fuel had been contaminated with water. After returning to base, the platoon was told to take the fuel to a base in Taji, Iraq, north of Baghdad.

The 343rd is a supply unit whose general mission is to deliver fuel and water. Their trucks have a top speed of forty miles per hour, and a combination of factors, including improper maintenance, have made the trucks extremely unsafe, and they were generally considered "deadlined." Armed Humvees and helicopter escorts are standard on missions, but that support wasn't provided for this particular assignment, even though it was generally understood that it wasn't a matter of if they'd be ambushed, but when.

For all of these reasons, the soldiers refused the order to attempt the delivery of tainted fuel that had been declined once already. That decision could result in the soldiers being charged with the willful disobedience of orders, punishable by dishonorable discharge, forfeiture of pay, and up to five years confinement.

The military command calls the action "An isolated incident confined to a small group of individuals." But those of us with soldiers on the ground know the truth about the continuing pattern of faulty equipment, a lack of protective gear, and the unarmored Humvees that put our loved ones at risk, and contributes to their deaths.

Retired Lieutenant Colonel George Isenberg and his wife, Beverly, have been MFSO members ever since their grandson, Sergeant Benjamin Warren of the Oregon National Guard, was killed on patrol by a roadside bomb that tore through his unarmored Humvee. Military Families Speak Out steps up immediately to support the 343rd, and the incident thrusts the longstanding equipment and supply problems faced by Guard and Reserve units into the national spotlight.

The weekend warriors seldom have access to the most contemporary military equipment. Post-Cold War planning was based on the premise that the Guard would be used in the later stages of battle, after they had received the necessary equipment, personnel, and training. During peacetime, Guard units do not have the resources required for wartime missions, and are not ready for rapid deployment. So when the call came to fight in the global war on terror, Guard units either transferred large amounts of equipment in various stages of operability, shifted personnel, or went to combat without it. Some of the 81st's vehicles were undrivable when the Brigade deployed and had to be dragged onto the carriers headed for Kuwait. In 2004, there was an eleven point three percent, or $15.7 million, shortage in funding for the required equipment. Sending them into an armed conflict with substandard equipment directly increases the mortal danger faced by these troops. In the early days of the invasion, National Guard Lieutenant General Blum said, "The resourcing and equipping of the National Guard is indistinguishable from that of the active duty soldiers."

More recently, the military has been forced to acknowledge there have been shortages, after being deluged with complaints. Claiming the lack of supplies was primarily due to the rapid deployments, the Army maintains that it has worked to quickly improve the situation. But National Guard and Reserve soldiers are still being deployed with defective radios, undependable trucks, and an insufficient number of soundly armored vehicles. Such was the case with the 1544th Transportation Company of the Illinois National Guard.

Relatives of the soldiers offered to cover the costs of welding steel plates on the unit's trucks when they were preparing for their February 2004 deployment. They were turned down by the Army, which told the soldiers and their families that they would be given up-armored vehicles in Iraq. Seven months later, many of the trucks remain unarmored, or minimally outfitted. The company, which conducts some of the most hazardous missions in the Sunni Triangle, is sustaining more deaths and injuries than any other Illinois unit presently deployed.

Five soldiers have been killed and thirty-two wounded while delivering mail and supplies, and escorting civilian convoys. Most of the trucks in the 1544th have been outfitted, but only with the steel plates that would have been installed had the families been taken up on their initial offer.[14] The Army calls the trucks armored, but there are three levels of armoring.

Up-armored is the top of the line, factory direct vehicle, and provides the best protection for soldiers. Next, in terms of safety, are the armor kits, prefabricated pieces that are welded onto the chassis. The last alternative leaves the soldiers to fend for themselves and salvage scrap metal and whatever they can get their hands on to bolt, staple, or tape to the floor and sides of their vehicles.

The House Armed Services Committee indicates that there are plans to produce armor kits for a minimum of 2,806 midsize trucks. As of last month, just 385 of the kits had been made and shipped to Iraq. The Army is also investigating methods to manufacture armor truck cabs more efficiently, and has placed an order for almost seven hundred armored Humvees with special weapons platforms that can provide protection on convoys.[15]

In the meantime, soldiers are manning the gunner's turrets lacking the cover of metal protective shields. Karma Kumlin's husband, a .50 caliber gunner, went on numerous missions without the shield. At six-foot-five, he made for a rather large target. The men in her husband's Minnesota Guard

---

14. "Along with Prayers, Families Send Armor." *New York Times*, October 30, 2004.

15. "Lack of vehicle armor keeps troops on edge." *Seattle Times*, October 21, 2004.

unit spent two hundred dollars out of pocket on radios to take with them. Their radios are more reliable than the standard Army issue; however, they're also less secure.

But, as Lieutenant General Christianson, the Army's deputy chief of staff said in an interview with the *New York Times,* "War is a come-as-you-are party. The way a unit was resourced when someone rang the bell is the way it showed up." It seems the military wasn't expecting the invitation.

The Director of Support Operations reports problems with communication and infrastructure, and the grit and sand interfere with the functionality of equipment and wear it down faster than it can be replaced. At times, it has taken fifty-three days to get critical equipment to the battleground. The Army has never achieved its goal of fourteen-day delivery, in part because of the attacks on convoys and the efficiency of IEDs in destroying dozens of vehicles. The ones that aren't damaged beyond repair are being pushed far past their intended performance levels.

An *Associated Press* article recounts Pentagon reports that "Humvees are being driven six to eight times their training rate, and helicopters are used at two to three times the usual rate." It also cites that "The Army's wheeled Stryker vehicles, now deployed in Iraq from their base at Fort Lewis, are driving an average of 1,200 miles a month, nearly six times the average of 208."

A recently returned member of the Washington Army National Guard's 1161st Transportation Company spoke of driving trucks with "hillbilly" armor and windshields, doors, and seats riddled with bullet holes. There are plans to add armor kits to 1,600 heavyweight trucks, but so far only 446 have been sent. The Army states that the entire job will be finished in March of next year. When I ask Lorin about it, he says his unit has completed the upgrades, but others are still waiting, and no one is willing to predict when their kits will arrive.

You asked me the other day about armor, and here's why it's so important. I was out on patrol, and we had been driving up and down dirt roads for several hours. When you're doing that, you just wait for a loud boom, for the explosion, hoping that it's not you. As it was dark out, we were wearing our night vision goggles, and everything was green and gray. The Colonel was in the lead HMMV, the one that got hit. They were about a hundred and fifty meters up front, driving down the road next to a canal.

All of a sudden a big flash of light, followed by a loud boom and lots of dirt and smoke. My driver jumped, "What the fuck was that?!!"

"IED." I yelled, "Stop!"

We waited for the dust to clear and then listened on the radio to see if the lead HMMV was okay. Word came over the radio that everyone was okay, just shaken up. It was then a matter of slowly looking around our area for more IEDs, since sometimes they are daisy-chained together, and then getting security out, in case there were bad guys in the area.

Once that was done, we walked the medic down the road, following the tracks of the HMMV in front to check on the exploded HMMV. Then, with helicopters flying overhead scouring the countryside, we settled in and waited about four hours till the QRF [quick reaction force] and the wrecker could come to us to tow the HMMV out, since it had its front wheel blown off. The QRF had to come to us from a different way. Once they were within a thousand meters of us they got the minesweeper out and walked slowly down the road in front of their HMMVs looking for more IEDs, then lead the wrecker in to tow the broken truck out.

I have been waiting for this to happen when I am out on patrol. It was going to happen sooner or later. It is really not different from being inside the wire. Inside the wire rockets just fall from the sky with no warning, outside the wire IEDs explode without warning. Six of one, half dozen of another.

Actually, I stand a better chance of living through an IED than having a rocket or mortar hit close by, because we are in protected HMMVs. I've had 3/8-inch steel plating put on the bottom of my HMMV, along with ballistic windows, and the sides were armored up. Here inside the wire I have no protection like that. I am exposed to the sky. Especially when I am sleeping in my trailer.

Also, and I know this is harsh, but I don't mind having the stress release that this gives me. If given the chance to fire my weapon, it is very therapeutic. I just want to have the people who are trying to kill me and my troops stop and one way is to kill them, or at least try. Right now, and many of us feel this way, though they may not say it, but this is not for us about weapons of mass destruction, or fighting terrorism, but about fighting for ourselves, to keep ourselves alive and to protect one another.

Being here in Iraq is sometimes worse than being in the worst part of New York City . . . there is some truth to the comic thing I sent you the other day, you move to the middle of the ghetto, fully armed, with all sorts of weapons, take over a place and then say we are there to help.

How would Americans react if we had another country's army occupy us, and drive around fully armed, just stopping people and searching them, reducing them to nothing? It is sad in so many respects, and yet I can see why some of it has to be done.

The bad guys dress like every one else, you can't tell them apart from the civilians. They will wave at you, come and talk to you, then throw bombs at you and shoot at you. You just don't know who to trust and who not to.

I send you my love, lots of my love, and kisses. Know that I respect you and honor you for all that have done, been though and are living right now. You are my strength . . . my love and my joy.

Reading this after the fact does little to diminish the terror. I wonder what the hell the administration was thinking, and what it's gotten this country into. Then I place a slew of calls to politicians, wanting to know what they're doing to support the troops and provide armor and equipment. The only response is from the Washington State Kerry campaign, and we set up a meeting at my house with Puget Sound MFSO members and Moms with a Mission.

The latter group consists of military moms and wives who are traveling across fifteen states to talk about how President Bush's decisions have affected their families. Their forty-city tour kicked off in West Virginia, and they have met with congressional members, local politicians, veterans, and other military families.

Like us, they've supported their husbands, daughters, and sons, bought body armor, and watched as the campaign in Iraq worsens—all while the President continues to mislead the nation about the war.

We squish into the living room and introduce ourselves, sharing our links to the war. Lietta Ruger is a minister and MFSO member with a long family history in the military. She's married to a Vietnam War veteran, and for the first time in her life, is opposing the government's decision to invade a country. Today, she talks about how difficult it's been for her to break the taboo amongst the military families by speaking out against the President, and her commitment to pressing for real support of the troops, regardless of who is elected.

We discuss what more we can do to get out the vote, and I ask them how their trip is going and how they've been received. I'll be doing something similar, but much more confrontational, when I join the Band of Sisters for the Chasing Cheney tour next week to show people the human cost of the war.

The Band of Sisters will follow Vice President Dick Cheney as he campaigns in four different states. Cheney was picked because he's the chief apologist and profiteer for the war, and because the sheer size of the President's security detail would make it impossible to tail him.

I'd recently seen an ad featuring Brooke Campbell, whose brother, Sergeant Ryan Campbell, was killed in action in Baghdad on April 29, 2004, number 832 in the death tally. He was on an unarmored foot patrol when a suicide car bomber targeted him and seven other soldiers. The ad was sponsored by Win Back Respect, a campaign created by a group of leading experts on national security, and American citizens who share a deep concern about the negative impact that the Bush administration's policies have had on America's standing in the world.

Win Back Respect is focused on restoring America's reputation in the international community, and is convinced that entails new leadership. They're backing the Band of Sisters, a group of approximately thirty women with loved ones in Iraq, and Brooke is our official spokesperson. General Wesley Clark introduced the group in Wisconsin, and the Band is ramping up for two tours: one in the Midwest, the other in the South. I'm so moved by Brooke's spot that I contribute to the cause, and send a little note expressing my support and condolences.

Two phone calls later and I'm on the tour, too. The first person I see when I get off the plane in Des Moines, Iowa, is Karma Kumlin. She's lost about twenty pounds since her husband was deployed, and is beginning to look gaunt. I hug her, and ask how she's doing, and she relays her activism in Minnesota, much of it with veterans' groups.

Then she says, "You know Brad and I got married right before he left, but the military still hasn't processed our marriage license. I've been trying to get them to register me as his spouse for eight months, so that I can get medical benefits. They still haven't done it, but at least they corrected his pay. Who knows when we'll get the back pay he's owed."

Kara Hollingsworth overhears our exchange in the small, otherwise deserted motel lobby, and introduces herself as one of our fellow Sisters. She's a gorgeous, bright-eyed young woman, and her husband is Army enlisted, stationed at Fort Bragg. He's completed one tour of duty in Iraq, and will be going back next month. The last time he went, his paychecks weren't automatically deposited in their account for a month, and Kara had to turn to family members to feed herself and their four-year-old girl until it could be straightened out.

Seventy-five percent of the wives I've spoken with have had some problems with getting their husbands' pay, and the military is excruciatingly slow to correct them. The General Accounting Office conducted audited case studies of mobilized units, and found that during an eighteen-month period from August 2002 through January, 2004, *ninety-five* percent of mobilized or deployed Reservists had at least one pay problem.

A General Accounting Office survey of 481 Army National Guard personnel from six states discovered that 450 of them had experienced pay problems. In one case that has yet to be resolved, thirty-four members of a Colorado Special Forces reserve unit were incorrectly consigned an average of $48,000 in debt, according to GAO. It is not uncommon for all or a portion of pay to be withheld for months after the soldiers have arrived at their overseas deployment.

Hundreds of Guard and Reserve soldiers and their families have been forced to spend considerable time trying to get the military to correct their active duty pay and allowances.

Brooke and Deby arrive in the next hour, and we have a quick dinner, then head off to bed. We're spending the next two days traveling to six cities and will have plenty of time to get to know each other on the small private plane, which has been paid for primarily through online contributions and a few donors with deep pockets.

Our morning press conference consists of one local television station at the terminal for private planes. While we're waiting for our plane to arrive, we talk about the Report on Pre-War Intelligence (October 21, 2004) just released by Senator Carl Levin, Ranking Member of the Senate Armed Services Committee. According to the document, high-ranking officials in the Department of Defense exaggerated the Iraq-Al Qaeda relationship, and Donald Rumsfeld, Paul Wolfowitz, Dick Cheney, and President Bush have been attempting to build a case against Saddam Hussein ever since Bush took office.

We're discussing the seeming lack of interest the American public has in the findings as we're ushered onto the waiting plane by the tour's volunteer coordinator, Megan Ceronsky, a Yale Law student with a head full of bouncy brunette curls and a laugh that should be patented. As we're getting settled into the cramped space, she introduces us to Rob McClarty, the owner of a public relations/political firm in Arkansas, who has worked with the Clintons and General Clark, and who will be our point man.

On the way to our first stop in Washington, Pennsylvania, Brooke smoothes her hands on the leather-upholstered seat and tells us her story.

"I learned my brother was dead during a graduate seminar at Emory University when my mom called my cell phone. At first, all she could say was, 'He's gone.'

"A uniformed officer had just come to the house. I left immediately, and all I could think on the long journey home was *No*. The last time I saw Ryan was in February, when he had his two weeks leave. He talked about how disillusioned he was, and that we'd all been led to believe that Iraq was a serious threat to this country. He thought they'd find weapons of mass destruction.

"He was supposed to be done on April 25, but two weeks earlier, I got an e-mail from him, telling me his tour of duty had just been extended. He also wrote, 'Just do me one big favor, ok? Don't vote for Bush.' He was killed on the twenty-ninth, four days after he should've been home."

Speaking so softly that we have to lean in to hear, Brooke continues, "This has almost destroyed my mom. She would've loved to be here, but it's just way too hard for her. Me, I've got to be here, ever since I saw President Bush speaking at a black-tie fundraiser, doing a comedy routine about the 'missing' weapons of mass destruction. He was looking behind curtains and under tables, acting like he was searching for hidden weapons, laughing as he did. His joke cost my little brother his life. I pray for the President, but I will not vote for him."

We're silent for the rest of the flight, and thirty minutes later, we're touching down in Washington, Pennsylvania. We take a van to the Washington and Jefferson College campus, only to find that we've missed Cheney by moments. Several local media crews are still packing up, but they unload quickly, and Brooke tells her story, with the rest of us standing behind her.

Collegiate Bush supporters are converging on the street and sidewalk behind us as we walk back to the van. We have to push our way through, and the scornful yells of the students linger in our ears even after the sliding door is shut.

I see the hurt in the eyes of the other women, and can't tell who it is that says she's gotten two hateful messages on her answering machine about what she's doing.

We check into another motel and get up early to do it all again in Schofield, Wisconsin, before heading up to International Falls, Minnesota. We land at the private airstrip in the northern Minnesota town just minutes in advance of the Vice President, barely avoiding the airspace lockdown. Cheney travels with several jets and helicopters, and a massive cargo carrier that holds the black vehicles used in his entourage.

We're refused access to the auditorium where Cheney will be speaking, and Rob, who is constantly on his cell phone, says they're on to us. The tension in our little cadre ratchets up as we contemplate just what we're doing, and whom we're dealing with.

Trying to lighten the mood, which has suddenly turned grim, Rob says, "Welcome to International Falls, you S.O.B.," as we pass the Vice President's motorcade on our way back to the airport. We all bust up laughing, and it becomes the standard phrase upon arrival in every other city.

We're ushered to our plane by a handful of Cheney's Secret Service personnel. Cheney travels with dozens of them, and most are sitting in a lounge off to one side of the terminal. Almost to a man, they're wearing black, or deep navy blue, and have headsets and all manner of electronic paraphernalia. The guys who are walking us to our plane seem decent, and I joke with them about women and bathrooms as the Sisters take turns in the single restroom.

Back on the plane, heading to Sioux City, Iowa, we talk about our husbands, or sons, and how they're doing. Deby Keller is from Oregon, and her husband was called back to service after twenty years in the military. He's been living in Virginia for the past year, working as a Captain in the Army's Casualty Office, tracking the deaths of soldiers in Iraq. He's one of the points of entry for new casualty information, and Deby says his job is breaking his heart.

Their son is in the Oregon Guard, and he took a forty percent pay cut when he was called up. His wife and their two kids are trying to survive the financial hardship, and Deby and her husband are making up the difference to the tune of five hundred dollars a month. There's not much they can do about their daughter-in-law's deteriorating mental state, which suffered another setback when they learned that her husband's long deployment has cost him his job as a restaurant manager.

We arrive in Sioux City before Cheney, but the tiny terminal is filled with Bush and Cheney supporters. We ignore them on our way through and have our biggest press conference of the tour. Brooke repeats her story, and each of us takes a turn at the microphone. I speak about the Bush administration's arrogant rush to war, and failure to plan for peace. Kara steps up to talk about the need for a true international coalition, and for us to reengage as a member of the United Nations.

The U.S. was instrumental in establishing the United Nations as an international forum to prevent humanity from destroying itself with nuclear weapons. In recent years, a surprising number of Americans have begun to view the U.N. as relevant only for Third World nations, and the unilateral decisions of the Bush administration have exacerbated the situation.

During the campaign, both sides have denied the truth: the U.N. weapons inspectors were right, and the top American political, military, and intelligence leaders were wrong. That gigantic error is being ignored on the Republican campaign trail, which is one of the reasons we're here.

The weather is unseasonably warm and humid, and it's all we can do to keep from swatting the flies swarming about our heads. We maintain our composure for the cameras, and once we're done, make a run for the van. Cheney's flight is approaching, so we can't get clearance to leave. We snack on free donut holes and talk amongst ourselves, keenly aware that the people wearing Bush-Cheney buttons are watching us closely. A Secret Service agent rushes in, asking if there's anyone here with the Band of Sisters, and we studiously ignore him.

Once he's gone, one of the elderly, blue-suited women who have been reclining in the airport chairs strikes up a conversation. When she learns we're the Band of Sisters, she goes back to her coven, which quickly closes ranks around her. The tension is the room is rising rapidly, so much so that one of the airport staff members suggests that we might want to go and sit in the pilots' break room. When we're finally given clearance to take off, the whole building sighs with relief.

Our final destination is in Eau Claire, Wisconsin, where we'll be speaking across the street from the Republican Party headquarters. Cheney is staying in the hotel a block away, and we debate whether or not we should have dinner there. Deciding it's asking for trouble, we pile into a van and go off on what seems like a three-hour tour, trying to find the restaurant that was recommended by the desk clerk.

We reconvene in the lobby the next morning, which is filled with guests, seated at small tables enjoying the continental buffet. I leave my luggage at the desk, and join the others who are obviously upset.

"What's going on? Is everything all right?"

Brooke gets up, saying she needs another cup of coffee. In her absence, Kara whispers, "We were talking and a lady came up to us and asked what group we were with. When we told her, she pulled her little boy away, and said, 'Let's go, Tommy, we don't want to be around *those* people.'"

I can tell the words cut close to the bone, reminiscent as they are of what Kara's grandmother heard as she was trying to be accepted as an African American woman in the early sixties. She and I had discussed race relations, among other things, as we were hopping from city to city.

When we get to our corner of the busy intersection the next morning, about a hundred sign-waving supporters greet us. Unbeknownst to us, state Democratic supporters had heard about what we were doing and rallied support. In rural Wisconsin, some people had driven for three hours to get here at 8 a.m. There's a black and white blowup cow, as tall as a two-story building, courtesy of the dairy farmers who are organizing to support Kerry.

Some of the largest labor organizations in the country have passed resolutions demanding that the troops be brought home and the war ended. Union opposition to war is an about-face from their traditional stance. According to figures compiled by U.S. Labor Against the War, the combined memberships of regional, state, and national labor organizations that have officially come out against the war totals 9,564,800.

We say good-bye at the private airstrip, embracing tightly, with promises to stay in touch. The intensity of such deeply personal activism tends to forge powerful emotional bonds. Rob, Brooke, and I are worn out, and don't talk much on the short drive to the Minneapolis-St. Paul airport.

I attend Lorin's brother's wedding the following evening, and recite "The Invitation" by Oriah Mountain Dreamer during the brief, sweet ceremony. It's the same reading we had when we got married, and I'm wishing Lorin were here tonight. Dan proposed to Julie a few weeks before Lorin left, and asked if Lorin wanted them to wait to get married until he returned. Lorin was adamant that they not postpone the wedding for him, but he paused before he answered, perhaps wondering how much he would miss in the time he was gone, or whether his temporary absence would be permanent.

10

Acceptable Losses

NOVEMBER 2004

I WENT ONLINE YESTERDAY to find the location of my polling place. It's a junior high school in my neighborhood, and the dog and I go by it several times a week. If the kids are at recess, they run to the fence and say hi to the dog. The school is the halfway point of our walks, and several of the houses that we pass as we make our way home have signs staked in their yards, No WAR IN IRAQ.

Overwhelming evidence has forced the government to admit that there's no clear, compelling link between the events of September 11th and Saddam Hussein. The sad truth is that we could've gone another way in the aftermath of 9/11. Actually, for a few months, we did.

Our initial reaction to the very worst of human behavior was to demonstrate the very best of it, both in this country and abroad. We answered the call to hate with a call to love. We opened our arms, and our hearts, to one another and to the world. As great as the horror and tragedy of that day was, the equally great and horrific tragedy of our time has been our unwillingness to sustain the outpouring of genuine love and profound human compassion that emerged in this country. The travesty is not only that we didn't maintain it. It is that we have *actively chosen* not to.

Once we'd established that the persons around us were safe (if indeed they were), and that *our* jobs weren't in jeopardy (if indeed they weren't), the vast majority of Americans, at the behest of the President, went back to business. As usual.

There has been no love between the political parties during this campaign; at times, the animosity between those who condone the war in Iraq and those who don't is almost tangible. There is no real empathy evidenced for the families who've lost their soldiers, or the countless civilians killed in Iraq. We have reverted to measuring body counts in terms of "theirs" or "ours," a distinction that disappeared in September of 2001.

But then it's almost as if something (or someone) came along, and said, "You have seen that it is possible to bind love as a social force. Now, will you?"

And we said no. Because we already had the tools and tradition of using military force, brute force, unilateral force. Because our government provided a fear-o-meter that was telling us to be very, very afraid, and for a lot of other reasons, too, we said, no to love. And not for the first time.

It is not a coincidence that the unhealed specter of Vietnam has come home to roost in the final days leading up to the 2004 Presidential election. We were to have gotten it that time.

We were supposed to have said no then, and mean it. We were supposed to have begun to live as if the catchphrase of the era, "all you need is love," wasn't just an ad campaign. Instead, we decided that perhaps money could buy us love. We have seen now that it cannot.

Yet, we dismiss love as a possibility, saying it's impractical, and simplistic. Love is for children. Instead, we trot out theories and defenses, offering all kinds of reasons why love just won't work. But I think what we're most afraid of is that it will. I suspect we know that to practice an *agape* love, a free and flowing love, will not only change the rules, it will introduce a whole different game on this planet.

The only cure for terrorism is to eradicate the underlying causes that bring it into being. If we genuinely want this country to be safe, we must work with the global community to attain goals that help the impoverished and the wealthy, northern and southern hemispheres, developing and advanced nations, and our common humanity. The end of terrorism will occur when the reign of terror has been replaced with the rule of love.

In the weeks following the attacks on America, the world wept with us. In the long months and years of the invasion of Iraq, America should be weeping still. It is unbelievable to me that we aren't. I cannot comprehend how the soul of this nation can survive the knowledge that one of its sons, a Marine Reservist, was sent to Iraq, was shattered by what he'd seen, returned home and was denied treatment by the Veteran's hospital, and later hung himself in his parents' basement. Is not each life precious?

That's what they tell the kids at Totem Junior High, where they teach the children that violence is not okay, and being a bully is not how you make friends. And that's what I'm thinking about when I go there to vote on November 2.

Lorin says he voted a while back, and I don't ask for whom. But I do ask if my activities of the past few weeks have caused him any problems, because some of it was on news programs that are seen in Iraq. He writes:

> I haven't really been harassed at all, but I did have one nice comment from the JAG. He said that he liked the article, told his wife about it. He said if he were home he would be very involved with the Kerry campaign. He said to his wife that here was a soldier who is a complete professional Non-Commissioned Officer (NCO), and look at what his wife is doing. He had good comments. But I did get harassed by some of the other guys.

I'm relieved to know that the latest articles about my activism are not creating waves with his superiors, but am sorry that he's getting flak from some of the guys. Then again, we've both somewhat grudgingly accepted that anytime I speak out, he's going to hear about it. People will sometimes say things to him that they never would to me, although they tend to reserve the harshest remarks for when they think we're out of earshot.

I ignore or avoid negative comments aimed toward me, but seize on an e-mail that's forwarded by Lorin's sister, Liahann, who'd written some of her friends about the Chasing Cheney tour.

> Hi there,
>
> Reading this has made me think so much of my mom, and what she would think of this election. Her brother, my uncle John, joined the Air Force in 1965, figuring he'd be drafted at some point and he'd rather choose how he'd go to Vietnam. He was shot down in 1966 and is one of approximately a thousand service members still MIA in Vietnam.
>
> My mother was never especially political in her life—and certainly not radical in any way. But she became radicalized because the government was so clearly lying to the POW/MIA families, and to the country as a whole, about what really was going on.
>
> Some of my earliest memories are of going to meetings on military bases and to antiwar rallies organized NOT by hippies but by military families. In our generation we all grew up in the shadow of that war in ways that made us suspicious of government, especially its leadership in war. But I grew up knowing that in a really personal, direct way, and yet I still can't even imagine what it feels like for your family now.
>
> I think a lot about you and your family these days—and what a great role model your sister-in-law is. While we never think we should have to chase our

leaders across the country to tell the truth, good for her for doing what needs to be done now! I am grateful that people like her are continuing the tradition of people like my mother and the other family members I remember so clearly—people who never imagined that they would stand up to generals and air force commanders to demand truth and justice for their brothers, husbands, sons. And Stacy is standing up to the Vice President—yay!

Now, time to watch the returns . . .

I was invited to Congressman Smith's election night party in Tacoma, but decide to stay home, reluctant to fly solo at such a big social event where I don't know anyone. I watch the returns on TV, and check in with other MFSO members throughout the evening via phone calls and e-mails, turning in shortly after reading this message from Nancy and Charley:

> It's going on 2 a.m. here on the East Coast, and things are looking pretty grim. We keep reminding ourselves of something Dave Cline, national president of Veterans for Peace and a Vietnam Veteran, frequently reminds us of: that we are Winter Soldiers, not sunshine patriots, and are in it for the long haul. And then there's the Martin Luther King Jr. quote: "Let us remember that there is a creative force in this universe working to pull down the gigantic mountains of evil, a power that is able to make a way out of no way, and transform dark yesterdays into bright tomorrows . . . the arc of the moral universe is long, but it bends toward justice."

I want to believe that's true, but Bush's reelection, particularly in light of the mounting death count and the just-released report in the *Lancet,* a highly regarded British medical journal, makes it difficult. Les Roberts, a public health expert at the Johns Hopkins Bloomberg School of Public Health, compiled the report. His team, which included investigators from the Columbia University School of Nursing and Al Mustansiriya University in Baghdad, surveyed households in thirty-three regions of Iraq and then compared civilian mortality rates before and after the invasion. It found that the risk of death was two and a half times greater after the U.S. arrived.

After reviewing the methodology, independent statisticians confirmed the rigorous and thorough nature of the study, and speculated that the civilian death count of a hundred thousand might very well under represent the true mortality rates, rather than the much lower numbers being reported by the American media. In the first eight months of 2004, there were three thousand gunshot-related deaths in Baghdad alone.

More than half of those who have died are women and children. At the twenty-month mark, the war in Iraq has become the deadliest conflict since Vietnam. And like Vietnam, dubbed the first "modern" war, ninety percent of casualties are civilians.

The most conservative estimate is that twenty thousand Iraqi people have been killed. It's been reported that Saddam Hussein oversaw the killing of at least three hundred thousand of his subjects, but only a small fraction of that number has been verified. If it is accurate, it took Saddam decades to reach it. Coalition forces may have arrived at a third of that total in just eighteen months, making it more murderous than Saddam's regime by any measure, greatly weakening the challenge of war proponents asking, "Would you rather Saddam was still in power?"

John Hari of the *Independent* is one of many pro-war commentators and politicians who've played the numbers game, citing figures of how many people would have died if Saddam had been in power, using it to call the war morally correct. The *Lancet* report nullifies that thesis, as well as any argument that this can be called a "moral war."

Exit polls indicated that it was President Bush's moral values that got him reelected, and the National Annenberg Election poll of military members and their families indicated that the majority felt that Bush was a more trustworthy commander in chief than Kerry would be. However, at least a third of military spouses feel that things are going badly in Iraq, and twenty-seven percent disapprove of Bush's performance as the commander in chief. That probably explains the twenty-five percent of the military who voted for Kerry, the overwhelming international preference.

An *Associated Press* article on November 3rd quoted Wagner Markues, a Brazilian, as saying, "We don't understand Americans now. Are they getting different news than us about the scandals in the Iraqi prisons and the children and civilians who are getting killed?"

At least fifty percent of the military is registered as Republican, twenty percent as Democrat, and twenty-seven percent claim to be Independent. Commentary about the election zings across the MFSO listserve. Member Sabrina King writes:

> Since my husband is in his third deployment to the sandbox in three years, I was so angry [about] the election results I nearly hyperventilated, quite literally. I know it means he will spend the next four years gone, just like this last

four, never home more than six months. I know it means I will continue to raise two children by myself, and that despite what the public says of supporting families I will still be fixing my roof alone, mowing my yard alone, changing my oil alone and every other thing I do alone.

I am tired of people voting for wars, it's easy when you don't have to go. And when you aren't left behind. Our son is nine years old. He came home Tuesday and said he wanted to make a sign for the yard that said, "Thanks to all the Republicans for keeping my dad gone another four years." It is amazing to me that a party supposedly cloaked in "family values" would do this.

More and more I hate this country, I hate the Army, and I can understand why the rest of the world hates such selfish arrogant ignorant asses. And I still want to know where my slice of the oil pie is since my husband has spent eighty percent of the last three years procuring it and we still live below the poverty line.

She's one of thousands of temporarily single parents barely scraping by because of this war, and hundreds of military families in Thurston County, Washington, home of Fort Lewis, have had to enroll in the WIC nutrition program to qualify for food stamps to feed their children. Between thirty and forty percent of Reservists draw lower salaries during mobilization and deployment. This creates financial chaos for the families left behind, and adds yet another post-deployment stressor, as it will likely take months, if not years, to crawl out of the money pit.

A few months ago, America's Second Harvest, a national alliance of food banks, collaborated with the National Guard to launch a program providing information about emergency food support to families of activated National Guardsmen and Reservists.

Food banks around the country have had a surge in demand from Reservist families, and the Army Emergency Relief organization reported that requests for assistance from active duty National Guard and Reserve troops shot up several hundred percent in 2003. The Department of Defense has been fielding calls from around the country from states wanting the Defense Department to educate military families about how to apply for food stamps and other relief programs.[16]

Homeland security experts are worried that having 60,000 Guardsmen in Iraq is weakening the nation's ability to defend itself now and in the future. Rather than complying with the recommendation of the Phase III Report of the U.S. Commission of National Security/21st Century issued

16. "Hungry U.S. Families Can't Be Defended." *The Oregonian*, June 2, 2004.

February 15, 2001, which urged that "The National Guard be given home-land security as a primary mission, as the U.S. Constitution itself ordains," the administration is methodically stripping away the first lines of defense offered by the National Guard and Reserve. And at the very time military families need it most, the government is in the process of slashing their benefits.

Speaking to the government's proposed funding cuts to schools on military bases, Lieutenant General Edward Hanlon, commander of the Marine Corps Combat Development Command, stated: "To win battles, you'd better have a good family foundation." Destroying this foundation has harmful implications for the effectiveness of the army.

Further undermining the short and long term capacity of the military, Chief Helmly of the U.S. Army Reserve says, "We have not, in the Army Reserve, applied the positive leadership necessary both in terms of how we treat people but also in our personnel practices and procedures to entice them to feel wanted, respected, admired."

According to an Annenberg Survey released by CBS News in October of 2004, the number of regular enlisted soldiers who said they were properly trained and prepared was just more than six in ten, but for Guard and Reservists, it was only four in ten. One informal survey showed that Reservists have registered ninety percent of the complaints about equipment shortages. According to the Army Guard's publication about the history of the Guard, the same type of complaints were heard in 1917, when the first of 433,478 Guardsmen were mobilized to fight in World War I.

> The extent and effectiveness of training varied widely. On Long Island, the Rainbow Division implemented a training regime that emphasized unity cohesion, physical fitness, and basic combat skills even though most of the troops lacked uniforms and shoes.

Pentagon officials have long denied any equipment shortages, but Congress just authorized the Department of Defense (DOD) to order reimbursement of service members filing their claims within one year of the purchase of body armor. The amount was capped at that $1,100 per item and the equipment purchased must be certified as usable for personal protection.

I tell Lorin about the new policy, but he still stubbornly refuses to acknowledge there've been problems with supplies. I've been sending him information about this for months, telling him about the website Karma set up to raise money to buy body armor for her husband's platoon. But Lorin continues to maintain there aren't any problems, regardless of how much proof I provide. Or what's being reported in the news.

Watched over by just a dozen National Guard and Reserve soldiers, 380 tons of explosives were looted from the al-Qaqaa ammunition site. Soldiers from the 317th had sent messages to commanders in Baghdad, requesting help to secure the site, but they were denied reinforcements. When Iraqi looters arrived with dozens of pickups, the badly outnumbered soldiers were unable to prevent them from loading up their vehicles and driving off.[17]

Three days later, the Fallujah offensive begins, and nine Reservists are killed on the first full day of fighting—the highest single-day death toll for part-time soldiers since the war began. An e-mail from Lorin follows:

> I knew Fallujah had started when helicopters began flying overhead around-the-clock, on the way to the hospital on base. Then I woke up at 0530 to the alarm telling us we had been attacked. I rolled over and went back to sleep. I wish I could be there to hold you in my arms and just be with you right now.

His leave is scheduled from November 14 through December 4, but I want him out of there now, a feeling that intensifies when I get a message from Dianna, one of the women in the Band of Sisters, about a twenty-one-year-old Marine's wife with a daughter who just turned three. During her daughter's party, right after singing "Happy Birthday," she answered a knock on the door. Standing on her front step was the same Chaplain that informed Dianna that her husband was dead.

Smoke from the candles was still wafting in the air when the young woman learned that her twenty-four-year-old husband had been killed in the first days of the Fallujah offensive. His tour of duty was set to end in three weeks. Fallujah is becoming a slaughterhouse when Lorin calls to tell me he's driving to Baghdad to drop off some papers.

I am appalled that he's being sent out on a mail delivery mission, and ask why they can't just put the documents on one of the planes that make regular trips to Baghdad. He doesn't know; all he knows is he's got to go.

"Don't worry, it'll be fine." He says soothingly. "I'm taking three other vehicles, so we'll have a little convoy."

"Well, I still think it's ridiculous. Please be careful, and call or send an e-mail when you're back." I'm fidgety and restless for the rest of the day.

---

17. *Los Angeles Times*, November 4, 2004.

Lorin phones the following morning, assures me that he's okay, and then says, "Something happened on the way. When you hear about it, it was the truck behind me by about twenty minutes."

The next day's paper mentions that a member of the 81st was killed after a suicide bomber penetrated his convoy as it was approaching Baghdad. Two California members of the 81st have been killed by IEDs in the past week, and another soldier who was riding shotgun in one of the HMMVs had both of his feet blown off. I e-mail Lorin, and ask how he's doing.

> Not too much to report right now. I am very tired. Haven't got a lot of sleep, last night we had to place several caskets on a plane so they could make the trip home. . . . more sadness in California. It's is just a sad reminder of where we are and what we face . . . I wish that the ones who have decided how this is playing out were the ones who had to experience it instead of hiding behind bulletproof cars and inside brick buildings in D.C.

Dear God, please just let him make it home. Lorin's next call is from Camp Doha in Kuwait, where he's been waiting for hours, along with several hundred other soldiers scheduled for leave. The contract plane that will take them to Dallas, by way of Ireland, has finally arrived. On November 15th, at six in the morning, he calls with his flight number and says he'll be at Sea-Tac airport at noon.

The remaining hours go by quickly, and I get to the airport with twenty minutes to spare. I show my military dependent ID at the American Airlines counter, giving them my husband's name and flight number. Commercial airlines are required by federal law to provide free flights to soldiers during a time of war. The clerk issues me a gate pass, and I scramble to security, stopping short when I see the line that triples back on itself.

I briefly consider ducking under the barricade, but suspect that would detain me for hours, if not days. Trying not to appear frantic, I approach one of the checkpoint personnel, and explain the situation. She scrutinizes my pass and ID before escorting me through.

His plane is still a few minutes out, and I sit by the window, shaking from nervous anticipation. After what seems like a ridiculously long time, I see a shaved brown head at the back of the line.

I'm crying when he wraps me in his arms and lifts me off the floor. We stay like that for a very long time. When he sets me down, there's mascara on his uniform and lipstick on his face. I kiss him properly, and he grabs my hand and his rucksack. I stop in the restroom on the way out, and call my father to let him know that Lorin was safely in Seattle. The answering machine picks up, and I say, "I've got him."

I drive home with one hand on the wheel, keeping the other on his leg or arm. I ask, "So, how was your trip? Did you get any sleep?"

"It wasn't bad, I slept some. Took a shower in Dallas. They've got a lounge area set up for soldiers."

"How did people in the airport respond to you?"

"Well, it was really interesting. Everybody was really nice, and respectful, some people came up to me and said thank you. That surprised me. I thought maybe I'd get some comments like 'baby-killer' or something. But I did notice that a lot of the men, particularly guys in business suits, could barely look at me. They'd see me coming and look away, almost like they were embarrassed."

"Why do you think that is?"

"My guess is those were the guys who were all pumped up about going to war, but were too afraid to go themselves."

We have an MFSO meeting at the house on Lorin's third day back. I want to introduce him to some of the people I've been talking about, and give him a better sense of what the group is about. He agreed to it, but he's got some reservations, and as we're arranging chairs in the living room, he asks, "Are you sure it's okay if I'm here? I don't want any antiwar people getting mad at me because I'm a soldier."

"No, honey, they won't. Remember, they've all got soldiers of their own. They want to hear what it's like, and if there's anything the troops need over there that they're not getting. Besides, part of the reason we decided to have the meeting at our house is because they knew you'd be here. I don't think you understand how important it is for us to be able to see you guys in person. Even though you're not their soldier, you give them hope that they will see theirs alive again, too."

"Well, okay, but if I don't agree with something, I'm going to say so."

"That's fine, I expect you to."

After Lorin is introduced to Judy Linehan, Cathy Schop, Sherrie Tillstra, and Meg Hamner and her mom, Judy, we discuss what we've heard about Halliburton and Kellogg, Brown, and Root having a five-year plan to remain in Iraq. When the conversation segues into the military's role in Iraq, Lorin interrupts, saying adamantly, "You all need to be really clear about the fact that the decision to invade Iraq was an administrative one, and a lot of military officials advised against it. If you're going to be talking about this stuff, then get your facts straight."

"Okay, then you tell us: what's the situation with body armor and armor for trucks?"

"You people really need to let that go. My guys have body armor, and the units I know about do, too."

"But what about some of the soldiers who've had to use the old flak jackets?"

"What about it?" He replies hotly. "That was at the beginning of the invasion. And the Guard never trained with flak jackets or body armor because we didn't think we'd ever need them. Besides, the insurgents are coming up with ways to defeat the armor, so unless you're driving a tank, there's really not a whole lot you can do."

I jump up from my seat, and say, "Okay, folks, let's remember that we're about supporting the troops here, not interrogating them. Anybody want something to drink?"

I pour coffee and we pass around some cookies, moving on to talking about upcoming events and debating whether or not it's wise to go door-belling at the housing around Fort Lewis. Most of us weigh in against it, not wanting to create problems for active duty personnel and their spouses.

I say, "We've got to respect where people are at, and Nancy and Charley have never been about in your face member recruitment. If and when people are ready, they'll find us. After all, isn't that how we all got here?"

People nod in agreement, and we bring the meeting to an end. Meg and her mom stick around for a few minutes afterward. Meg asks Lorin, "So, how's my husband doing?"

"Oman? He's okay. Plays a lot of video games. Why? Haven't you heard from him?"

"No. The last time we talked was a few weeks ago, in the middle of the night. He said he'd call me back later that morning, but I haven't heard from him since. I send him e-mails, too, and now he's not even answering those."

Shaking his head, Lorin says, "Do you want me to talk to him?"

"If you wouldn't mind, just please ask him to call home when you see him." When she starts to cry, Lorin hugs her, letting her weep on his shoulder for a while. Drying her tears, Meg pulls away, giggling in embarrassment.

"Oh, God, I'm sorry. I can't seem to stop crying."

Before the tears start again, her mother whisks her out the door. The following days are an endless series of lunches, dinners, and cocktail gatherings with friends, as well as several of Lorin's coworkers who've been fired or laid off since he was deployed. In the middle of the week, we load up the car and head to Coeur d'Alene for the Thanksgiving holiday. I don't ask Lorin about what he's seen, and he doesn't volunteer. I set aside my questions, just wanting to enjoy him for these few weeks, knowing he's going right back into harm's way when it's over.

Passing through Spokane, we swing by Helen's junior high classroom, where Lorin talks to the kids and shows a clip of video footage that one of his guys taped over in Iraq. The computer screen explodes in bursts of light, followed by billowing smoke as round after round of mortars are fired. I'm watching this from a seat in the back of the room when Ginny, a school counselor, approaches with a handout entitled "Washington State Operation: Military Kids."

In light of the large number of kids whose parents are suddenly being sent to a war zone as fulltime soldiers, the military is presenting half-day seminars meant to help educators and counselors support the students who are "coping with the stresses of knowing their parents are deployed and in harm's way."

Some of the training topics are: "Military culture and the impact of war," "The cycle of deployment and its effects on military families and youth," and "Post-deployment reunion and reintegration issues."

Ginny tells me about some of the kids she's begun working with, and how their school absences have jumped and their grades plummeted since their parents were sent to war. I want to know more, but the bell rings, indicating that class is in session.

Lorin and I say our good-byes, and on our way out, Helen gives me a letter written by one of the other teachers. He served with Lorin in the eighties and early nineties, and they spent a summer fighting fires.

We were there in all kinds of weather, often under stressful conditions. In all of those circumstances, Lorin stood out. He did his job and helped others do theirs. He cared about the men he led and directed. There is a phrase of honor in the Guard: "A man I'd go to war with." Lorin is such a man. Knowing him and having served with him is a privilege. My heart weeps that he and others like him find themselves where they are today. Perhaps that will change before long. I share your burdens and concerns and pride. L———

Thanksgiving at my dad's house is packed with family and friends, more than twenty-four of us around the table, all vying for time with my husband. Lorin and I get together with his family at Helen and Paul's place in Cheney the following day, returning home the day after that.

During his last few days of leave, we go to matinees and do a little shopping, and one of our neighbors shows up at the door with his six-year-old boy. Hayden bashfully hands Lorin a bound, laminated booklet of cards made by all fifteen of his classmates. After prompting from his dad, Hayden asks Lorin if he'll come to his kindergarten class at Star Lake Elementary.

We show up at the school the next day, and tap on the glass panel of the classroom door. The teacher motions us in, and the kids' eyes widen when they see Lorin, crew-cut and camouflaged, an action hero come to life. Hayden's wearing a camo shirt and pants, and Lorin sits on the floor with him and the other kids, talking about what it means to be a soldier. He teaches them how to salute, and before we go, everybody stands and recites the Pledge of Allegiance.

As we're leaving, the teacher says, "Thank you so much for coming. The kids loved it, and Hayden's going to be the most popular boy in class for the rest of the week."

Sitting in the classroom of perfectly formed, healthy little kids made me think of the soldiers in this war, and the first Gulf War, who are bringing Depleted Uranium (DU) back to the States in their bodies, and passing it on to their wives, girlfriends, and children.

A study group of 251 soldiers in Mississippi who had all fathered normal babies prior to deployment found that sixty-seven percent of the post-Gulf War children they had were born with acute defects such as missing eyes, limbs, and internal organs, or serious blood diseases and immune disorders. The children's immunological problems frequently mirror those of their parents, and the offspring of dozens of Iraq war veterans have been born with the same series of abnormalities as seen in the children of soldiers after the first Gulf war.

What's particularly astounding this time around is how rapidly soldiers exposed to DU are displaying symptoms. An *American Free Press* article announced a forty percent malignancy rate in one unit that served in Iraq in 2003. Figures from the Department of Veterans Affairs show that there are presently 518,730 "Gulf-era veterans" on medical disability, even though only 7,035 have been reported wounded in Iraq. Those numbers are inclusive of *all* soldiers who've served over there since 1991, and roughly correspond with the 1998 map released by the Department of Defense, which verifies that up to 436,000 troops had entered areas heavily contaminated by DU radioactive dust.

Four hundred sixty-seven of the 580,400 soldiers who served in Gulf War I were wounded, but by 2000, 11,000 were dead, and 325,000 had been put on permanent medical disability, a shocking fifty-six percent of the total number of soldiers who served. Exposure to depleted uranium is ultimately lethal, and ironically, it meets the U.S. government's definition of a Weapon of Mass Destruction.[18]

Depleted uranium is a radioactive toxic waste product used in armor and to coat bullets and tanks. When hit or fired, the material gives off a fine mist of chemical that coats everything in the vicinity and is distributed by air currents, seeping into the soil and groundwater, causing permanent contamination.Depleted uranium has a radioactive life of around four point five billion years. And it destroys the genetic code.

The U.S. government states that being exposed to just .01 gram of D.U. in a single week can cause health problems. Every DU round fired by an M-1 series tank generates up to 3,100 grams of dust on impact. The dust is insoluble, and stays in the body for decades when inhaled. DU exposure is cumulative, and problems often take years to manifest.[19]

The levels ingested and/or breathed in by soldiers and civilians in the Persian Gulf War and during Operation Iraqi Freedom are so staggeringly high that symptoms are appearing within months of absorbing the particles. The sufferers aren't considered casualties of war.

One hundred and thirty-six U.S. soldiers were killed this month, more fatalities than any other month of the invasion. The official casualty counts of Operation Enduring Freedom are 1,102 dead and 7,782 severely wounded American soldiers, more than half of them so badly that they're unable to return to duty. The number doesn't include the estimated twenty thousand troops—not publicly reported by the Department of Defense—medevaced out of Iraq for "non-combat related injuries."

Coalition partners are departing Iraq in droves, and families of British and Scottish soldiers are banding together to launch an antiwar campaign. Modeled after Military Families Speak Out, the group includes bereaved parents and families of those still serving, and Dante Zappala is in London for their first event.

Several parents in Military Families Against the War (MFAW) have accused Prime Minister Tony Blair of "morally unacceptable conduct," disparaging his relationship with President Bush as an "unhealthy liaison."

They went to Blair's residence at 10 Downing Street with wreaths and photographs of three dead Black Watch soldiers, because, according to one

---

18. "DU: Dirty Bombs, Dirty Missiles, Dirty Bullets." *San Francisco Bayview,* March, 2005.

19. National Gulf War Resource Center.

MFAW member, "The responsibility for this carnage lies at the doorstep of Number 10."

Public opinion in Britain and other European nations has been against the war in Iraq since before the invasion. The latest polls in the U.S. show that support for the occupation has diminished, and pressure is mounting to bring the troops home. But rather than put together an exit strategy, the administration is going to send more troops over.

The increase is being arranged through a combination of early and additional deployments and extensions that will bring the total troop strength to 150,000 in the days leading up to the January election. The official word is that the units scheduled to return in March and April of 2005 will not be effected, but I'll believe that when I see it. Lorin maintains his Brigade is coming home on time, even though some military analysts have begun to suggest it might not be. Driving him to the airport in the early morning fog, I wonder when, or if, I will see him again.

11

All I Want for Christmas

DECEMBER 2004

GLOBAL POLICY EXPERTS are projecting increased violence prior to the Iraq elections, but there are fewer coalition forces on the ground to deal with it. Six members have pulled out within the last few months, Hungary has indicated it will leave by March of 2005, and Poland is considering reducing or completely cutting its commitment of 2,500 troops. Scrambling to pick up the slack, an additional 12,000 U.S. soldiers are preparing for deployment, and 10,400 military personnel in Iraq are being extended for at least two more months. The number of soldiers who've been forced to serve under the stop-loss order now exceeds twenty-five thousand, impacting seven thousand at any given time.

Army officials claim that the stop-loss policy is the result of lessons learned during Vietnam, when troops were rotated out of combat just as they were getting used to fighting in dangerous conditions. Authorized by Congress, it was first implemented during the Persian Gulf War, but on a considerably smaller scale.

The unprecedented scale of enforcement has generated at least six lawsuits contesting both the legality of stop-loss and a parallel policy relating to members of the Individual Ready Reserves. Characterized as a breach of contract, and a violation of the National Guard's implied promise of state-based service, the first challenges to the stop-loss policy were invoked by two former active duty soldiers who enlisted with the California National Guard.

They came in under the Try One program, which gives combat veterans a one-year trial stint as a citizen soldier, but they ended up serving tours of duty considerably longer than twelve months. Some of the 5,600 Reservists forced back into service have also contested the Individual Ready Reserves policy. The activation of the IRR is another Band-Aid solution that is proving ineffective and insufficient. In September 2004, the *Army Times* reported that just one-third of the civilians called back through the IRR had actually shown up.

Jay Ferriola, an Army Reserve Captain who served in Germany and South Korea while completing his contract, filed suit after he was ordered to return to active duty four months after resigning his commission. Arguing that the orders were a breach of contract and a violation of the constitutional protection from involuntary servitude, he won his case and received an honorable discharge.

According to an article in the *New York Times* on December 6, the Center for Constitutional Rights filed a lawsuit on behalf of GIs stationed in Iraq affected by stop-loss. There are eight plaintiffs of record in the groundbreaking court challenge by a group of soldiers. At an injunction hearing on the ninth, U.S. District Judge Royce C. Lamberth declined a request to allow the complainants home on leave to remain in the United States.

Arkansas National Guardsman David Qualls signed up under the Try One program and is the only soldier identified in the suit. The judge determined that the other seven couldn't proceed as John Does and required that they provide their name, rank, unit, and address. Due to the considerable risk involved, those soldiers withdrew from the suit rather than go public.

Staughton Lynd, the attorney spearheading the complaint, said, "David Qualls signed up under the most fraudulent of all the different forms of enlistment." Lynd expects the case will drag out for months because it's the most viable challenge yet against the policy.

The case is one of a series of problems facing the Pentagon that have recently come under public scrutiny. Shortly after Specialist Thomas Wilson, Tennessee National Guard, confronted Defense Secretary Rumsfeld about the lack of armored equipment, figures released by the House Armed Services Committee indicated that almost two-thirds of the Humvees are still vulnerable, and the vast majority of the transport and supply trucks in Iraq aren't armored at all.

Eighty-five percent of the 4,314 heavy transport vehicles lack armor, as do ninety percent of the medium-weight transport trucks. When questioned by soldiers preparing to move into Iraq from their station in Kuwait, wanting to know why U.S. forces were being sent into combat with insufficient protection, Rumsfeld's response was, "You go to war with the army you have, not the army you want."

Upon hearing Rumsfeld's remark, Paul Rieckhoff, a former infantry platoon leader with the Florida National Guard stationed in Iraq, and the founder of Operation Truth, an advocacy organization for soldiers and veterans, stated: "Rumsfeld shows that he fails to understand what goes on on the ground. . . . Complacency, incompetency, or negligence . . . when [those] guys screw up, we bleed."

Pentagon military officials registered no surprise that it was a member of the Guard who brought up the issue, and acknowledged that their system for training, equipping, mobilizing, and deploying Reservists wasn't ready for the post-9/11 call-ups. Twenty-one months after the U.S. invaded Iraq, the Defense Department is just beginning to address equipment shortfalls.

The cost of up-armoring is $58,000 per vehicle, but apparently Rumsfeld thought that the assembly lines installing armor kits were already running at maximum capacity, because he told the troops, "It isn't a matter of money. It's a matter of production."

Two days later, the Pentagon placed orders to boost production by a hundred trucks per month, and at least one company indicated that it could increase its output even more, if necessary.[20]

The administration never publicly chastised Specialist Wilson, or the Idaho Guardsman who also took Rumsfeld to task in front of the international media. But shortly afterward, the military began instructing deploying units and soldiers already in the country that any further public challenges to the administration or its representatives may be punished by an Article 15.

Under the Uniform Military Code of Justice (UMCJ), an Article 15 is a nonjudicial punishment, which refers to disciplinary actions that can be implemented in the instance of minor offenses. Article 15s are typically invoked to deal with misconduct, such as disrespect to superiors, disobedience of military orders, and "a particularly gross absence of self-discipline amounting to a moral deficiency."

Soldiers contesting their orders, or filing for Conscientious Objector status, can be subjected to much more severe punishments, as Camilo Mejia discovered when he was sentenced to a year in jail. Mejia is one of the steadily climbing numbers of military personnel who have applied for Conscientious Objector status since the September 11th terrorist attacks.

---

20. "Army will Add Humvees." *Los Angeles Times*, December 11, 2004.

The Quaker House in Fayetteville, North Carolina, helps coordinate the GI Rights Hotline, which provides counseling and referral services to members of the military who are exploring options for leaving the service. They received almost six thousand calls in 2004, virtually doubling the earlier record set in 2001.

"After September 11th, our organization was getting about one or two calls a week," said J. E. McNeil, director of the Washington-based Center on Conscience and War. "Now, it's closer to two or three a day." More than 5,500 U.S. military personnel have deserted during the Iraq war, a spike in a trend that began in the mid-nineties. Between 1995 and 2001, the number of desertions nearly tripled, but rather than forcing them to return to service, ninety-four percent were released with less-than-honorable discharges.

That changed in the aftermath of 9/11, when the Army introduced a new policy mandating the return of deserters to their original military units. Between 2001 and 2004, the number of soldiers calling the Hotline escalated from 17,000 to 33,000. Desperate to leave the service for reasons that are frequently personal than political, the number of Conscientious Objector applications has increased threefold since the beginning of the war in Iraq. But the vast majority are denied.[21]

One exception is twenty-year-old National Guard Specialist Petra Salazar, who joined the 3631st Maintenance Company of the New Mexico National Guard as a senior at Espanola Valley High School. Shortly before she was scheduled for discharge, Salazar got orders for deployment. She refused them, and after signing a mountain of paperwork, and meeting with members of the clergy, she was honorably discharged. There are approximately five thousand New Mexico National Guard members, and Salazar is one of a handful of that have been granted CO status in the past few years.

"Ever since the shift of focus from Osama to Saddam, I knew he was going to exploit 9/11, and I knew the day would come when I was going to have to leave," Salazar said. "It was an oil war to begin with. It had nothing to do with freeing the Iraqi people. How many people profited from 9/11 and this war? It's Bush and his people who are profiting off of blue-collar military labor."[22]

Salazar is a working-class girl who joined the Guard because it covers the full cost of tuition at any state university. Having refused to fulfill her military service, the Defense Department could force her repay the college

21. "AWOL in America," *Harper's Magazine*, March 2005.
22. *Rio Grande Sun*, September 16, 2004.

tuition money she's gotten for the past three years, and she can still be called up and deployed as part of the Individual Ready Reserves. If that happens, Salazar probably won't have the option of serving with the unit she knows and has trained with, a standard practice with former Guard members who are recalled.

Military Families Speak Out has publicly advocated on behalf of Camilo Mejia and other soldiers seeking CO standing, but we walk a very fine line in doing so. We've gone around and around about endorsing counter-recruitment efforts, but vetoed the idea. MFSO is adamant that it's not anti-military; it's anti-War in Iraq. Although it's not a factor in the decision, there are a couple of seldom-enforced laws that make any attempt to entice or procure members of the military to desert, or to aid or harbor deserting service members, punishable by up to three years in prison, a fine, or both.[23]

Sanctions allowed under Section 2387, which covers activities potentially detrimental to morale or inciting insubordination, include up to ten years in prison and a fine. Anyone convicted of violating #2387 is also "ineligible for employment by the United States or any department or agency thereof, for the five years next following his conviction."

Thousands of Americans, and hundreds of Canadians, are actively violating these edicts. I'm one of them, but since I couldn't even keep my own husband at home, I doubt they'd have a very strong case against me.

Apparently the case against the twenty-three Army Reservists who refused a mission transporting fuel along one of the most perilous highways in Iraq wasn't too strong, either. None of them will be court-martialed, but they're all being given Article 15s for refusing to follow orders. The trials of the seven Reservists from the Maryland-based Military Police Company involved in the Abu Ghraib prisoner abuse are continuing, and Staff Sergeant Frederick pleaded guilty as part of a deal with the military court.

Army Specialist Graner filed for the dismissal of charges on the grounds that any military jury would inevitably be biased, but was denied. The judge in the case also ruled against the defense's request to call Lieutenant General Ricardo Sanchez, former U.S. Commander in Iraq, as a witness. The decision was made on the grounds that Sanchez's testimony would have "nothing to do with what happened" at the Abu Ghraib prison.

The disconnect between leaders and actual events and any culpability of the former in the latter seems to go all the way to the top, even though reports show that Rumsfeld slashed the training time for National Guard

23. The United States Code, #18, Section 1381.

units prior to their deployment, including the soldiers that have been brought up on charges for abuses at Abu Ghraib. But for the most part, the administration, military tribunals, and the court of public opinion, shaped by the media, keep the spotlight fixed on the people on the ground. One of the few articles about the possible culpability of the Commander in chief stated, "Repeated references in an internal FBI email suggest that the President issued a special order to permit some of the more objectionable torture techniques used at Abu Ghraib and other U.S.-run prison facilities."[24]

Virtually all of the torture and intimidation techniques used, including enforced nudity of detainees, putting black hoods on prisoners' heads, using Army canines, etcetera, were itemized in an internal FBI memorandum dated May 22, 2004. The memo mentioned an Executive Order—a presidential edict introducing particular laws or directives that supersede or complement existing legislation—ten times.

After the American Civil Liberties Union publicly released the e-mail, officials from the Pentagon, the White House, and the FBI said that the order came from the Department of Defense, and was not an Executive Order. The White House has refused to respond to repeated inquiries about the origin and veracity of the document.

President Bush has said he has only authorized interrogation techniques that "would conform to U.S. law and would be consistent with international treaty obligations."

What he did not mention is that any interrogation procedures issued by a President in an Executive Order are made legal under U.S. law.

I've been trying to get into the Holiday swing, but the spirit of the season eludes me. Lorin's told me that there's a decorated tree on base, and that Christmas dinner will be served, but it's just another day at war. There are a couple of community drives and activities geared toward fulltime military and families with kids, which obviously doesn't include me.

Alisa invites me over to help the boys build gingerbread houses, and we spend a couple of hours trying to get the icing to cement the walls and sides together before resorting to toothpaste as an adhesive.

Just after we've put the boys to bed, her husband, Michael, comes in, and after asking about Lorin, the conversation quickly turns to Iraq. He's a

---

24. "President Authorized Abu Ghraib," December 23, 2004, Z-Net.

staunch Republican, and we've had a number of talks about Christian val-ues, moral wars, and the pros and cons of our respective political parties. In the past we've kept it pretty light, but it's been a tough week, and I'm sad, and lonely, and weary of war.

"I really admire Lorin for what he's doing. I think we need to be over there."

"If you're so supportive of the war, why haven't you joined up?" I ask pointedly.

"Who, me? They wouldn't take me," He says, seemingly dumbstruck by my suggestion.

"Well, actually, I think they would. Recruitment's *way* down, and the Guard and Reserve are hurting for soldiers. Didn't you see the article on the front page of the *Seattle Times?*"

Scrambling to stop the hemorrhage of officers, the Reserve has rejected almost half of the resignation requests from captains and lieutenants, invok-ing the stop-loss. They're even turning down requests from soldiers who aren't currently on active duty or scheduled for deployment.

The Reserve can deny resignations if an officer's specialty is in short sup-ply, and as of September of this year, over forty percent of the captain slots were vacant. They've added hundreds more recruiters to their payroll, and are drafting a policy that would prevent company-grade officers who haven't yet served in Iraq or Afghanistan from resigning, except in cases of extreme hardship such as the death or disability of a spouse.

In response to my question, Michael says, "No, we don't get the paper." Alisa's getting a little nervous about where this conversation is going, but I'll be damned if I'm going to rein myself in tonight.

"Well, I've got it. The war in Iraq has depleted the Guard and Reserves, which has had resignation requests from officers go from fifteen in 2001 to 370 this past year. They've lowered their standards, and estimate that they'll take two thousand new enlistees that wouldn't have made the cut before. So I'm sure they'd take you."

"He's not going anywhere," Alisa interjects.

"Why not? He says he supports the war, and it's a good idea for us to be over there. He says it's a Christian thing to help the people of Iraq. If he means it, then I think he should seriously consider signing up."

Both Michael and Alisa are frowning, and looking extremely uncomfortable.

I want to ask if they understand that when Michael says he supports the war, but refuses to enlist, the unspoken message is that Michael's life is more important than Lorin's. But I've already said too much, and call it a night, returning to my dark, deserted house.

I am one of 138,000 American households that will have empty plates at their tables this Christmas. Twelve hundred American families will have a vacancy forever, as will anywhere from twenty to a hundred thousand Iraqi households. In keeping with the Missing Man table, I plan to set a place for Lorin when I go to Dan and Julie's on Christmas Eve.

The Missing Man Table and Honors ceremony is an historic tradition of setting a table for six, each empty place representing Americans missing from the five branches of fulltime service (Army, Navy, Marine, Air Force, Coast Guard) and civilians. Guard and Reserves are not specifically recognized. They've fought and died in previous wars, but in nowhere near the numbers.

I contact area churches, inviting them to consider asking their congregants to bring a plate with them to their Christmas Eve church service, and set a table for the absent, the wounded, and the dead. I suggest that the plates could be collected and given to local food banks and shelters, as a reminder that we are all connected, and hunger for peace.

Four days before Christmas, fifteen American soldiers were killed, and sixty-six wounded, when an explosion ripped through their mess tent at Forward Operating Base Marez in Mosul, about seven hours from Anaconda. Two of the soldiers who died in the blast are from the 133rd Engineer Battalion of the Maine Army National Guard. The 133rd had its first casualty when a roadside bomb killed newly married specialist Christopher Gelineau, twenty-three, two months into his deployment. Another dozen Maine Guardsmen were wounded in the mess tent attack, and now even their Chaplain, David Sivret, is saying, "It's time for all of us to come home."

National Guard Specialist John West, of the 81st Brigade, has been recuperating at home since early September, after suffering multiple fractures, broken bones, lacerations, and torn and ruptured organs. August 4th is seared in his mind, and in the aftermath of the explosion that took the life of the gunner, he recalls thinking, "So this is what it's like to get blown up."

The IED took a chunk out of his lower back and buttocks. One of the first men on the scene remarked that the glob of flesh he found on the seat of the truck looked like a couple of pounds of hamburger.

After two months of bed rest, multiple surgeries, and intense physical therapy, West is ambulatory again, with the help of a walker. He continues to struggle with the acute stress that includes depression, delusions, and flashbacks. His wife was pushing him in his wheelchair when an amusement ride backfired at the Pullayup County Fair, and West began crying and trembling violently, screaming, "Get down! Get the kids down!"

The memory of two soldiers killed while on foot patrol haunts him as well. West's unit was following in a HMMV a few paces behind when shots rang out. They were unable to move forward because kids begging for food swarmed their vehicle. West watched helplessly as one soldier was shot in the face, and a bullet found its way through a gap in the armor of another, killing him, too.[25]

Almost two hundred Guard and Reserves troops have died since the war began. Pentagon statistics show that the losses sustained by Army National Guard soldiers in Iraq are thirty-five percent higher than that of regular enlisted. The elevated mortality rate of citizen soldiers is unparalleled. Of the 58,209 U.S. deaths in Vietnam, ninety-four were Guardsmen, and no Guardsmen were killed in the Persian Gulf War. Both wars had an overall injury mortality rate of twenty-four percent.[26]

According to the *New England Journal of Medicine* December issue, U.S. military surgical teams "have saved the lives of an unprecedented ninety percent of the soldiers wounded in battle." The survival rate of troops sustaining serious combat injuries in the Vietnam and Persian Gulf Wars was seventy-six percent. The increase is due to a combination of factors, including surgical and technological advances, soldiers and medics that are better-trained in life-saving techniques, improvements in body armor, and a four-day delivery time in getting soldiers off the battlefield and back to U.S. medical facilities. A *Seattle Times* article on December 9th reported that during Vietnam, it took an average of forty-five days to get soldiers into stateside hospitals.

Soldiers who would have died in earlier conflicts have survived with bodily damage, including amputations and traumatic brain injuries that are generally irreversible, and will seriously affect, if not completely alter, the rest of their lives.

The Army Reserve is being altered as well, and "is rapidly degenerating into a 'broken' force," according to Lieutenant General James Helmly's December 20th memo to Army Chief of Staff General Peter Schoomaker. In a section entitled "US Army Reserve Readiness Discussion, Past Dysfunctional Practices and Policies," he writes: "The Army Reserve is hamstrung

---

25. *Seattle Times*, December 5, 2004.
26. "Army NG Has Highest Death Rate." *USA Today*, December 13, 2004.

in its ability to effectively manage its force. Manpower and personnel management policies and practices . . . were designed for 'peacetime.'"

Helmly cites the remobilization of eight thousand Reserve soldiers within
three months of having been demobilized as an illustration of the problems
plaguing the Reserve and severely limiting its capabilities. He also expresses
concern about differential deployment policies, the incremental and
extended mobilization of units, and the cobbling together of personnel from
various units.

Helmly questioned "a policy which precludes RC (Reserve Component)
soldiers from performing inactive duty training for sixty days and annual
training for six months . . . after demobilization . . . precludes timely initia-
tion of resetting actions. Further, it fails to renew the soldier's bond with his
or her unit, thus harming retention."

Army National Guard retention rates are also being damaged by frequent
redeployments. An assessment conducted by the Pentagon indicates that
part-time soldiers are serving the highest percentage of multiple tours of
duty in Iraq and Afghanistan. Nearly forty percent of Army National Guard
soldiers have been called up more than once, almost half of the Air National
Guard called to active duty have served two or more tours since September
11th, and almost thirty-five percent of Army Reservists mobilized in the last
three years have been redeployed.

In 2003, the Guard and Reserves put in almost sixty-three million cumulative duty days, more than five times the annual total clocked in the late
nineties. People who thought they'd signed up to be part-time soldiers
are being pressed into fulltime service, often overseas. The repeat tours of
combat zone duty are putting a particular strain on citizen soldiers and their
families.

The National Military Family Association found that although there are
programs and services in place to support military families, they're implemented inconsistently. The lack of a comprehensive and reliable support
system is undermining the resiliency of the families left behind, and contrib-
uting to plunging rates of recruitment.

Fifty percent of Guard personnel have traditionally been built of soldiers
leaving active duty service. But since Guard service is quite likely going to
mean a quick trip back to Iraq, the number has dropped to about thirty-five
percent in recent months. In response, the Guard has increased the number
of recruiters from 2,700 to 4,100, and shifted its advertising to target a new
pool of potential recruits.

Taking their cues from corporate America, recruiters are working to establish the Army as an instantly recognizable "brand" with positive associations in the minds of potential consumers/enlistees, much like Coca-Cola. They are hosting parties with free food and "America's Army" video game tournaments to attract teens. The Guard has also begun aggressively seeking civilians with relatively few work and domestic obligations, in the hopes that they'll be more willing to serve extended overseas deployments. Can informal open houses at foster facilities, prisons, and detention centers be too far away?

Nine out of ten regular Army divisions are currently in Afghanistan or Iraq, or have returned and begun readying for their next deployment. Currently, 185,732 National Guard and Reservists are mobilized, and more than 247,181 have already served in Operations Iraqi Freedom and Enduring Freedom. Temporary duty lasting up to three months is not included in these figures.

Rumors about the possible reinstatement of the draft were quelled during the presidential elections, but they continue to rumble in the consciousness, if not the conversations, of many Americans. Eighteen-year-old males are still required to register, and the Selective Service System is securing personnel to sit on appeals panels and staff thousands of local draft boards. All in preparation for the coming day when it dawns on America that the United States' all-volunteer Armed Forces have become another casualty of this war.

12

Keeping the Faith

JANUARY 2005

THE DEATH TOLL from a massive tsunami in Southeast Asia on December 26 has surpassed 160,000, and donations and assistance have poured into that corner of the world. After initially designating $35 million for relief assistance, President Bush increased the amount tenfold when members of the media and world leaders opined about the lack of generosity from the wealthiest nation on the planet. A nation that, according to Project Billboard in New York's Times Square, sponsored by the Center for American Progress, is spending $177 million a day to wage war in Iraq.

The initial shock and horror felt in the aftermath of the gigantic wave was quickly translated into compassionate action, the channeling of funds and resources to heal the wounded, recover the dead, and relieve the suffering of millions. Much like the days following the terrorist attacks of September 11th, national boundaries dissolved, and humanity lost its mind (in the best possible way) and remembered its heart.

Watching this unfold, I can't help but think we've got it backward. People everywhere are talking about the tsunami, the loss of life, and the devastation of the natural landscape of a handful of nations. Some are asking how God could allow this to happen, others want to know why more wasn't done to prevent it, or, at the very least, warn people. The destructive forces of nature dismay us, yet manmade destruction continues.

The projected death toll of soldier and civilian casualties in Iraq will reach between fifty and a hundred and fifty thousand this year. Hundreds of thousands have been wounded or permanently disabled, and millions of Iraqis are without homes or jobs, engaged in a daily struggle for food and water.

The country's landscape has been irrevocably changed by bombs and poisoned by depleted uranium, and I suspect the before and after photos of Fallujah and the seaside cities of Southern Asia have much in common. Yet no one speaks of the dead in Asia as merely collateral damage. *That's* a tragedy; *this* is war.

If we have a spiritual, moral, and humanitarian mandate to alleviate suffering, then surely we are ordained not to inflict it.

But contemporary religious and spiritual leaders have for the most part been silent about the war. Why have they not taken a stand for peace, not called for a genuine demonstration of moral authority from the Bush administration and American voters? Where is God on Iraq? What *would* Jesus do?

President Bush claimed his decision to invade Iraq was a directive from God, but the message from Pope John Paul II, delivered to the President by Cardinal Pio Laghi, was indisputable: God is not on your side if you invade Iraq.

According to Bush's perspective, God's either with us or against us. If President Bush receives the occasional communication from God, I figure the Pope's on speed dial, so I'm going with the Pope.

Pope John Paul II has been the most reliable and frequent promoter of peace and human rights for the past two decades. He spoke out against the first Gulf War at least fifty-six times, admonishing President George H. W. Bush for the first attack. President W. Bush, reelected because of his purportedly strong stance on moral values, ignored the highest-ranking U.S. Bishop in Rome, Francis Cardinal Stafford, who said, "War would be morally unjustified."

American media omitted the persistent calls for peace from the Vatican in its coverage of the first Gulf War, and they're doing it again. The Pope has repeatedly stated that there were not sufficient reasons to initiate a war in Iraq, and has questioned the very idea of a "just war."

Addressing thousands of worshipers at the Ash Wednesday Mass in 2003, days after the first American strike, the Pope proclaimed: "There will be no peace on earth while the oppression of peoples, injustices, and economic imbalances . . . endure. For the desired structural changes to take place, external initiative and interventions are not enough; what is needed above all is a joint conversion of hearts to love."

The sentiments evoke the words of Dr. Martin Luther King Jr., who called for quantitative change, as well as "a qualitative change in our hearts."

But in the interests of pursuing our personal, private good, which is often greed, we have discarded even the possibility that there might be common goals and values, common issues and concerns. We have limited our aspiration to the realm of the material. We have deflated, and possibly sold, the Dream. We have lost the address for the beloved community, and it can no longer be found on our social map.

Monday is the national Dr. King holiday, which kicks off a week of events in his honor. I'm on a panel of speakers at a teach-in sponsored by Students Against War at Seattle Community College. I meet up with Judy and her partner Wes, a Vietnam War veteran and member of Veterans for Peace, outside the conference room in the campus administration building.

After a round of hugs, we move toward the room and Judy remarks, "I guess the Seattle Community College has the most active antiwar student group in the area. That surprises me. What about Seattle University, or the University of Washington? They're huge."

After a moment's consideration, I reply, "Actually, I suppose it makes sense. After all, most Community College students are poor or working class, and I bet a lot of them are here under the G.I. Bill. These are the kids that joined the Guard or Reserves to pay for school."

"That's what Lorin did, and he went to a community college. I bet more of the students here have brothers, or even parents, in Iraq, than the kids at more expensive schools. Besides, this is where the military recruiters set up shop. For these guys, the war is hitting a whole lot closer to home."

Judy's on the agenda first, and she talks to the audience of three dozen or so students about her involvement with Military Families Speak Out, and about having her son in Iraq.

Before returning to her seat, Judy says, "I recently heard another MFSO member say it was like living in an emergency room for a year. I instantly understood what she meant. For one year, I waited, and worried constantly. I never knew what was happening, if my son was wounded, or if he was going to make it out alive."

It's one of the most accurate analogies I've heard. I'm grateful that, if things go according to plan, I've only got a few more months in the emergency room, because I feel like I'm living in amber.

The next speaker is a young man with a slightly overdeveloped upper body and a blue-tipped Mohawk. Turning toward Judy, he says, "When I was over there, I always knew when I was safe, and when I was in danger. But back here, you never know. Most of the moms only hear from their sons every few weeks, and for only a few minutes at a time. In a lot of ways, I think it's the people at home who have the most courage."

He's the same age as most of the kids in the room, but after serving in both Afghanistan and Iraq, the patina of his youth has lost its sheen. Riley signed up for, and served, two years. He's no longer active in the Army Rangers, but he can still be deployed. The fine print of the military contract states that regardless of the initial length of service, once they've enlisted, soldiers can be called back and forced to serve for a total of eight years.

He expects the call will come next month, and I expect he's right. He rambles for ten minutes, sharing stories, exposing himself, perhaps more than he realizes.

"One of the guys, about my age, was in an explosion, and he fell into a ditch and bled to death. Now, this was a really great guy, he had a steady girlfriend and everything. Me and the other guys, well, we're not always so nice, and, you know, it's just us, I mean, we don't have girlfriends or nothing. So why him? Why not one of us? Why did we live?"

Behind me, Wes whispers, "Survivor's syndrome." He did a tour of duty in Vietnam, so he knows what that's about.

The ex-Ranger continues: "When I first got back, all I did was drink. That's what most of the guys do, just take a year off and drink. After what we've seen and done, we figure we deserve it. But I had to stop because I'd be at bars, and I'd be drinking . . . and think I was back in combat. So it wasn't good."

Shaking his head, he goes on, "What I can't believe is that some of these guys want to go back. What pisses me off, though, is that there's this one guy, from a wealthy family, lots of money, lots of opportunity, he could do anything, but after one tour of duty, he says, 'I've got to go back. It's all I have.' And I think, *Yeah, right, it's all you have. Whatever.*"

He finishes, "The people who are sending us to war have never been there. If Bush was in my unit, I don't think he'd be right there in front, fighting with me. He'd be the guy hiding in the back and hogging the porn."

He's so honest and politically incorrect that I can't help but chuckle, even as I hear the disapproving gasps of the young women around me. Apparently, he hadn't seen the pamphlet for today's event, proclaiming opposition to Bush and his racist, sexist, classist, homophobic corporate administration. Pornography and war are inseparable, always have been.

There's a brief question and answer session, and then I take the podium, turn to Judy, and say, "You said that this generation is the hope for the future, and that's true to an extent, but we can't put it all on their shoulders. And in a way, I think we've failed them."

Trying to ignore Judy's embarrassed grimace, I press on, "You came of age during the Sixties, when there was a lot going on in terms of protests and movements. How do you explain the fact that things in this country actually seem to have gotten worse on your watch? And what have you learned that might prevent this generation from making those same mistakes?"

After a moment or two, she replies, "Wow, well, I don't know, exactly. For me, I got caught up in having children, and then work, I guess, and all of my activism went by the wayside. I think a lot of us got complacent because we were comfortable. But I'm back now, and I'm not going away this time."

During the shuffle of speakers, she approaches me and adds remorsefully, "I've actually talked to my daughter, who's thirty-six, about this, too. For a long time, I've been telling myself that I didn't prepare my children for war, but I guess I did, because I failed to prepare them for peace."

Turning back toward the students, I say, "What happened to the energy of the civil rights, feminist, and antiwar movements? Very simply: we went shopping. Sure, there were other things. I think the murders of Dr. King and the Kennedys scared the bejeezus out of people, and they were lost without their leaders. But mainly, the great force for change that was alive back then went away because we went shopping. And let's not pretend we don't all have some responsibility in that. We've got to make that mirror big enough to reflect a nation. We *all* went shopping."

I spend the next few minutes talking about specific things they can do, ideas for broader scale, sustained activism, and how critical their involvement is.

"This is not halfhearted work, and it's not easy. If we're going to be as effective as we need to be, we've got to have the same passionate commitment to peace that Bush, Cheney, Rumsfeld, and all the other hawks have to war."

On my way out, I remind Judy of tomorrow's meeting with Congressman Smith at his home office in Tacoma. While we're talking politics, these kids, along with hundreds of others, are going to walk out of their classrooms and protest the presence of military recruiters on campus. Then they'll take to the streets, joining thousands of Seattleites as they converge downtown to protest the second inaugural ceremony for President Bush. Four more years.

Immediately after the election, I was so disheartened that I wanted to become one of the Not My Problem people, because pretty soon, none of this will be. Lorin will be home, and out of the Guard, and we don't have kids, so no worries about the possibility of a draft or the escalation of domestic and international violence.

As long as the environment holds out for another thirty or forty years, we're set. But to drop out now would make me a hypocrite, and besides, there were those who told me that racism wasn't really my issue, either. Even so, I vacillate about participating in the huge peace rally and antiwar events planned in Fayetteville, North Carolina, on the second anniversary of the invasion, since Lorin will have just gotten home.

I run it by him to see if he wants to go, but he says, "No. The last thing I want to do after spending a year over here is come back and hang out by a military base for the weekend."

After a couple of phone calls to Charley and Nancy, I decide to go to Fort Bragg in March. Military Families Speak Out, United for Peace and Justice, Iraq Veterans Against the War, Veterans for Peace, and the North Carolina Council of Churches are among the groups spearheading the Fayetteville protest on the twentieth, the second anniversary of the Iraq invasion. North Carolina hosts five of the nation's largest military bases, including Fort Bragg, ground zero for the 82nd Airborne Division and many of the Army's elite units.

Fayetteville is also home to a growing base of antiwar activists and organizations comprised of military folks, veterans, and families of active duty soldiers, students, homemakers, clergy, and teachers. They are part of a developing statewide network opposed to the continuing American presence in Iraq, and questioning how the elections, scheduled for January 30th, can be deemed legitimate with the daily insurgent attacks that will assuredly undermine voter participation.

Now, I am committed to the core principles of a democratic system, and am grateful to be living in an approximation of one. But there's an inherent contradiction in dictating democracy, the rationale *du jour* for the ongoing presence of American troops in Iraq. The trumped-up justification given back in 2003 for invading Iraq evaporated months ago.

Having found no weapons of mass destruction in Iraq, the search was declared over on January 12, 2005. Celeste Zappala wept at her kitchen table when she heard. Any shred of hope she may have harbored that Sherwood did not die in vain was annihilated.

It's been more than a year since the invasion was deemed a success, Saddam Hussein was captured, and President Bush crowed, "Mission accomplished!" Current polls show that American support for the war continues to dwindle, and only forty-four percent of respondents believe the invasion was worth it. One might think the U.S. troops would be packing their duffel sacks and loading up the Conexes. Not so fast, soldier.

The Pentagon intends to keep armed forces in Iraq at least through 2006. The government has numerous contracts with civilian companies to assist in building up to fourteen bases, and the timeline for completion is five years out. Republican Senator John McCain is one of many politicians who've said U.S. troops will stay another ten to twenty years. Mothers, lock up your sons.

Bush and Company have continually denied they will reinstate the draft, but they may have to if they want to maintain anything near the current troop strength over the next several years. The official word is that the military is planning to reduce the number of soldiers from 150,000 to 120,000 sometime this year, but the Administration recently began considering a plan to extend call-ups for Reservists in order to meet the combat demands in Iraq. The change can be made with just Rumsfeld's approval, and it would negate the earlier policy of the Bush administration, which held the cumulative maximum for Reserve deployments at twenty-four months. The move is the result of the military's growing difficulty in recruiting and retaining Guard and Reserve members.

National Guard recruiters in Los Angeles schools and other American inner cities have taken to telling parents not to worry about their kids signing up, because there's a greater likelihood that they'll be killed on the mean streets of their neighborhoods than in Iraq. Army and National Guard recruiters have also called thousands of inactive Reservists, encouraging them to reenlist in the active reserves or join their local Guard units, warning that, if they don't, they could soon be headed to Iraq.

Active duty numbers are holding relatively stable, but National Guard soldiers who've served in Iraq are leaving the service at unprecedented levels. Annual recruitment has fallen nearly thirty percent in the Guard and ten percent in the Reserves. Part of the reason for the mass exodus is the military's continuing violation of its own policies, one of which states that Reservists are not supposed to be on assignment for more than twelve months of every five to six years.

That's just one of the items on the agenda for today's meeting with Congressman Smith. Seattle MFSO member Sherrie Tillstra is seated in the reception area when I arrive at his relatively austere Tacoma headquarters. After a brief wait, we're ushered into his office.

As we're getting settled, I tell him that Judy should be along shortly and say, "I want to congratulate you on your reelection, and thank you for your efforts to support the troops. One of the reasons we're here is to request that you contact Democratic Senator Maria Cantwell and join her in calling for hearings regarding the plan to extend call-ups for Reservists."

He replies, "I'll take a look at it."

"Thank you," I say. "I would also like you to ask for a hearing and subsequent vote of confidence/no confidence on Rumsfeld. I know you called for his resignation after the Abu Ghraib catastrophe, but I think that a sufficient number of issues have come up since then that merit investigation."

Congressman Smith says something about looking into it again, but I get the sense he's not too optimistic.

"We spoke in D.C. about the proposal to create a Department of Peace, and I know you had some reservations, but it's going to be reintroduced in September. I would really like to see you get behind it, and here's why."

I pull forward in my chair so that I'm leaning over the table slightly, and say, "I appreciate your concern about creating more bureaucracy, but clearly the State Department is not doing its job. One of the costs of the invasion of Iraq is the significant damage to this country's reputation and international relations."

Smith sits on the International Relations Committee, so I'm hoping this gets his attention.

"Furthermore, the Bush administration has demonstrated that it's got no plan whatsoever for securing the peace, and it certainly didn't consider nonviolent options prior to invading the country and initiating a war. Now, more than ever, it's critical for the future of this nation, and the world, to support the bill to establish a Department of Peace."

After a moment's consideration, the Congressman replies, "I tell you what, I'm going to take a look at it, and give it some thought."

"Thank you, that's what I wanted to hear."

Adam invites Sherrie to speak, and she tells him about a friend of her family, a young woman with three small children, all under the age of six. Her husband was killed in Iraq less than two months ago, and the grieving widow and her kids have moved into cramped quarters at the homes of their in-laws. It was that or homelessness.

Like far too many bereaved military families and spouses, they have been forced to go to shelters, food shelves, and welfare offices. The one time "death benefit" of $12,420 paid to the family of a soldier killed in combat disappears quickly, leaving thousands of women and children to fend for themselves.

The military gratuity has remained at $6,000 for more than a decade. In 2003, it was doubled to $12,000, and made fully tax deductible, with subsequent adjustments to keep pace with inflation. The current proposal before the House and the Senate would pay $100,000 to families when the service member was killed in a war zone, and some Congressmen are advocating that it be expanded to include all active duty service members.

The legislation has a clause providing an additional $150,000 in life insurance, above and beyond the $250,000 standard carried by most military personnel. In the aftermath of the September 11th attacks, the government paid an average of $2.1 million to the families of those killed in those attacks.

Congressman Smith thanks Sherrie for the personal testimony and assures her that the increase will almost surely be approved. I suggest that perhaps the gross tax cuts for corporations and the very wealthy could be revoked as a way to pay for this and some of the other costs of this war.

He's checking his watch when Judy tumbles into the room. He remembers her from our meeting at the Capitol, and asks if there's anything she would like to address. I brief her on what we've already covered, and she does the close.

"I am grateful for your efforts to support the troops, but the best way to support our troops is to bring them home from this reckless, ill-conceived war based on lies."

Smith diplomatically tells us that the United States has a responsibility to see the transition through, and there's still a small window of opportunity to turn things around. MFSO members have heard the Pottery Barn defense—you break it, you fix it!—so often that Nancy and Charley have a ready response.

In one of our last conversations, they pointed out, "Actually, if you break something in a store, you don't fix it. You pay for it. What's more, if you are walking through the store smashing things with a hammer, they call the cops and remove you from the building. Then they talk money."

After thanking us for our time, and assuring us he will follow up on our other requests, one of Smith's interns leads us out of his office.

Judy, Sherrie, and I debrief quickly, agreeing that we can count on some action from him, with one painfully obvious exception: getting out of Iraq.

"I was afraid he was going to say that," I grouse, "even though the window of opportunity has shattered."

The cold winter rain is penetrating our coats, and Sherrie asks if we want to have dinner. I'm seriously tempted, as I've been starved for company, but remind her that it's Not One Damn Dime Day, a twenty-four-hour boycott of all spending, initiated by Bill Moyers. It's a sort of civil disobedience for a consumer culture, and while nobody imagines we'll bring the economy to a screeching halt, maybe we can slow it down during the inaugural events.

I tell Lorin about this when we talk, and picture him shaking his head at me and the hundreds of thousands of Don Quixote types fiercely clinging to hope. Bush's reelection, and today's inauguration, is meaningless in the landscape of Lorin's current life; nothing would've changed for him regardless of who was elected. At least with Kerry I thought there was a chance for something better, eventually. But every key military yardstick indicates the opposite.

The Sunni-led insurgency, initially projected to number about five thousand strong, has ballooned to two hundred thousand, at least forty thousand of which are considered hard-core fighters. U.S. fatalities now average eighty-two per month, an almost five-fold increase since March of 2003. During the same time frame, the number of soldiers wounded in combat has escalated from 142 to 808 per month, and it's estimated that fifty thousand troops have been evacuated.

The mounting casualties are one of the platforms contained in the House Congressional Resolution #35, presented by Representative Lynne Woolsey and cosponsored by two dozen other Congressmen. Presented on January 26, the Resolution "Express[es] the sense of Congress that the President should develop and implement a plan to begin the immediate withdrawal of United States Armed Forces from Iraq."

The paper comes on the heels of Senator Ted Kennedy's calls for an exit strategy, accompanied by a detailed five-point plan for a phased withdrawal. But both the Congressional Resolution and Kennedy's high-profile politicking are overshadowed by the President's new budget proposal.

The supplemental appropriations bill for Fiscal Year 2005, which requests another $81.9 billion, will bring the running cost of the Iraq war to more than $200 billion. This is the President's fourth supplemental spending request for the war, and economist Doug Henwood has estimated that the war will cost each American household at least $3,415. An article published by the Center for American Progress states, "The supplemental request will include funds for several unexpected demands, such as the eighty-four percent surge in the need for heavily armored Humvee transport vehicles."

The document also addresses the likelihood that troops will remain in Iraq for another four years: "Based on the Pentagon's spending to date, the operational and maintenance costs of a projected four-year requirement would amount to $259.2 billion." Bush's supplemental budget doesn't include the $18 billion that will be necessary to restore military vehicles, jets, and other equipment damaged or exhausted in Iraq.

Nowhere does it address the anticipated $34 billion projected for reconstruction plans through 2007. But it does contain proposed cuts to the Veterans Administration budget and scales back health benefits for veterans.

The VA is the second largest federal bureaucracy (the Department of Defense is number one), with almost two hundred forty thousand staff members who oversee pension and disability payments and health care programs for nearly 25 million veterans. It operates 171 medical centers; more than three hundred fifty outpatient, community, and outreach clinics; 126 nursing homes; and 35 domiciliaries. The House Budget Committee released figures showing that funding for VA programs has risen seventy-seven percent since 1995, while costs have increased eighty-five percent.

The $68.3 billion VA budget requested by President Bush for fiscal year 2005 is a meager one point one percent increase, and the projected annual increases over the next five years amount to approximately two point three percent, at a time when the national average for yearly inflation increases in health services is twelve percent. The cost saving measures introduced in the new budget proposal come directly out of the pockets of veterans.

One plan up for consideration requires that all veterans without service related disabilities pay an annual enrollment fee of $250; the other more than doubles the pharmacy copayment, raising it from seven dollars to fifteen. But these measures, even if approved, will not begin to generate enough revenue to meet the present and future needs of the nearly one million veterans of the "War on Terror."

Defense Department data released this month shows that ninety-five percent of the troops wounded in action sustained their injuries after May 1, 2003. Since then, the monthly mass casualty bombings have gone from zero to thirteen, and attacks on coalition forces have jumped from 735 a month in November of 2003, to upwards of 2,300 one year later.

Lorin just needs to hold on and keep his head down for a few more months, and he'll be out of there. His latest e-mail is succinct:

I am just very tired right now. I got up at 12:30 a.m. and went on a mission last night from 2 a.m. till about 8 a.m. Had to go raid the houses of the people that murdered one of our interpreters, they cut his head off in his front yard, and then dumped his body's at his mother's home. That was for working with the Americans. So we had to go get them.

Lorin makes a quick phone call a few days later, and I ask him why, as a Mortars man, he was out on that kind of mission.

"Well, actually, I've been kind of bored, so I, uh . . . I volunteered."

"Are you kidding me?"

"Well, no. I'm tired of just sitting around here."

"Be tired, honey. Better tired than dead," I say sharply.

Lorin mentions he's been recommended to receive several medals, including a Bronze Star. The medal dates back to December of 1941, and is awarded to any person serving in the United States military who has distinguished him or herself by heroic or meritorious achievement or service while engaged in military operations involving conflict with a foreign enemy.

He's seen the paperwork, but when I ask him what the medals are for, he changes the subject.

"Hey, listen to this! I was sitting outside my trailer drinking my morning coffee when a truck loaded with explosives blew up at the front gate of the base. It was about half a mile away, but it still made my uniform move, like there was a really strong wind."

I am once again caught between wanting to know and not wanting to know, realizing there are some things I never will know about his year at war.

Since he went back, our communication has been shorter and less frequent. I think we're both holding our breath in a different way than before, hoping he'll make it through these last months unharmed. We only speak once a week now, whereas before it had usually been twice.

I don't press him the way that I used to; now isn't the time to ask him to delve too deeply into the ramifications of what he's doing. But sometimes I forget, like when he asked me about the 100,000 and Counting event I'd gone to a few weeks ago. The demonstration was intended to heighten public awareness of the number of Iraqi civilians since the invasion and express sympathy and solidarity from Americans.

"You do know that the vast majority of people who've been killed in Iraq are innocent civilians, unarmed women and children?" I ask.

"Yeah, I know. Believe me I know. I've been responsible for some of them."

"How do you feel about that?" Then, catching myself, I say, "Wait, forget it, don't think about that now. We'll deal with it when you're home. It's going to be okay."

And I will it to be true.

When he resumes talking, he tells me, "I am going on a trip down south this weekend, to Baghdad, and some of the outlying areas."

"How many times do I have to tell you not to volunteer? Russ will be really pissed off if you keep doing that." I sense my father's ire is more of a preventative than mine.

"The Brigade Sergeant Major wants me to go with him to look at and visit some other units. He told me he wants me to go. Don't worry, I'll be fine, I'll call you when I get back."

I spend the next thirty-six hours with an escalated fear level. Why don't they track that, along with the national terrorist threat levels?

Lorin calls the day before the elections. "They're going to cut off all communications for the next day or so. I don't know what they're expecting, but we're not going anywhere. Sounds like the most powerful Army on earth is just going to hunker down and hide, which is kind of sad, really."

Perhaps, I think, but maybe it'll keep them alive. He sounds better, clearer, than he has in weeks, like the man he was before. I ask how he's doing, and he says, "I'm pretty good. They told us we're leaving for Kuwait at the end of February, and I could be home by March 10th."

"Really? That's fabulous! It's even earlier than expected. How's everybody else doing?"

"Well, you won't believe it, but Ozmer's back. He just got in."

"What?" I ask. "You've only got a month or so left. Besides, I thought he got beat up pretty badly."

Captain Tim Ozmer was severely injured on August 4th when an insurgent's bomb exploded under his Humvee outside Logistical Support Area Anaconda. He was returning from several hours of patrolling the dusty farm country around the base when one of the front wheels of the heavily armored rig he was in ran over a piece of plywood buried in the dust.

The plywood was attached to a pressure-triggered detonator, which was hooked up to three antitank mines.

Ozmer's rig—number six in the convoy—was tossed onto its roof, and his seat slammed onto the upturned ceiling, shattering his L-4 vertebrae.

Even before he went into surgery, Ozmer began lobbying to return to duty. He enlisted in the Army in August 1986, and after an active duty stint, has been in the Guard ever since. The surgeon said they'd have to wait and see how things went. Ozmer's spine was fused with titanium, and he spent a month at Landstuhl Army Regional Medical Center in Germany before he was stable enough to travel. He received additional treatments at Madigan Army Medical Center at Fort Lewis, followed by four months of physical therapy. He began running laps at the Y while wearing his body armor, and was ultimately cleared to return to combat. His wife, Connie, understood his desire to join his unit, but didn't much like it.

Lorin says admiringly, "I love this guy. He said he wasn't going to let Iraq beat him."

Insurgent attacks in the days leading up to the Iraq elections are targeting civilians in an effort to deter people from voting, and dozens of Iraqi election workers have been killed or wounded. So many people are afraid to vote that some nations question the legitimacy of the election. U.S. political leadership has no such concerns, and pictures of smiling Iraqis displaying purple-inked index fingers, the proof of having cast a ballot, inspire counter-protesters to create a new slogan. In the days following the election, counterprotestors at rallies calling for an end to the war gleefully chant: "Seven million Iraqis gave you people the finger!"

13

Bring Them Home Now, and Take Care of Them When They Get Here

MILITARY FAMILIES SPEAK OUT members in Vermont, Washington, and Oregon are mobilizing efforts to bring the National Guard troops home. The state-based campaigns are being tailored according to each state's political system, and will include town hall and city council meetings, and hearings at the State Legislatures about the multiple impacts of National Guard deployments, which are averaging about three hundred twenty days. Some units are being sent on second and even third tours of combat duty, with just eight months in between deployments.

The unprecedented reliance on the Guard is devastating its ability to respond to local emergencies, a situation that's exacerbated by the increasingly common practice of bringing understaffed deploying units up to appropriate levels by pilfering personnel and equipment from other units, rendering stateside units ineffective. In addition, returning units are leaving much of their equipment in Iraq for use by their replacements, or because it has been destroyed. The cost of reorganizing the Guard is projected to be in the billions.

Veterans for Peace member Wes Hamilton is spearheading the Washington state proposal, and we make plans to get together in Olympia on Saturday.

On my way to meet Wes and Judy, I stop in Puyallup, about thirty miles south of Seattle, to visit my six-year-old thoroughbred. She's a Christmas gift from Lorin, who had heard me reminisce about how much I'd loved having horses when I was growing up in North Dakota. Temper is being stabled on a three-acre spread, where the wife of one of one of Lorin's men lives with their four kids. Sharon* has a dozen other horses on the land, and between them and the kids, she's running ragged. Her life has been a series of accidents, literally and figuratively, since her husband was deployed, and it's catching up with her.

She unloads while I'm grooming Temper, telling me that she hurt her back in the most recent collision, which nearly totaled her truck. She says, "I've started seeing a counselor, and she put me on anti-depressants." Mixed in with the relief is an undertone of somehow having failed, a feeling I know all too well.

"Good for you. Maybe you won't keep having all those accidents, and things will slow down for you. You've got a lot to cope with, what with the kids and all. And the winters here are so gray and miserable, I'm surprised more people aren't on anti-depressants."

She's called away to another minor childcare crisis before I can tell her that I just got a prescription, too.

Seated at a table in a little café in Olympia, Wes brings me up to speed on the proposition that he's been working on with several attorneys. Focusing on the President's latest Executive Orders, which proclaimed that there is no threat in Iraq or Afghanistan, the various state proposals are asking that the President's 2001 declaration that the country is in a state of national emergency be officially revoked, and that the Guard brought home.

More than eight thousand Oregon National Guardsmen have been mobilized since 9/11, and about 2,700 have been to Iraq or Afghanistan. Washington state has nearly four thousand Reservists overseas, and the 81st is scheduled to begin a massive restructuring after they return, becoming the first National Guard Unit to transition into a "Unit of Action."

The move is part of the Army's plan to reorganize the Army National Guard into thirty-four brigade-size units by fiscal year 2007. The revision is the largest since World War II, part of a comprehensive overhaul that's coming at one of the most stressful points in Guard history. But if it's not done now, there is virtually unilateral agreement that the Guard will not survive.

Lorin maintains that the timeline for making the changes will prevent the 81st from being redeployed until at least 2008. Not willing to take their

---

*Name has been changed.

chances, some of the guys in his unit plan to get out of the Guard as fast as they can. There are others who might've been willing to stay, but their wives have talked them out of it.

Searching for new ways to bolster its diminishing ranks, the Army National Guard is pushing for Congressional approval to raise the $5,000 reenlistment bonus offered to active duty soldiers once their contracts have expired to $15,000, which is tax free if the soldiers re-up for six years while still in Iraq. Bonuses for first time recruits are being bumped from $6,000 to $10,000, and there's talk of moving the age limit for recruits from thirty-four to forty.

Six months ago, Vermont was second in the nation in National Guard recruitment, but now it's scraping the bottom. On a per capita basis, Vermont recently passed North Dakota as the state with the highest number of deployed troops. Hawaii, Oregon, and Vermont have had upward of fifty percent of their state militia deployed or federally activated. The state by state percentages of mobilized Guard units contradicts the promise made by Lieutenant General Steven Blum, chief of the National Guard Bureau, that he would not mobilize more than fifty percent of Guard forces at any given time. At least fifty-four percent of the Guard has been deployed since 2001, and unit readiness has decreased by nearly twenty-eight percent since July 2002.

According to the Army National Guard's Annual Financial Report for fiscal year 2004, there were 81,000 ARNG soldiers mobilized at any given time during 2004, with a total of 149,790 Guardsmen on active duty. Utah has deployed over fifty percent of its soldiers since 9/11, and seventy-eight percent of the Rhode Island members have gone overseas at least once. More than half of the South Dakota Army National Guard had served in the Middle East by February of 2004, with seventy-four percent of its members mobilized for Operations Iraqi Freedom, Noble Eagle, and Enduring Freedom.

Pennsylvania has one of the largest Guard units in the nation, and is also among the most frequently deployed. Almost all of New Hampshire's citizen soldiers have been alerted or mobilized, which is also true for Oklahoma. Maine started 2004 with a twenty percent mobilization rate for the National Guard, but closed the year with over half of its force having been called up. New Jersey has sixty percent of its state Guard on federal active duty, sixty-two percent of the Washington Guard has been deployed so far, and eighty percent of Idaho's.

After discussing the proposal, Judy asks if I'm still attending the rally at Fort Bragg on March 19th, expected to draw around five thousand participants. The location was chosen to demonstrate that it's possible to support the troops and oppose the administration. Veterans groups, many in uniform, will lead the march in an effort to dispel the lingering memory of antiwar activists' sometimes poor treatment of Vietnam soldiers during the protests in the sixties.

I say, "Yes, I'm going. Are you guys?"

Wes tells me that he's participating in a rally in Olympia that day, and Judy will be speaking at antiwar protests in England. She recently received a four-month fellowship for a nursing program in London, and is leaving on March 6th. Wes will join her three weeks later, and they'll stay until the end of summer.

They've hooked up with Military Families Against the War and other activist groups in England via the Internet, and are obviously looking forward to their trip. As we're saying good-bye, Wes promises to send the declaration that was unanimously passed by the Central Committee Meeting of the Multnomah County Democrats in Oregon, in an attempt to leverage the National Democratic Platform.

I contact Washington State Congressman Jim McDermott's office to ask if he will support a similar resolution in Washington. Jane Sanders, his Seattle-based District Director, puts me in touch with Julie Mock, the Board President of the National Gulf War Resource Center. It's a coalition of advocates, organizations, and members providing referrals and information about the pattern of health problems suffered by Gulf War veterans.

Julie and her husband are both Gulf War vets, and she was diagnosed with multiple sclerosis five years after being in the Gulf. Their two sons are facing an array of physical and mental health issues, and according to the Self Help Guide the organization published in November of 2003, "A survey of 1,200 ill veterans performed in 1994 by U.S. Senator Donald Reigle reported that seventy-seven percent of spouses and sixty-eight percent of children born after the war were experiencing Gulf War illness symptoms or birth defects."

Soldiers were exposed to so many toxins, including chemical and biological weapons such as sarin, depleted uranium, and nerve agents, as well as various vaccinations that were administered by the military, that it's impossible to isolate one single cause for the astronomical rates of illness and infection in Gulf War vets. Since soldiers who were given anthrax vaccines yet were never deployed are also symptomatic, it points to the possibility of the vaccination itself being a causal factor.

Investigative journalist Gary Matsumoto explores the phenomenon in his book, *Vaccine A* (Basic Books, 2004), which reveals that between May 1986 and September 1989, the United States sold anthrax to Saddam Hussein, suspecting it would be "weaponized." Not surprisingly, a background paper written in the late eighties by the Defense Intelligence Agency, led by Paul Wolfowitz and Dick Cheney, concluded, "Iraq is assessed to have the biological weapons agents anthrax and botulism toxin." Secretary of Defense Cheney made the protection of the Persian Gulf oil supply the top priority of the Defense Department in 1989.

As the likelihood of war in the Gulf began to grow, so did the Department of Defense's concerns about the immunization of its troops. The approved anthrax vaccine required a series of six shots, and the "time to immunity" (before it could be considered effective) was up to nine months. None too practical when mobilizing and deploying for war. However, government researchers at Fort Detrick, Maryland, had been experimenting with several variants of a "second generation" single-shot anthrax vaccine for years.

All four of the formulations included squalane or squalene, an oil derivative used as an adjuvant[27] in order to improve the immune response to the vaccine. This oil was known to cause debilitating illnesses and severe autoimmune reactions in tests that were previously restricted to relatively small case studies and animal experiments.

On January 5, 1991, as the United States military was gearing up for Desert Storm, it began immunizing troops against anthrax, and conducting clinical trials of the vaccine prototypes. These vaccinations were either not documented on soldiers' medical records, or were classified "Secret." This covert medical experimentation was made possible by several key pieces of legislation and interdepartmental agreements, including a 1974 "Memorandum of Understanding between the Department of Defense and the FDA

---

27. An adjuvant is a substance that, when added to a medicine, speeds or improves its action. In immunology, a substance that is added to a vaccine to improve the immune response so that less vaccine is needed to produce more antibodies. Such adjuvants apparently work by speeding the division of lymphocytes and by keeping the antigen in the area where the immune response is taking place. (Biotech dictionary)

that permits the military to administer investigational drugs to its personnel without their consent and without public disclosure."

The document is supported by FDA rule 23(d), issued immediately prior to Desert Storm, which permits experimental drugs to be administered without informed consent, as it was "not feasible in a specific military operation involving combat or the immediate threat of combat."

The Gulf War syndrome is a constellation of symptoms that can be classified as autoimmune disorders. These are extremely rare in men, and virtually absent in young, previously "healthy" males. Yet, nearly a hundred thousand Gulf War vets have reported problems, including some soldiers who were immunized but who never served in the Gulf. Coincidentally, there were roughly a hundred thousand soldiers involved in the study.

In 1994, Major General Blanck, Commander of the Walter Reed Army Medical Center, said, "Anthrax vaccine should continue to be considered as a potential cause for undiagnosed illnesses in Persian Gulf military personnel because many of the support troops received anthrax vaccine, and because DOD believes that the incidence of undiagnosed illnesses in support troops may be higher than that in combat troops."

It should be noted that "support troops" are primarily Guard and Reserves. A 1999 survey of Air National Guard and Reserve personnel, conducted by the General Accounting Office, indicated "thirty-seven percent of Guard and Reserve personnel received one or more anthrax shots. Of these, eighty-four percent reported side effects or adverse events."

A preliminary survey of randomly chosen Guard and Reserve members done by the GAO the following year found that a quarter of pilots and aircrew personnel in the Air Force Reserve and Air National Guard had left the military or transferred to inactive status or non-flying duty because of concerns about the anthrax vaccine. Another eighteen percent indicated that they planned to leave within six months, citing the anthrax immunization as the determining factor. Pentagon officials challenged the findings, and the Department of Defense's denial continued through a series of hearings, which included testimony from three National Guard pilots. Lieutenant Colonel Tom Heemstra (Retired), former commander of the 122nd Fighter Wing, said that, "Military officials have 'coerced, intimidated, threatened, and punished' Reserve pilots who refuse to volunteer to take the vaccine.

"Captain Daniel Marohn, an F-16 pilot in Heemstra's unit who accompanied him to the hearing, was given an Article 15, fined, and threatened with jail time. Lieutenant Colonel Ross said that he was not allowed to resign from his unit when he refused to take the anthrax shot."[28]

Fort Lewis, Washington, where Lorin trained prior to deployment, is on the list of military bases, hospitals, and training centers where the test lots were administered, according to recently declassified documents. I recall Lorin mentioning that he had to get a series of vaccinations, and the next time he calls, I ask him if one of them was for anthrax.

"Yeah, everybody got it. Why do you want to know?"

"Because there might be a problem with it. You may have been given a trial vaccine, one that isn't approved, and seems to be linked to some health problems. Did you get a series of shots?"

"No," he says. "I was supposed to, but after the second one, I didn't go back."

"Why?"

"I had a funny feeling about them. Besides, by then, a federal court had ruled that the Army could no longer enforce the administration of the anthrax vaccine. The judge said the vaccination program was illegal."

I relay this in a conversation with Lieutenant Thomas Barnes, the Managing Director of the Homeland Security Policy Institute Group. He served in Desert Storm, and speculates that Guard members and Reservists were specifically selected for the clinical trials.

Barnes says emphatically, "Tell him not to sign off on anything until he's a hundred percent physically fit. They've got to keep him on active duty until all of his medical issues are fully resolved. And make sure he asks for copies of all of his medical records."

A review conducted by the General Accounting Office in the fall of 2003 revealed that thirty-eight to ninety-eight percent of personnel records were lacking one or both of the pre- and post-deployment health assessments. The gaps in the records will make it extremely difficult, if not impossible, for soldiers, especially citizen soldiers, to readily and easily obtain medical care.

When Lorin was home for his two-week R&R, he had a couple of strange skin conditions (one of the hallmarks of the test vaccine) that doctors have yet to diagnose. The 2003–2004 Veterans Administration reports on the health status of returning Iraq war veterans reveal a significant rise in the number of unidentified skin disorders of returning veterans.

---

28. "Survey: Reservists Leaving Because of Vaccine Concerns." *Stars and Stripes*, October 13, 2000.

These rates are fifteen percent higher for Guard and Reserve than for regular enlisted, a figure becomes even more significant when considering that: (1) even at their highest rates of deployment Guardsmen and Reservists have represented no more than forty-four percent of overall troops strength; (2) Guardsmen and Reservists have no systematic medical follow-up, but regular military do; and (3) a number of studies conducted at Walter Reed Military Hospital don't even include Guard and Reserve soldiers.

Twenty-three percent of the Iraq war soldiers receiving services at VA clinics have been diagnosed with mental health issues or symptoms of PTSD, and more than 5,100 soldiers have sought treatment as of December 2004, a number that is expected to triple. The markers of post-traumatic stress include nightmares, avoidance of anything that could be a reminder of the traumatic event, and hyperarousal, a physiological response to stress that can lead to irritability and restlessness, drug use, and alcohol abuse.

Among soldiers who develop PTSD, the study says, "There was a strong reported relation between combat experiences, such as being shot at, handling dead bodies, knowing someone who was killed, or killing enemy combatants."

Entering into combat is like walking through a one-way door; once you've been through it, you can never go back. It's learning how to go forward that's presenting a problem for the approximately 87,000 veterans currently receiving treatment for PTSD. It's a figure that many health care officials expect to more than double in the coming years.

For National Guard and Reserve soldiers, whose mental health benefits apply for a maximum of two years after their service, with full medical benefits terminated six months post-deployment, it is anticipated that PTSD rates will be even higher. Because citizen soldiers have less training and preparation for deployment, and less cohesive units, they are at significantly higher psychological risk.

National Guard members are increasingly exposed to more combat than regular soldiers, but rather than rotating back to military bases for medical treatment and monitoring, they return home. Once there, the separation from other soldiers creates a feeling of isolation at a time when support and connection with others who are going through the same emotional adjustments is critical.

Adding to the pressure is that many mental health officials believe that the nature of urban street fighting, civilian combatants, and insurgent warfare, coupled with heavy reliance on Guard and Reserve troops in combat roles and on extremely dangerous missions, will result in higher rates of post-traumatic stress disorder amongst this group of veterans than those in previous conflicts.

Post-traumatic stress disorder is the result of subtle biological changes in the brain chemistry as a response to severe stress. Researchers believe that extreme stress alters the way the brain stores memories, and during a particularly intense episode, the body releases massive amounts of adrenaline, and the physiological alterations associated with the intense emotional reaction create memories that disrupt normal life. It's likely that some people are genetically predisposed to the disorder, and persons who have undergone earlier traumatic experiences have a lower resistance to PTSD.

Given that Guardsmen and Reservists are more likely to hold jobs in the police, fire, and emergency medical departments, their higher rates of PTSD will potentially undermine the delivery of those services once the soldiers are home. Nearly fifty percent of police departments have had officers deployed to Iraq, and local fire departments have also been depleted, effecting things like the response time for 911 calls.

Medical experts also anticipate that PTSD may be far more common in female vets than their male counterparts, since women deplete serotonin, a brain chemical that helps ward off depression, much more quickly than men, and replenish it more slowly. The ratio of female to male veterans suffering from PTSD was two to one after the first Gulf War, which was a much shorter conflict that used far fewer citizen soldiers.

Women are much more likely to sign up for the Guard and Reserve than for active duty, and figures released by the Office of Army Demographics showed that in 2004, there were approximately 93,570 women in the Guard and Reserves, compared to 74,140 in the active component.

Lieutenant General Steven Blum, chief of the National Guard, expects that a full eighty percent of National Guardsmen will be combat veterans by 2006, the majority having served in Iraq.

Findings by the *New England Journal of Medicine* (July 1, 2004) show that while seventy-one to eighty-six percent of soldiers deployed to Iraq engaged in a firefight, only thirty-one percent of soldiers deployed to Afghanistan reported being in actual combat situations. Of those who were, the median number of firefights during deployment in Afghanistan was two; in Iraq, it's five.

Iraq veterans are reporting significantly higher rates of post-combat PTSD than soldiers returning from Afghanistan. This has instigated an unprecedented outreach effort by the Department of Veterans Affairs, which has sent letters to 10,860 vets, including Guard and Reserve, urging them to seek medical services.

But many veterans' advocacy groups say it's not enough, and with the protracted ground war, some military and mental health experts are warning that we're just seeing the tip of the iceberg. Studies indicate soldiers are suffering from post-traumatic stress disorder on a scale not seen since Vietnam, if even then. Without treatment, PTSD can actually jeopardize survival.

Epidemiologists conducting long-term studies of combat veterans have discovered that five years after the Vietnam War, veterans who saw combat were almost twice as likely to die from car accidents and inadvertent poisoning than non-combat veterans. Three decades later, a study published in the *Archives of Internal Medicine* (2004) found that those same combat vets continued to have higher mortality rates, and were particularly at risk for drug overdoses and accidental poisoning.

According to federal government statistics, veterans comprise thirty-three percent of the nation's homeless men. More Vietnam veterans have committed suicide than were killed in action during the war.

"Iraq is Vietnam without water," said Rick Weidman, a spokesman for Vietnam Veterans of America. He believes that one-third of the more than one million soldiers who have served in Iraq will be faced with psychological problems, and initial findings support his position.

Part of the reason for the escalating mental health challenges is that while soldiers were typically sent for one tour of duty in Vietnam, more and more troops are serving two, and occasionally three, rotations in Iraq. Another challenge is the moral ambiguity of fighting a war without front lines, and where the combatants are, or are dressed as, civilians, some of them women or teens. Iraqi law allows the use of children as soldiers, and at least a thousand youth are believed to be serving in the Iraq military, a figure that doesn't account for the adolescents providing assistance to insurgency forces.

There is considerable psychological distress associated with going into a country under the auspices of liberating and helping a people, only to have those people rise up against you, and it lingers long after the war has ended. Yet, with all that's known about PTSD, military attitudes haven't changed much since Vietnam, and the vast majority of soldiers with PTSD don't seek help.

The Army has tried to circumvent this in recent years by requiring all returning soldiers to complete mental health evaluation forms while they're waiting to be reunited with their families. Not wanting to delay the homecoming, the vast majority of soldiers won't disclose symptoms.

Colonel James Polo, medical director at Fort Carson in Colorado, admits that's the wrong time to look for signs of the illness, and the Department of Defense has begun assessing soldiers three to six months after their return, which is when PTSD typically begins to manifest. The Army has initiated a deployment psycho-support program and an extensive suicide prevention program, spurred in part by the findings of an Army team of mental health experts that was sent to Iraq after five soldiers committed suicide in July of 2003.

The resulting study, printed in the *New England Journal of Medicine*, was one of a handful of investigations that discovered that up to twenty percent of soldiers serving in Iraq showed signs of major depression, generalized anxiety or post-traumatic stress disorder.

The majority of soldiers with psychological problems told researchers they were afraid to seek counseling because of the stigma amongst their peers, or the potentially detrimental impact on their careers. In addition, mental health workers serving on bases in Iraq felt they didn't have the skills or training necessary to effectively treat the soldiers.

The multiple barriers to receiving care lead many experts to believe that the number of soldiers in Iraq suffering from combat-related psychological problems is considerably higher than reported. The home front impact of untreated PTSD includes addiction, a new generation of homeless war veterans, domestic violence, mental and emotional abuse, suicide, and divorce. Post-Persian Gulf War studies showed divorce rates at three Army bases that sent troops overseas rose by thirty-seven to fifty-six percent.

Long deployments also disrupt the parent-child relationship, and when infants and toddlers are left behind, their reactions to the loss of a parent may include some of the classic signs of depression, such as a loss of appetite, irritability, and apathy. After bonding with a new caretaker, they sometimes exhibit stranger anxiety when unfamiliar parents finally come home.

Preschoolers may regress to such behaviors as bed-wetting, and, just as with divorce, frequently blame themselves for the absence of a parent.

Sergeant First Class Merle McLain, a thirty-six-year-old father of twins, thinks there's a fifty percent chance that the 130 citizen soldiers from Ephrata, Washington, population 6,980, will have to return to Iraq. They have been home now for nearly seven months, after almost a year and a half deployment. That's three months more than the stated Pentagon policy, and is the longest deployment of any Washington Guard unit since World War II.

The small 1161st Transportation Company, consisting of men and women ages eighteen through sixty, landed in Iraq in the early days of the invasion, and completed more than fourteen thousand missions, covering over a million miles in unarmored vehicles with severe equipment shortages. Soldiers served without body armor for months, had to improvise extra protection for truck cabs, and spent the better part of the year driving truck convoys without the customary security against insurgent attacks—a truck mounted with a .50-caliber gun to escort them. The 1161st was extended twice, learning of the last one only when someone read about it in the military newspaper, *Stars and Stripes,* as they were waiting to board the plane.

Everybody eventually made it home, and the unit sustained relatively few physical injuries. But the psychological impact is just beginning to be felt, and some of the soldiers are being treated for PTSD. The military coached soldiers and spouses on possible reintegration problems, but few were prepared for the reality of coming home to find themselves unemployed. Little was said about returning husbands unable to engage with their wives and children. No one told one of the women that she could expect to be woken up in the middle of the night by her husband, holding an imaginary gun to her head.[29]

I'm worried, but don't say it, the next time I speak to Lorin. Instead, we talk about his welcome home party, refusing to broach the possibility that it could be postponed if his unit gets extended.

After putting in his menu requests, he says, "I was talking to the other guys about coming home, and we just want people to leave us alone. We were thinking we should get T-shirts made up that say IRAQ? DON'T F***** ASK!"

We're joking about it, but between the tightness in his voice, and the stories I've heard, I'm worried. I don't seriously think Lorin's a candidate for suicide, but I can't be sure, and I don't want to miss the warning signs.

---

29. "They're Back from Iraq, But Are They OK?," *Seattle Post-Intelligencer,* March 7, 2005.

Soldiers who have served in Iraq are killing themselves at higher percentages than in any other war where such figures have been tracked. A Native American girl, barely in her twenties, has tried to kill herself several times since she got back to her Wisconsin reservation. An MFSO member told me that the young vet's most recent effort to destroy herself involved taking a large butcher's knife to her torso, slashing and gouging herself repeatedly, before passing out from blood loss and shock.

A different type of casualty is the women who are murdered by their returning husbands, as was the case with the wife of Matthew Denni, a supply sergeant with the Oregon 671st Engineer Army Reserve Company, who served in Iraq and was shot and sent back home to heal.

Driven, in part, by the trauma he'd experienced, catalyzed by his wife's infidelity, he murdered his wife and packed her corpse into an Army regulation footlocker. He was sentenced to twenty years in the state penitentiary.

> We cannot stress the importance of attending reunion training. Units that have returned home have experienced serious challenges and difficulties with relationships. The focus of the trainings is to equip families with tools to most effectively deal with the transition back home. It is very critical to attend reunion training.

The message about upcoming Family Reunification Trainings is sent to the wives of the 81st. We were given no guidance or preparation prior to mobilization, and scant support during deployment, and now the Guard has the gall to use what amounts to a scare tactic to induce us to come to this meeting? They put our spouses in a war zone for which they are ill equipped, psychologically and otherwise, and then bring them home and dump them back into their families, with the expectation that we will pick up the pieces.

During the World Wars, Korea, and Vietnam, soldiers took a slow boat home, and there was a *de facto* decompression time. Now that the military is using commercial airlines, it's not unusual for soldiers go from combat to cul-de-sac in eighteen hours. Which is part of the reason that, during a six-week period in the summer of 2002, Army wives at Fort Bragg, North Carolina, suffered more casualties than the soldiers: four women were murdered by their husbands, three of whom had recently returned from Afghanistan.

"Coming Home: A Guide for Service Members Returning from Mobilization/Deployment," doesn't mention the dangers of post-deployment domestic violence. Since the Iraq war began, monthly calls to the Miles Foundation hotline for domestic violence victims in the military have jumped from fifty to more than five hundred. The one-page pamphlet reads, "Readjustment may cause stress. This may be especially true for demobilizing Guard/Reservists who are transitioning back to civilian life."

Although it's not named as such, there's also a paragraph that refers to PTSD:

> You may have seen or experienced some things that were very upsetting. Some normal reactions to these abnormal situations are fear, nervousness and irritability, fatigue, sleep disturbances, startle reactions, moodiness, trouble concentrating, feelings of numbness, and frequent thoughts of the event. Talking with others who were there and/or counselors trained in crisis stress reactions is very important.

This same paragraph is included in the version distributed to spouses, but where the soldiers have ten points about reuniting with a spouse, those of us who've got a service member coming home have thirteen.

We are told what to watch out for, and how to deal with our husbands' insecurities and bring him back into the family fold. The 2004 Department of Defense guide for spouses reads like nothing so much as a marriage manual for happy homemakers, circa 1950: "Reassure your spouse that they are needed, even though you've coped during deployment. . . . Your spouse may need to hear that it wasn't the same doing things alone . . ."

I messed that up in our last conversation, when I unthinkingly said, "You know, I've completely reverted to living alone, and the other day, I realized that when you get back, nothing's really going to change for me in terms of cleaning house, figuring the taxes, making sure the bills get paid, taking the garbage out, and all the other stuff I've been doing."

After a short silence, Lorin replied forlornly, "I take the garbage out sometimes."

We're provided with a list of resources, names, and numbers we can call for assistance, but the military's definition of "assistance" is worlds away from mine. I am angered at the presumption and the irresponsibility of the government and its henchmen in the Department of Defense.

They take our loved ones for a year or more and then throw them back to us, chipped, cracked, or broken, and say, "Here. You fix him."

Better yet, pretend nothing's wrong.

Case in point is an account from a National Guard wife, posted on the MFSO Website:

The last year has been really rough on us as a family. My husband came home a different person. We all needed counseling. Our marriage fell apart. We're still talking divorce. My kids are heartbroken. Sixty days after a reserve soldier's terminal leave ends the government drops them from their health insurance. The Army has washed their hands of our problems!!

Even though it is illegal, he was bypassed (by his civilian employer) for a big promotion. We took a big financial hit while he was gone and now we're still taking the hit because he should have been promoted. I thank God that my husband came home. He's due to deploy to Iraq within the next year, this time for eighteen months.

I want to stay married to him, because I love him, but this deployment business is devastating to soldiers and their families. Since we're a reserve family, we don't live near any other soldier's families. We don't have close contact with any bases where there could possibly be support groups. When our medical insurance changes we go through a costly nightmare. We are pretty much on our own.

Even more isolated are the nearly three hundred wounded Guard and Reserve soldiers who have been mistakenly removed from active duty military payrolls, even after filing the necessary paperwork. Injured citizen soldiers must apply for active duty extensions in order to receive regular military pay and benefits during their recovery. But thirty-four percent of the soldiers who did so were still dropped from the system, resulting in months of wading through paperwork and bureaucracy trying to get reinstated while recuperating without any means of financial support for themselves or their families.

Unable to pay the rent, some citizen soldiers have found temporary housing with friends or family members, but the number of hurt and homeless Iraq war veterans is growing. The National Coalition for Homeless Veterans reported that Iraq war veterans have begun to show up at shelters in New York and California.

There are upwards of three thousand injured or ill Guard and Reserve soldiers assigned to the Army medical hold at any given time, and the peacetime structure of the Department of Defense is admittedly insufficient for dealing with them. The U.S. House Government Reform Committee is investigating the problem, which has been equated to "financial friendly fire" by Committee Chairman Tom Davis.

A much larger, and longer-term challenge is how the Department of Veterans Affairs is going to handle the disability and retirement benefits of the nearly a hundred and fifty thousand National Guard and Reserve veterans of the global war on terror who became eligible as of August 1, 2004. VA accounting indicates that 26,633 (sixteen percent) of the 166,334 veterans of operations in Iraq and Afghanistan that have separated from military service have filed claims for service-connected disabilities, but less than two thirds of those claims have been processed.

Although sixty to seventy thousand new claims are submitted each month, President Bush's budget for 2005 calls for cutting the Department of Veterans Affairs staff that handles benefits claims. Disability Review Boards, typically comprised of active duty personnel, review the files of injured soldiers and make a determination about their eligibility for benefits. Those who qualify for disability compensation typically don't begin receiving payments for another six months to two years after that.

Firsthand accounts from the wives of Reservists and volunteers at Fort Madigan Medical Center in Washington point toward an emerging pattern of Guardsmen and Reservists being granted decidedly lower benefits than active duty enlisted for comparable injuries. 81st Brigade Specialist West's back injury required the fusion of spinal vertebrae, the attachment of two eight-inch titanium rods, secured by two-inch screws, and two six-inch bolts in his pelvis. His gallbladder was removed, and the broken bones in his heel and leg have mended, but he will never walk normally again, and back pain is his constant companion. For this, West was granted a ten percent disability.

Washington State Guard and Reserve soldiers who were pulled away from their regular jobs to serve in Iraq are also encountering obstacles in receiving retirement benefits from civilian employers. Apparently, when the laws covering military service credit were passed, no one imagined that a reservist approaching retirement would be mobilized for an extended period of duty.

There is a law barring employers from denying benefits to employees that are forced to leave work for military service, but the current Iraq conflict isn't listed as one of the military operations that are qualified for the classification of veteran status. Bills in the Washington State House and Senate have been introduced to update the list of qualifying military conflicts to include Iraq and Afghanistan as part of the global war on terror.

The military doesn't pay retirement benefits to Guardsmen and Reservists until they've turned sixty. After some debate about lowering the age limit, the government deemed it too expensive. Near as we can tell, Lorin's about a year away from qualifying for retirement benefits, if in fact he's accrued sufficient points in his twenty-plus years to qualify. He's looked in to it, and thinks he is, but isn't one hundred percent sure. Right now, he's not even sure if he'll have a job waiting for him when he gets back.

14

I Got the Call Today

MARCH 2005

I AM BARRAGED by questions from people wanting to know, "Aren't you excited about Lorin coming home?" Of course I am, but I'm holding my enthusiasm in check until he's actually on the plane. Coupled with the anticipation of his return is the worry that his deployment could be extended at the last second, and an unpleasantly persistent annoyance at how our lives have been disrupted, the time forever lost. But it's not something I can articulate to anyone outside of Military Families Speak Out. Even there, I feel vaguely guilty talking about it, since more and more of our members are getting their loved ones back in a box.

Vermont has one of the highest per capita rates of National Guard casualties in Iraq. A predominantly rural state with a population of 619,000, Vermont has lost eleven soldiers in Iraq, four of them Guardsmen. Twelve hundred National Guardsmen from two hundred of Vermont's 251 towns and cities have been shipped to Iraq, and more have been placed on alert. This, coupled with the long history of social activism, has made it the flagship state for the presentation of an initiative calling on the Governor to bring the Guard home.

Vermont Military Families Speak Out members were instrumental in the drive to get an antiwar resolution on the ballot in one fifth of the state's two hundred and fifty one towns. Fifty of the fifty-six towns passed some version of the resolution calling upon state legislators to study the local impact of Guard deployments, asking the congressional delegation to reassert state authority over Guard units, and requesting that the federal government bring Reservists home.

The resolution carries no formal weight, but it has initiated conversation about the significant social costs of the war in Iraq. It was unanimously adopted by United for Peace and Justice, a coalition of over a thousand anti-war groups, and heralds the first time in American history that military families and people concerned about the federalization of citizen soldiers have joined with pacifist and antiwar groups to demand accountability from the government, effectively challenging the President's authority to order members of the National Guard to be deployed.

There is a 1980 precedent for gubernatorial action, which involved several governors protesting the deployment of National Guard troops for training missions in Central America. Congress passed the Montgomery Amendment in response to their objections, forbidding governors from opposing the deployment of Guard troops for training missions based on "location, purpose, type, or schedule of such active duty."

A 1990 U.S. Supreme Court ruling determined that the Montgomery Amendment was constitutional, but specified that "under the current statutory scheme, the states are assured of the use of their National Guard units for any legitimate state purpose. They are simply forbidden to use their control over the state National Guard to thwart federal use of the NGUS for national security and foreign policy objectives with which they disagree."

The language of the Amendment, and of the subsequent Supreme Court ruling, has a considerable gray area and leaves open to legal and political debate several issues pertinent to Guard deployment in the occupation of Iraq. Of primary consideration is that the Governor can and should challenge the federalization of the Guard since the President himself confirmed that the rationale for the federalization is invalid, and the Supreme Court has stipulated that the use of the Guard would be only for legitimate state purposes. The Supreme Court has never ruled on the legality of the occupation of Iraq.

Furthermore, the Montgomery Amendment refers only to training missions; it does not address wartime protocol, active duty mobilizations and deployments, or long-term overseas occupations. The Montgomery Amendment does, however, guarantee states the right to protect themselves and take back control of the Guard from the federal government if it is proven necessary for state safety and security.

Finally, the question of priority, or first rights to use of the National Guard when there is a conflict between the federalization of the Guard and the legitimate state use and need, for instance fire fighting, border patrol, and homeland security, has never been directly addressed by the courts.

With nearly sixty thousand National Guard and Reserve troops currently in Iraq, almost four hundred thousand deployed so far in the "War on Terror," more than three hundred killed, and no end to the occupation in sight, there is a growing likelihood that at some point, the courts will have to. Given that all three of the states' congressional delegates voted against invading Iraq, Vermont might just be the place.

Back in Washington State, most of the soldiers from the 81st Brigade Combat Team have begun the journey home. Some have elected to remain at their posts for another six to twelve months, offering reasons such as a sense of duty, the tax-free paycheck and signing bonuses, or, most often, that their wives or girlfriends have left them, and they've got nothing to go home to. Troops are being rotated off base and flown to Kuwait, where they spend a day or two waiting for the carriers that will take them to Ireland or Germany. From there, they board planes that will land at Fort McChord Air Force Base, just south of Tacoma, after about twenty-one hours in transit.

Once they're in the air, the Brigade Family Support Lead Volunteer is notified, and given the flight information and a roster of the battalions on board. At that point, the Family Support Program phone trees are activated, and a family member or designated contact person is called with the details of their soldier's arrival.

Some of the units have already returned, and planes are landing daily. After spending several hours going through customs and getting processed, the soldiers are bussed to the Soldiers Field House at Fort Lewis for what the Army promises will be a very short welcome ceremony before they're released and reunited with their families.

Brigade General Hilman has secured passes allowing soldiers three or four days with their families before they have to report back to Fort Lewis for the five to seven day demobilization process. Once completed, the soldiers have thirty days of paid leave. I hear stories on the news about the returning soldiers almost every day, but I'm still waiting for mine. Lorin and I thought he'd be flying back with his Platoon, but he's held over.

Dear Wife:
    Just when I thought I was out of this place, surprise! The airflow got bumped back one day. This is the Army, nothing goes as planned. Hardball. Well you were on okay, and I guess so was I. The first person that told me about it was the Brigade Sergeant Major. Not so good. It would have been fine if MY PICTURE had not been plastered all over the international news, not once but four times. Too many people saw it and let's just say that I've been trying to explain it.

I am so glad that I was not in the chow hall when it came on. I love that you do these things, but at times I do not like having my picture all over the news, mostly because of the fact of where I am at and what I am doing right now. I heard it was good, that you looked good. Okay enough on that.

I'd done a segment on MSNBC's "Hardball with Chris Matthews" a few nights earlier, talking about the military's treatment of wives, and the reprehensible lack of support for the Guard and Reserve families that are left behind. The show aired in the mess hall at Camp Anaconda while hundreds of soldiers were having lunch.

Lorin wasn't there at the time, but he's gotten a lot of flak about it. I've had it with people crabbing about me speaking out, especially when they're complaining to my husband. I have heard too many soldiers, my husband included, saying that the people in the States either need to pick up a protest sign or a gun. Wartime is no place for armchair quarterbacks.

In my e-mail back to him, I write:

You tell the people who are complaining to you that I'm a taxpayer, and an American. I'm exercising my First Amendment rights. If you're over there supposedly defending democracy, what is the problem with the people who are engaging it? If they want military wives to shut up, tell them to recognize us as the unpaid resource we are. They've got no business bothering you for what a private citizen is saying. And you tell them that. Or God knows, I will.

His next reply:

Hello my love. I'm still in Iraq; I won't be leaving till the eighth now. The good part is that I will spend little time in Kuwait. I am so bored, no TV, nothing except magazines and a few books to read plus take naps.

Don't fret too much on the "Hardball" thing. I've had people say good things about it, like good for you for speaking your mind, saying what you believe in and not being afraid to speak out. I have not been in trouble and I won't be. I think the worst for me is just that there are 25,000 people here and a lot of people saw it. I know that you are nutty in love with me, but please, try to use some restraint with the picture.

So, don't worry about it, you are doing the right thing. I am over here fighting so that the Iraqi people can have the right for freedom of expression, the same right that you have. Shuts them up every time. Just a few more days and I will be home. I am looking forward to seeing you and holding you in my arms, sweetie, being able to kiss you. Yummy.

I get word of his tentative return date and time to friends and family, inviting everybody to a welcome home party on Saturday night, the day after he arrives.

I can't wait to see him, but I'm also apprehensive about what the next months will bring.

Lakewood County, Washington, is home to a lot of Guard and Reserve members, and has had an eighty percent rise in family counseling since soldiers started rotating home through nearby Fort Lewis in October. Five million dollars have been allocated to make post-deployment couples counseling available for Guard families, but it's clearly not enough. An article in the *Fort Lewis Ranger* addressed "the rocketing rate of couples in crisis linked to the war on terror . . . citing divorce rates as high as fifty to eighty percent in some units returning from yearlong deployments."[30]

The "Courage to Care Reintegration Roadmap," part of a new health promotion of Uniformed Services University, provides a four-step guide that couples should use to "reestablish a shared sense of purpose," as though there's a tidy little formula for healing the wounds of war.

Angela Blickenstaff mentions the difficulties of reintegration during our meeting with Antonio Ginatta, Governor Christine Gregoire's Executive Policy Advisor. Angie is an MFSO member who is also in the Washington National Guard. She's heard from numerous wives, as well as their husbands, about the problems they've encountered post-deployment: unabated bickering, snide remarks, fights over kids and money and household chores, hostile arguments over things done, and left undone, during deployment. At the other end of the spectrum are the returning spouses who are effectively AWOL from their families even though they are back at home.

Angie never found out firsthand because she became a widow at twenty-three when her husband, Joe, was killed in an accident in Iraq. A few weeks ago, Angie's unit was alerted that they might be deployed to Iraq. Mr. Ginatta, the Executive Policy Advisor to Washington State Governor Christine Gregoire, listens to this, shaking his head ever so slightly.

We're in a conference room at the Insurance Building on the Washington State Capitol grounds in Olympia, along with Susan Livingston, Wes Hamilton, and Lietta Ruger. Between us, we hold memberships in two Veterans for Peace Chapters, Military Families Speak Out, Gold Star Families for Peace, and the Fellowship of Reconciliation.

---

30. Dunkelberger, March 3–9, 2005.

The topic of medical benefits comes up almost immediately in the meeting with Ginatta, and I say, "As soon as the soldiers are taken off active duty status, typically within thirty days of returning, they lose their dental benefits, and the family members do, too. After the Tri-care coverage runs out, there's typically a lag time before their employers put them back on the company health plan, which can leave families without any health care whatsoever for months. Soldiers who remain in the Guard or Reserves are entitled to an additional 180 days of medical benefits, but fewer and fewer doctors or health care providers will even take Tri-Care. If soldiers have unresolved medical issues, the military is supposedly obligated to care for them, but a lot of soldiers get ignored. Besides, PTSD symptoms typically don't manifest for months, and often years, after the fact."

We request that a task force be established to investigate post-deployment health care, but the main reason that we're here is to call upon Governor Christine Gregoire to challenge the ongoing deployments of Guardsmen and Reservists, and to seek their withdrawal from Iraq. So far, 1,516 American soldiers have been killed in action, and 11,344 wounded. The monthly casualty average has gone from 449 to 748 since the June 28, 2004, transition of power, a sixty percent increase.

Support for the occupation is declining in the U.S. and abroad, not that the international community ever signed on with overwhelming enthusiasm. The latest figures from the Institute for Policy Studies show that just thirty-nine percent of Americans now believe it was "worth going to war," and sixty-five percent think it has worsened this country's standing in the world. Polls in twenty-one countries revealed that fifty-eight percent of the respondents consider the reelection of President Bush to have made the world more dangerous, and an overwhelming eighty percent of Iraqis indicated that they had "no confidence" in American officials or coalition forces.

Susan hands Mr. Ginatta a copy of the proposal, which has been fashioned after similar proposals tendered in Vermont and Oregon. As he's skimming the one-page document, Susan hits the main points:

"What we'd like the Governor to do is ask President Bush to justify the continued use of Washington National Guard in Iraq. Congress gave President Bush permission to take National Guard Troops to Iraq on two premises, the first being that Iraq poses a threat to the U.S. as a terrorist nation, the second that Iraq has WMDs, in violation of U.S. sanctions. Both have been nullified by the President's own Executive Orders."

As Antonio is mulling this over, I offer, "The Department of Defense and the State legislatures can argue about who's responsible for taking care of the citizen soldiers once they get home. After all, it was the Department of Defense that created the conditions our soldiers are coming back with. But a long debate about who is responsible doesn't help the soldiers and their families, and they need help now."

I relay some of the statistics about the downward slide in National Guard recruitment, including the thirty percent decline in enlistments in February. The Army Reserve tracks recruitment figures in major metropolitan areas, and over the past six months, the Seattle office has only been able to sign up twenty-five new soldiers, badly missing its target of approximately a hundred recruits. Oregon recruitment is down forty percent, and several battalions have lost more than half of their members. One Reserve unit saw seventy percent of its members leave within a few months of coming home. The normal attrition is one fifth.

I talk about how this war is affecting the families of weekend warriors, and the stress-related health problems of some of the wives. Brenda Winkler is married to Major Ed Winkler, Oregon National Guard, who served a brief, three month tour of duty in Iraq. While he was there, she contracted Meniere's disease, an affliction of the inner ear that causes bouts of extreme nausea and dizziness lasting for up to twelve hours. Doctors attributed the diagnosis to extreme stress, and fitted Brenda with a hearing aid, which she'll be wearing for the rest of her life.

I also tell him about how the lack of preparation for sustained ground combat and a long occupation is depleting Guard manpower and gear faster than they can be replaced. The number of Guard units that have the minimum amount of equipment required for ready deployment has dropped to an all-time low of sixty percent. This is due to the transfer of nearly 100,000 pieces of equipment from nondeployed units. Much of this material cannot be accounted for or has been left overseas to support ongoing operations. Supply shortages in Guard units returning from Iraq are so severe that some are unable to conduct training. There is currently no plan or funding to replace the equipment, estimated to cost over $1.2 billion. Reserve units being rotated back home are rated at the lowest level of readiness (C4), as they don't have the necessary training, equipment, or manpower—an even greater concern for border states, especially those who have declared drought emergencies, or are on the brink of doing so.

As General Richard A. Cody, Army Vice Chief of Staff, put it, "The real stress on the system was the fact that no one envisioned we would have this level of commitment for the National Guard."[31]

---

31. Truthout.org, March 19, 2005.

The Guard has been deployed in significant numbers before, but was a comparatively small part of the total troop strength. According to the United States Census Bureau, 2,509,550 soldiers were deployed during World War I, 379,071 of them Guardsmen, slightly more than fifteen percent of the soldiers sent overseas. A spokesperson from the DOD Public Affairs office stated that 300,034 of the 11,762,490 soldiers that fought in World War II were in the National Guard, just 2.55 percent of deployed troops. By comparison, about forty-one percent of the million soldiers who've served in the war on terror have been citizen soldiers, according to statistics from the United States Military.

Pentagon spokesperson Lieutenant Colonel Pamela Hart said that the Guard's stop-loss policy has affected approximately fifty thousand troops so far, sometimes for almost two years after their contracts expired, including 412 of Washington's 81st Brigade.

If Vietnam veterans felt betrayed by the American public when they came home, the sense of betrayal that soldiers are expressing in this war is directed toward the government. More and more soldiers are talking with their feet, and refusing to report for duty. Perhaps what speaks loudest is that thirty-seven of the six thousand soldiers who are currently AWOL are military recruiters.

Susan jumps in and tells Mr. Ginatta that Governor Gregoire's friend Oregon Governor Kulongoski is considering the same resolution. Almost forty Oregon Guard members have been killed in Iraq, representing one out of every 210 Oregonian citizen soldiers. This doesn't include the deployed soldiers who've died as the result of infections, motor vehicle accidents, and other nonviolent causes. One hundred nineteen have been wounded in combat; others have suffered heart attacks, psychological trauma, and a growing array of casualties not considered combat related.

Mr. Ginatta replies, "Well, two governors standing together on this are certainly stronger than one."

"And there might be a third," says Wes, pulling out a copy of an article that ran today on CNN. "Montana's Governor just asked for part of his National Guard to come home with his fire fighting equipment—he is concerned about Montana Forest Fires this summer."

According to Montana Governor Brian Schweitzer, "It's going to be a bad fire year. . . . Somebody's going to have a blowup. Is it northern Idaho, is it eastern Washington, or is it Montana?"

At one point during the past year, fifty-five percent of the Montana National Guard had been mobilized or alerted. Approximately a thousand of Montana's Guard troops are on extended duty in Iraq, along with ten of the state's twelve Black Hawk helicopters, traditionally used for firefighting because they can hold about twice as much water as commercial carriers.

The Mississippi Guard is facing a similar scenario, as the unit assigned to deal with hurricane damage has shipped twenty-one copters to Iraq, forcing them to make do with just five choppers for post-storm rescue and transport of cargo and troops in case of state emergencies.

Mr. Ginatta has been taking notes virtually nonstop, and says, "The Governor is also concerned about our state's readiness and the drought. She's already begun thinking about that, and has been talking about National Guard integration issues. I can't speak for her, but I know she will be very interested in this. I believe you can expect follow-up meetings and continued dialogue with the Governor's office."

Cautiously optimistic, and wanting to close the deal, Angie presents each of us with a letter she's gotten from a National Guardsman currently in Iraq.

> Having a stable Middle East is in the world's best interests. What we have to decide is how much we are willing to pay into this. We need to set a definite date to leave and stick to it. We will not be able to change everybody's hearts and minds. While doing pre-deployment training at Fort Hood, Texas, the entire Brigade was put on lockdown (no going off post, no visits to family, that kind of stuff).
>
> This does not happen to active duty units. . . . Apparently this is the first time a deploying unit has been treated this way, and we were given no explanation as to why or what we may have done to deserve it.

The four-page document has additional accounts that highlight a number of problems, and dovetails with the questions we'd asked about the lack of health insurance and the long lag that troops wait for disability to kick in— their families going without income for months at a time. It also puts the topic of job placement once troops return front and center, which is critical since almost ten percent of Guardsmen and Reservists are self-employed, and eighteen percent work for very small businesses.

A report issued by the Congressional Budget Office in May 2005 found that up to fifteen thousand businesses headed by deployed Reservists have had severe management and scheduling problems, or financial losses. An article published by the *New York Times* on August 25th stated that "other experts estimate that anywhere from 8,000 to 30,000 mobilized reservists held crucial jobs at their small businesses."

The latest statistics from the U.S. Labor Department reveal that about forty percent of the seven hundred Oregon National Guardsmen just returned from Iraq and Afghanistan are unemployed, as compared to the state's overall unemployment rate of 6.4 percent. According to the Bureau of Labor Statistics, slightly more than twenty percent of twenty- to twenty-four-year-old male veterans who were separated from military service in 2004 were jobless in the first quarter of 2005. The figure is almost double the unemployment rate for twenty to twenty-four-year-old civilian males, which was 9.4 percent in 2004, as compared to 13.6 percent for young veterans. Some of the soldiers are reenrolling in college, and others didn't have work prior to deployment, but most lost their jobs while serving overseas.

The Uniformed Services Employment and Reemployment Rights Act of 1994 (USERRA) guarantees that members and former members of the Armed Forces are entitled to go back to a civilian job they held prior to military service. The same isn't true for those who were on the government's payroll prior to deployment.

Operation Guardian began in 1989 as a federal program targeting broadscale drug trafficking, and employed National Guard members in several states on a fulltime basis. Those Guardsmen were in Iraq when they got a letter from the Guard's joint director of military support, Colonel Norman Redding, telling them they'd be out of work when they got home.

The federal law, which doesn't apply to government employers, contains fine print that provides exemptions to civilian employers. Caveats include economic hardship on the business, or a change in the soldier's ability to perform his or her job once they return, which could present a problem for the 212 members of the 81st who were wounded in action.

If national statistics hold true in Washington State, approximately seventy-five members of the 81st will have problems with returning to their previous employers. Even though the Department of Labor says that Veterans get WorkForce priority, and the Pentagon operates state-based Employer Support Programs for Guard and Reserve, calls to a national job assistance hotline for returning Guard and Reservists have jumped from 125 to 400 calls per week in the past three years.

Our time is up, and Mr. Ginatta promises that we'll hear from him after he informs the Governor. We promise that he'll hear from us if we don't. He moves down the corridor to his office, and the six of us quickly debrief on the sidewalk outside the building, welcoming the sunshine after almost an hour in the basement.

After discussing plans to follow up with Ginatta, Angie says, "I went to the Veterans Memorial before the meeting, and one of the Republican Senators was there. So I gave him a copy of the resolution, and talked about my service in the Guard. It seemed like he was listening, but then, when I showed him my husband's picture, and told him how he'd died, he refused to look at the photo or even shake my hand. He just walked away."

None of us have words for that, beyond saying we're sorry. Forty-eight hours later, I get a voice mail message from Lorin, telling me he's in Kuwait, and might be home in less than two days. The time and date of his return has been revised so often that I've taken to telling people I won't know for sure when he's going to be home until I know for sure. And then finally, I do.

"This is the United States Army calling about Sergeant Lorin Bannerman. May I speak with Stacy Bannerman?"

Thinking this is the call I've prayed would never come, my heart stalls as I furtively look out the picture window, fearful there is a black car pulling into the drive. Mentally talking myself down, I hear the woman say, "I am calling to inform you that your soldier, Sergeant First Class Lorin Bannerman, will be arriving at Fort Lewis. You can meet him at the Reception Ceremony at the Soldiers Field House at nine o'clock this Friday morning, March 11th. Do you have any questions?"

"I just want to make sure I got the information right." After repeating what she's told me, I thank her and hang up.

I contact Lorin's folks, who will drive over from Spokane tomorrow, and let his siblings know the details of the reception. The countdown to his return begins, and it feels as though everything's going in reverse. On my way to Fort Lewis Friday morning, I recall driving this same stretch of highway a lifetime ago.

Lorin's military sticker is still on the lower left windshield of his car, and although it's good through the summer, I stop at the gate for the ID check. The young woman peers at my driver's license, and then looks at the sticker, repeating the motions several times with a look of growing consternation. She finally waves me through, and it's not until I've parked the car that I understand why: I'd propped a "Bring Them Home Now" postcard next to the base sticker.

Helen, Paul, Dan, Julie, and her son, Brandon, wave me over from their place about halfway up the bleachers that run along one side of the gymnasium wall. I ask how the drive was, and listen to them talk about mundane things while keeping my eyes glued on the large rolling metal door in the far corner of the hall. The air is filled with a steadily rising combination of excitement and apprehension, as though we won't believe they're actually back safely until we see them ourselves.

It's almost half past nine, and the ceremony hasn't begun. The small military band that's been playing for the past thirty minutes takes a break, and a uniformed speaker steps behind the podium that's positioned off to one side of the gym floor.

"I appreciate your patience, folks. I know you've been waiting for this a very long time. If you can hold on for just a few minutes more, a plane full of Scouts arrived a few hours earlier, and they're being rushed through processing in order to get to the ceremony."

Helen leans over and says to me, "Scouts? Didn't know they we're taking them that young."

I reply, "No wonder it's been so hard to buy cookies."

Liahann and Hardy climb up the bleacher stairs to join us as an officer is prepping us to yell, "Hoo-ah!" as a greeting to the soldiers.

Moments later the band, in full dress uniform, launches into a reasonable rendition of "When Johnny Comes Marching Home Again" as the metal door rises slightly, revealing rows of nappy camel boots marching swiftly toward it. The crowd of several hundred yells and stomps on the bleachers, rising up with a roar as the door rolls to the ceiling, revealing legs, and shoulders, and then heads and hats.

Twelve dozen men in wrinkled, dusty desert camouflage advance toward the stands, coming to a halt in formation, front and center. We all stand for the national anthem, followed by a brief prayer. Resuming our seats, I mumble to Dan, "So much for the separation of church and state."

Intently scanning the troops, I quickly spot Lorin standing at attention in the front row. I jump to my feet and wave, yelling "Scooby!" His head lifts and his eyes pick me out, and a radiant smile bursts his stern face open. A couple of uniforms make brief remarks about the success of the mission, but nothing's said about the nine members of the 81st that were killed.

"Soldiers, you're free to go."

Quelling my impulse to shove my way through, I move quickly through the people who are just beginning to rise and gather their belongings. Lorin pulls me into his arms, and up in the air, and I nuzzle into his neck. When he eventually sets me down gently, I kiss his sweet, beautiful, sunburned face.

He keeps me tucked under his arm as he greets his family, and we pose for pictures. We pick up his duffel sacks outside, and walk to our vehicles.

Lorin has told his family that he wants time alone with me, so we say our good-byes, and I remind them that the party tomorrow starts around six.

We don't talk much on the way home, there's no need. But I ask him what he wants, and he says, "A shower. A shower and sleep."

Shortly after we get his bags unloaded, our doorbell rings, and Jourdan and Shannon fly at him, flinging their arms around him.

"Lorin's Home! Lorin's Home!" They exclaim, dancing around him, touching him, grabbing at his shorn hair and rumpled hat. Surrounded by his family at the field house, I failed to see the recognition of how much he's loved and been missed. But it's in his eyes now, which glisten as he ducks his head.

Alisa pries the boys off of him, "Okay, guys, that's enough. You can come over and see Lorin later."

She hugs him, and then they cross the lawn to their house, the boys tripping a bit, because they're looking back at Lorin rather than paying attention to their feet.

Lorin showers and naps, and we have dinner at a Thai restaurant. We talk about the party and if there's anything in particular he wants for it. I repeatedly tell him that part of the point of having a party for him is so that he doesn't do any of the work, but he insists on preparing a few appetizers.

It's not until the next day, when I'm watching him bustle about the kitchen, happy and content, that it dawns on me that he loves to do this, that this is one of the ways he feels connected to home. I kiss his cheek and pat him on the butt before getting into the shower.

The hot water must be loosening something, because the next thing I know, I'm curled into a ball in the tub, sobbing, overwhelmed with the relief of having him home and finally knowing that he's safe. I dry myself off and get ready for the party.

About twenty people are at the house, which is hung with streamers and posters and WELCOME HOME banners. We toast Lorin's return, and I read the citation he received for his Bronze Star Medal for exceptionally meritorious service:

SFC Bannerman's leadership, adherence to extremely high standards, and commitment to taking the fight to the enemy, have set an example of excellence for his soldiers and indeed all soldiers of the 81st BCT to emulate. Through his diligence, his platoon has maintained a ninety-nine percent readiness rating . . . this incredible speed and deadly accurate response is part of the reason that most mortar and rockets are now fired from much farther away from the LSA. . . . Hearing the report of outgoing mortar fire after being attacked has motivated American troops inside the LSA and often brings cheers from the soldiers.

Our little group cheers, too, but I'm still trying to navigate my way through my conflicted feelings. As we're cleaning up after the party, Lorin says, "I'm going to stay in the Guard for another year or so."

"Excuse me? What did you just say?"

Clearing his throat, he replies, "I said I'm staying in the Guard."

"Oh, God, no. What happened to what you said? Remember when you got over there? You kept promising me that as soon as you got home, you'd be done. You said you were getting out. Just last night, you told me that it wasn't worth a year of your life."

"Well, yeah," he replies, "but I just want to make sure I get my twenty 'good' years in for retirement benefits. Besides, there's no way we'll get deployed again. It just isn't going to happen."

And all I can think is *I've been told that before.* Does our marriage matter so little to him that he's willing to put us through another year and a half like the one we just spent? How can he be so cavalier about the fact that every decision he's made about the Guard since we've met has ended up wreaking havoc on my life, too? I don't want to be married to the military; I don't want to have to live not knowing when, or if, my husband might be called up, and sent off to fight in a war that I will never support.

He might believe the military and the administration when they tell him he won't be deployed again, but they've broken far too many promises for me to trust them now. I stalk off to bed, where he joins me half an hour later.

As he's dropping off to sleep, I sit up, and say furiously, "I suggest you get a very good divorce lawyer, because I won't do this again."

After a tortured sleep, I wake to find him getting dressed, and ask, "What are you doing?"

"I've got to go. I need some time to think. The last thing you said last night was that you wanted a divorce."

"Yeah."

"Jesus. I just got home, and you drop this on me!"

"You've dropped a lot of shit on me here, too! I absolutely refuse to live like this. I cannot live like this. I *won't.* And I can't believe you'd ask me to. Do you have any idea what this last year has been like for me?"

"Do you have any idea what it's been like for me?!!"

"No, I don't, and I never will. Nor will you. But I'm not the one choosing to put us through it again. You are, and that's not fair. Not to me, not to either of us. Do I mean so little to you? Does our marriage?"

"It's not about that. It's not about our marriage."

"Hell yes it is. When I was desperate for work, and had an opportunity in Portland, you refused to let me go, even for a few months. You said long distance relationships don't work. Remember?"

Lorin grimaces, and then replies, "Yes, I remember, but I didn't choose to get deployed."

"You chose to join the Guard, though, didn't you? And you're choosing it again, over me. How would you feel if I did that to you?"

Taking his hands in mine, I continue more gently, "Lorin, I love you. I *adore* you, but I need to know that I matter to you, that *we* matter. I need to be able to count on you to be here. Right now, I can't."

"Yes, you can . . . you can," he says adamantly.

"Honey, saying something loud enough or long enough doesn't necessarily make it true. Look, I can't talk about this anymore right now, but I think we need to. Would you be willing to see a counselor with me?"

His shoulders slump, but he says, "Fine, if you think we need to. I think we just need to give it time."

We tiptoe around each other for the next couple of days, trying to get used to being in one another's space again. He stays up until two or three in the morning, spending hours surfing the web, looking for articles and updates about the war in Iraq, watching video clips of footage that he got from other soldiers in Iraq.

When he finally comes to bed he sleeps so fitfully, almost aggressively, that I end up going to the guest room.

I want everything to be okay right now, but I haven't a clue as to how to do that. I relay this to the counselor when we finally get in to see her. I'm nervous, but Lorin seems pretty relaxed, and after we bring her up to speed on the situation, she asks, "So, tell me why you're here?"

Lorin says, "I'm not sure that we're actually having any problems, but I know Stacy's frustrated and worried that I'm going to be deployed again, even though I keep telling her that I'm not."

"That's what he says, but I don't believe it."

The counselor asks, "Why not?"

"Because he told me before that he wouldn't get deployed, but he did. We're not leaving Iraq anytime soon, and rumors have it that by the end of summer, over fifty percent of the soldiers over there will be Guard and Reserves. I just don't trust him."

"Is it him you don't trust, or the government?"

"The government."

"Well, that's understandable, but Lorin's already told you all of the reasons that they most likely won't be deployed again anytime soon, and by then, he'll be retired."

"I don't know. Maybe I just need to keep hearing that."

"Something else you both might want to consider is talking about what the last year was like for you. It will help you to understand each other better, but I think it sounds like you also need to grieve the loss of a year of your lives together. It seems to me that is what Stacy's really struggling with now. How does that sound? Are you willing to do that?"

Her words have triggered the heartache I've held, and reaching blindly across the loveseat, my hand finds Lorin's, and together, we say, "Yes."

The counselor offers me a Kleenex, and says, "You two can come back here whenever you need to. Just give yourselves some time, grieve for the past year, and remember what you love about each other. I think you're going to be just fine."

For the first time since this began, I think so, too.

Paper Crane I will write peace on your wings and you will fly all over the world.

Sadako Sasaki, age twelve

INDEX